THE REMOTE CONTROL IN THE NEW AGE OF TELEVISION

THE REMOTE CONTROL IN THE NEW AGE OF TELEVISION

Edited by *James R. Walker* and *Robert V. Bellamy, Jr.*

PRAEGER

Westport, Connecticut
London

Library of Congress Cataloging-in-Publication Data

The remote control in the new age of television / edited by James R.
  Walker and Robert V. Bellamy.
        p.   cm.
    Includes bibliographical references and index.
    ISBN 0–275–94396–8 (alk. paper)
    1. Television viewers—United States—Psychology.   2. Television—
Channel selectors—Social aspects.   3. Television—Channel
selectors—Psychological aspects.   I. Walker, James Robert.
II. Bellamy, Robert V.
PN1992.55.R46   1993
302.23'45'0973—dc20   93–6774

British Library Cataloguing in Publication Data is available.

Library of Congress Catalog Card Number: 93–6774
ISBN: 0–275–94396–8

First published in 1993

Praeger Publishers, 88 Post Road West, Westport, CT 06881
An imprint of Greenwood Publishing Group, Inc.

Printed in the United States of America

The paper used in this book complies with the
Permanent Paper Standard issued by the National
Information Standards Organization (Z39.48–1984).

10 9 8 7 6 5 4 3 2 1

Copyright Acknowledgment

An earlier version of chapter 5 appeared in the *Journal of Popular Film and Television* 18,
no. 2 (1990): 65–71. Portions of that article are reprinted with permission of the Helen
Dwight Reid Educational Foundation. Published by Heldref Publications, 1319 18th Street,
N.W., Washington, D.C. 20036–1802. Copyright 1990.

Contents

Tables and Figures

TABLES

FIGURES

Preface

Producing an edited volume about remote control devices (RCDs) invites a certain amount of ridicule. One friend said, "Is your next book going to be about the horizontal hold?" However, with a few good-natured exceptions, we received support and encouragement for our effort. Some of our contributors "signed up" for this project early in 1989 when we proposed that a panel of original RCD research be presented at the Speech Communication Association (SCA) convention that November in San Francisco. Louise Benjamin, Gary Copeland, and David Lavery joined Walker and Bellamy on that first panel. Larry Wenner provided an intelligent and supportive response to our initial efforts. We suspected that we might be onto something when twenty-five curious (crazy?) souls struggled to join us for our 7:00 A.M. *Sunday* session. We had expected no more than five. That rosy response led to a second SCA panel the next year with contributions from Jennings Bryant, Larry Wenner, Maryann Dennehy, Paul Traudt, and, this time, Bellamy and Walker. Sam Becker contributed a theoretically contextualized response. Although he claimed he "didn't know anything about remote controls," Sam focused the panelists and audience on a multitude of critical questions raised by RCDs. Our thanks go to these early contributors.

With eight papers in hand, a book seemed in order, but the project would likely have died without continued support from our institutions. In 1990 I received a Faculty Development Leave from Memphis State University. This precious gift of time allowed me to develop the proposal for this volume and become a visiting scholar at the University of San Francisco (USF). While at USF, I profited immensely from the insights of Larry Wenner and his colleagues.

Special gratitude goes to my co-editor, Rob Bellamy. I hate to think how much fun would have been drained out of this project, not to mention how much more work would have been added, if he had not agreed to co-edit. This is surely his volume as much as it is mine. My thanks to Paula Ashman for her help in preparing this volume. Finally, let me acknowledge the intellectual, emotional, and editorial support of my wife, Judith Hiltner. Without her, projects such as this one are empty efforts.

Although this volume is a scholarly quest, its preparation has stimulated the memories of our RCD past. My primal RCD experiences came during many visits to a favorite aunt and uncle's home in State College, Pennsylvania, during the 1970s. Somehow, I would always manage to capture the remote for a time and use it to graze across their ten-channel, cable-equipped color television. The gratification that I received from grazing was directly proportional to the annoyance it brought to my aunt and uncle. Clever ploys were devised to gain my attention, so that viewing control could be resumed by the rightful authorities. Although that was many years ago and I've grown more respectful of the group viewing situation, my aunt and uncle still take precautions. The moment I ring their doorbell, the RCD is discreetly hidden.

Jim Walker
Memphis, Tennessee

Our first remote control device (RCD) was included with a wired J. C. Penney model VCR purchased in 1984. After we quickly tired of the play-element of the RCD (e.g., watching people move and speak very fast both forward and in reverse), the RCD became the tool that enabled us to "zip" through the advertising and other extraneous material on time-shifted and rented materials. As our home-entertainment system evolved and we acquired multiple RCDs, we continued to experiment with the "forbidden fruit" (from the perspective of television programmers and advertisers) by grazing, zipping, and zapping a growing number of video (and audio) options. Of course, most of our friends were doing the same. RCD-derived behaviors were in fact becoming part of the currency of everyday life. The ability to instantaneously monitor multiple news or sports events or to watch bits and pieces of many different programs became a new means of using the television set (or system).

Of course, not everyone uses her or his RCD at the same rate or for the same purposes. Early on, for example, my friend and co-editor, Jim Walker, was a confirmed grazer. A typical viewing episode with him is an ever-changing kaleidoscope of images. Because my wife, Cathy, has worked an evening shift for the last three years, she is more a time shifter and zipper. Watching television with her means viewing programs but rarely getting to hear advertising, promotion, theme songs, and credits as they zip by. I consider myself more the casual grazer and dedicated multiple program viewer. Perhaps because I almost always have a radio or television set on while I am reading or writing, I am not apt to graze a great deal except during those rare times when I explicitly choose to watch television. Since when I do, I often feel like Bruce Springsteen (i.e., "57 Channels and Nothing On"), I do graze but only until I find "something on" or give up and go back into my "TV as background" mode. However, when breaking news stories or sporting events are on, I will use the RCD to go between two or more television sources for hours—not wanting to miss a thing.

Despite the different ways in which we use RCDs, there is little doubt that they are an essential part of our television life. Ask anyone who has lost or inadvertently destroyed one. Notice the increased attention to RCDs in popular media. Notice the trade press accounts (and watch the results) of how the television industry is attempting to cope with audiences who have more control than ever before. I hope that this volume, by bringing together a series of studies and essays on the impact of the RCD on the viewer and the industry, helps the reader better understand the RCD phenomenon.

Thanks to Anne Kiefer and Jude Grant at Praeger for their superb work on this book; Jim Walker for coming up with the concept of an edited volume on RCD research; Nancy Harper, who arranged for me to have a reduction in course load on two occasions at Duquesne University; and Charla Rylands for her assistance with the preparation of the book. I especially want to thank Catherine Cecil Bellamy for her unwavering support of this and other projects (although I would like to hear theme songs on occasion).

Rob Bellamy
Pittsburgh, Pennsylvania

Part I

Overview and Developmental Perspectives

1

The Remote Control Device: An Overlooked Technology

James R. Walker and Robert V. Bellamy, Jr.

On the evening of October 30, 1938, several million Americans tuned their radios from NBC's popular "Edgar Bergen and Charlie McCarthy" program (i.e., "The Chase & Sanborn Hour") to CBS's much-lower-rated "Mercury Theatre of the Air," which was presenting a dramatization of H. G. Wells's *War of the Worlds*. The subsequent panic on the part of some of the "Mercury" listeners and the massive attention paid to it by the popular and academic press is, of course, well known to historians and media-effects scholars. The end of Bergen's first "Charlie McCarthy" skit has been posited as the reason for the late tune-in to the "Mercury Theatre" (Cantril 1947). Latecomers missed the program's opening disclosure and many were convinced that they were listening to an authentic newscast. Thus, what is arguably the most famous example of a powerful media effect was partially the result of channel hopping.

The Martian panic was not the only effect of the "War of the Worlds" broadcast. Manchester (1973, 232) wrote that the incident led to the unpleasant "discovery" that the "audience will tune to another station when advertising or unpopular entertainment comes on." This was an early warning to the broadcast and advertising industries that the audience can be quite active, "zapping" undesirable programming and, most significantly, commercials. Following World War II, smaller table models made radio a more personal medium, shortening the distance between listener and tuning knob, and presumably increasing channel hopping. However, the diffusion of television during the next decade shifted the receiver back to the living room and control back to advertisers. Zappers trapped across the living room would have to wait a generation for electronic deliverance.

THE RISE OF THE RCD

Closely following the more publicized diffusion of cable television and VCRs, television remote control devices (RCDs) have constituted a more subtle revolution. Earlier books on new technology make little or no mention of the technology (Becker and Schoenbach 1989; Rogers 1986; Rogers and Balle 1985; Williams 1983). However, remote control devices, which were expected to be in 90 percent of U.S. households by 1993 (Klopfenstein, Chapter 3 of this volume), have been found to encourage new television viewing styles (Ainslie 1989; Walker 1992). "Grazing" viewers are able to use the remote control to redefine dramatically the structure of television programming by combining seemingly disparate elements of television content into individualized televisual episodes (see Traudt, Chapter 5 of this volume). For many viewers, a viewing session no longer consists of a few programs; rather, it has become a vast collection of program segments sequenced by the broadcast/cable networks and selected by the viewer. The notion of an "active" audience has taken on a new meaning, producing significant changes for advertisers and television programmers.

One of the most fascinating aspects of the RCD is its refinement by the user (Williams 1989). As Rogers (1986) suggests, one of the characteristics that marks the diffusion of new communication technologies is their "re-invention" by the consumer. Although remote control devices were designed to make existing television operations more convenient, the technology has been used by the consumer to facilitate grazing and multiple program viewing and to change the relationship of viewer to the television medium. Indeed, product manufacturers have begun to incorporate such re-inventions into later RCD designs (Heeter, Yoon, and Sampson, Chapter 7 of this volume; Klopfenstein, Chapter 3 of this volume), easing multiple program viewing and channel scanning for program selection.

RCDs AND THE TELEVISION INDUSTRY

Grazing, "zapping" (using RCDs to avoid commercials), and "zipping" (avoiding commercials by rapidly scanning recorded programming) are means by which the audience exerts control over television programming and, by extension, the television industry. As can be seen from the "Mercury Theatre" example, the audience's desire for and exertion of control have existed since the advent of broadcasting. As such, the increased level of audience control resulting from the diffusion of RCDs can be seen as consistent with historical patterns of the relationship between media outlet and user.

From a television programming and advertising industry perspective, the use of RCDs is a subversive activity in that it allows the user to move easily from one programming source to another. As such, the promotion of RCDs has been from the manufacturing sector of the television industry (see Benjamin, Chapter 2 of this volume; Klopfenstein, Chapter 3 of this volume), which originally saw the device as a premium product enhancement for top-of-the-line television sets. Although all manufacturers eventually offered RCDs with their sets, the only television set manufacturer who initially saw the television RCD as a tool for zapping and program grazing was Zenith. Zenith's long-time leader, Eugene McDonald, who was attempting to gain government regulatory approval for the company's Phonevision pay-per-view television system from the late 1940s through the 1960s, was convinced that advertising would "ruin" television (Bellamy 1988). Zenith's promotion of the RCD, then, can be seen as part of a strategy to hurt commercial television by allowing the audience to avoid advertising. However, as in the case of the radio RCD experiments (see Benjamin, Chapter 2 of this volume), early television RCDs failed to gain substantial penetration in the marketplace due to their cost and limited applicability in a time of limited television channels.

The Television Oligopoly

The limited number of television channels was the result of federal regulatory policies that allowed for a mixed VHF/UHF system. This resulted in a broadcast system dominated by CBS and NBC (and eventually ABC) with essential control over the major portions of their local affiliates' schedules. The economic behavior of the three major networks has been described as an oligopoly that resulted in similar behavioral (i.e., market conduct) patterns in areas such as management and operations, programming, promotion, and relationship to the advertising industry (Bellamy 1992; Gomery 1989; Picard 1989).

One of the primary market conduct results of the network oligopoly was the conceptualization of the television audience as basically passive. This belief was applied in programming strategy through an emphasis on the flow of viewers from one program to another through scheduling ploys such as hammocking a new or weak program between two successful programs, and a concentration on mass-appeal and "inoffensive programming." What media critics derided as bland and unchallenging "least common denominator" programming was celebrated and utilized by the networks through "theories" such as Klein's Least Objectional Program (LOP) (Klein 1978). The theory was that the audience, rather than being motivated to watch television because of a desire to seek out specific content, could best be captured by the show that it objected to least. Although Klein presented his LOP theory somewhat facetiously (something completely missed by many communications scholars), his belief that the audience "watches television rather than programs" was undoubtably a major strategic element in the network-dominated television industry.

As long as the television industry was dominated by the network oligopoly, there was little way for a viewer to exert any control in her/his relationship with the audience except to avoid watching television—an option chosen by very few Americans. With the minor exceptions of limited-appeal public or educational television and independent television in a few large markets (with schedules primarily consisting of off-network programming), U.S. television and the network/affiliate system were the same.

Changing Relationship of Television User and the Industry

The existence of the network oligopoly does not prove the theory of the passive audience. In fact, the diffusion of alternative means of program delivery and control beginning in the 1970s made clear that this was not the case. As Bellamy (Chapter 14 of this volume) argues, the move to a deregulation mode in the federal government under the prodding of the existing television oligopoly led to a new level of control on the part of the audience—a result clearly not foreseen or intended by the existing television industry.

The enhanced power relationship of the user to the television medium (which parallels the movement of much mass communication research to the uses and gratifications perspective) primarily is the result of the diffusion of three "new" television technologies: cable, VCRs, and RCDs. Of importance to the understanding of the increase in audience control is the fact that these technological innovations diffused at the same time and are in fact highly interdependent. The FCC's promulgation of the Cable and "Open Skies" decisions in 1972 was crucial to the diffusion of cable television. Although the 1972 Cable decision was highly restrictive (*Cable TV report* 1972), it did set consistent parameters for the spread of cable services to urban areas. Of no less importance to the cable industry was the "Open Skies" decision, which deregulated the domestic use of communication satellites (*Domestic communication* 1972). This decision was the catalyst for the development of cable networks—a near financial and technical impossibility with landlines and microwave delivery. Although much cable programming is controlled, scheduled, and structured like traditional broadcast television programming (and in many cases *is* off-network product), the ability of cable to provide programming flexibility for the user and to offer some specialized "narrowcast" services (e.g., CNN, C-SPAN, MTV) gave the audience a wide range of non-network viewing options.

Cable, RCDs, and Audience Flow

Because many conventional program scheduling strategies, such as block programming, hammocking, and tent-poling, are based on assumptions of substantial audience flow, any reduction in the lead-in or inheritance effects between programs has important implications for broadcast and cable programmers and promoters. Scheduling strategies of the past may be losing effectiveness in the era of remote controls and plentiful cable options. Some industry-related research has examined the relationship between increasing remote control penetration and cable television program selection. Using Webster and Wakshlag's (1983) Model of Program Choice as a starting point, Walker (1988) and Davis and Walker (1990) documented the impact that easy channel changing, facilitated by remote control devices, has had on the audience flow between network programs. The results for network (ABC, CBS, NBC) programming have been inconsistent. Walker found that inheritance effects declined for network series between 1979 and 1982, but Walker and Davis documented an increase between 1985 and 1988.

The implications of increased remote control penetration for traditional broadcast networks and stations are also significant. Remote control use is positively related to cable viewing (Ainslie 1989), suggesting that the remote control has contributed to the decreased audience shares experienced by broadcast networks in the 1980s (Bellamy and Walker 1990b). Cable networks and independent stations have expanded program options, and the RCD has made those options substantially easier to review and select.

VCRs, RCDs, and Advertising Avoidance

Even more important than cable to the increase in audience control is the diffusion of the videocassette recorder (VCR), complete with RCD. While the VCR was similar to cable as a programming conduit (through the rental of pre-recorded tapes), it also allowed the user to restructure her or his television viewing environment through time-shifting. With a VCR, the viewer was no longer restricted to the rigid scheduling methods of the networks or local stations. VCR users could watch programs in the sequence that they found most appealing, watch two programs scheduled opposite one another, and, most ominously for the television oligopoly, "zip" through the commercials on recorded programs (Secunda 1990).

This ability to zap or zip through undesirable programming and advertising was a major byproduct of the rapid diffusion of VCR and television RCDs in the 1980s and 1990s. As the manufacturing industries overcame the problems of haphazard and unwieldy performance that had plagued earlier RCDs through a movement to digitally based systems, and as most U.S. set manufacturers moved out of the United States (where they had little incentive to support the existing domestic television oligopoly by hindering the diffusion of new technologies), RCDs quickly became a standard feature of television sets and VCRs (see Klopfenstein, Chapter 3 of this volume).

The explosive growth in remote control penetration has received considerable attention in the advertising community (Fountas 1985; Frank 1984; Kaplan 1985; Mermigas 1984) and some study by advertising scholars

(Eskin 1985; Heeter and Greenberg 1985a; Levy and Gunter 1988; Yorke and Kitchen 1985). One of the more recent lines of academic and industry research in television is the contribution of cable, VCRs, and RCDs to the phenomena of zapping and zipping. This is because the commercial television industry can no longer "guarantee" a relatively captive audience to the advertising industry, which grudgingly pays higher rates for commercials that consumers can more easily avoid. Indeed, zap-proof programming and advertising, exploiting more action-oriented, unusual, and eye/ear-catching techniques, have become growth areas in the television industry.

THEORETICAL ISSUES

In addition to industry concerns, the user control offered by remote control devices and changes in viewing behavior that result from that empowerment have implications for several long-standing mass communication theories, including uses and gratifications, selective exposure/avoidance, play theory, and theories based on limited content choice such as cultivation theory, agenda setting, and demassification. Ultimately, the "clicker" may produce greater changes in mass communication theory than in the increasingly RCD-sensitive television industry.

Uses and Gratifications

The audience activity central to the uses and gratifications approach is clearly connected to RCD behaviors. At minimum, the physical activity of the RCD-equipped viewer is manifest. As the degree of control the viewer has over the medium increases, the potential for new sources of gratification appears.

The first job for researchers is to identify the unique gratifications obtained from RCD use. As Rice (1984, 80) notes in his general analysis of new technologies, "Research aimed at understanding human benefits from new media should focus on the unique strengths of each medium; rather than only on how they compensate or substitute for more natural media linkages." Encouraged by new technology scholars such as Rice and Williams, Phillips, and Lum (1985), survey researchers (Walker and Bellamy 1991a; Walker, Bellamy, and Traudt, Chapter 8 of this volume; Wenner and Dennehy, Chapter 9 of this volume) have identified six to seven specific motivations for RCD use. The gratifications in these studies have centered around the RCD's ability to increase the value of cable television, to enable audiences to avoid unpleasant aspects of viewing, and to control the viewing of others. These gratifications have, in turn, been related to background attributes including demographic, personality, and media use variables.

Selective Exposure and Avoidance

Selective exposure and avoidance are long-standing concepts in mass communication research (Katz and Lazarsfeld 1955; Klapper 1960; Zillmann and Bryant 1985b). Media audiences are seen as frequently selecting material that confirms their beliefs, values, and attitudes, while rejecting media content that conflicts with these cognitions. Although selective exposure/avoidance may influence media consumption, the form of a particular medium increases or decreases the probability of selective exposure/avoidance.

For example, print media can be randomly accessed, but television, until recently, was a more restrictive medium. As Hsia (1989, xx) notes, a "glaring drawback of the broadcast media is that no broadcast program allows random access, because they must be sequentially presented in accordance with schedules. With newspapers, readers can read the last page first and they can also skip, stop, and restart reading at their own will." However, VCRs and RCDs have changed television's accessibility. Viewers with RCDs are more likely to randomly access the various channels available to them (Bryant and Rockwell, Chapter 6 of this volume), while VCRs allow viewers to record broadcast and cable programming, which can be played back at any time and in any sequence. The RCD allows viewers to zap more than just commercials.

Indeed, uses and gratifications research (Walker and Bellamy 1991a; Walker, Bellamy, and Traudt, Chapter 8 of this volume; Wenner and Dennehy, Chapter 9 of this volume) has found that the selective avoidance of unpleasant stimuli, including politicians, political ads, news reporters, and others, is an important motivation for RCD use. These studies show that selective avoidance is significantly related to RCD use. Perse (1990, 693) speculates that the channel changing induced by RCDs may strengthen the audience's resistance to persuasive messages: "increased channel changing coupled with lower attention may weaken media impact. It may be that the higher levels of channel changing may be a sign of an obstinate audience not likely to be affected by media content." Obstinance may increase with each click of the clicker.

Play Theory

William Stephenson's (1967) play theory of mass communication argues that most researchers have ignored one of the most important reasons for media consumption: the enjoyment that comes from "communication pleasure." Stephenson contends that our first reaction to a communication phenomenon, such as the RCD, is to treat it as something potentially harmful, rather than to see it as an extension of our ability to play with the medium. Thus, the disturbances brought about by RCDs to advertisers (zapping) and family life (selfish grazing) are emphasized, rather than the benefits of the technology to the individual.

However, media consumers gain pleasure from the manipulation of media content as well as the content itself. Audiences often "play" with a medium before carefully attending to it. Thus, Stephenson, writing more than a quarter century ago, reported:

Most people on picking up a weekly magazine like *Life* or *Look* first skim or scan it, skipping from page to page, looking at the pictures first, examining the headlines and captions; nothing is read thoroughly. Only later, if they return to the magazine, or if a feature article has attracted them, do they settle down to serious reading. The initial and usual interaction is one of "milling" around, as people do aimlessly and yet pleasantly at a fair, a shopping center, or at the seaside promenade. All of this is "pure play attitude." (151)

Indeed, Ruotolo's (1988) recent typology of newspaper readers includes one group, scanners, who derive their primary pleasure from this "hop, skip, and jump" style of reading. The RCD transforms television into a browsers' medium as well. This playful approach to television is exhibited by the RCD grazer (Ainslie 1988) who may change the channel hundreds of times during an hour's viewing. Lavery (Chapter 15 of this volume) provides a description of one such chaotic television escapade. Play theory implies that the grazer's enjoyment comes not just from the images encountered but from the control he or she has over those images (see Wenner and Dennehy, Chapter 9 of this volume). The communication-pleasure that had been reserved for print and that Stephenson saw as part of the mature pattern of newspaper reading has come full force to television. A recent industry study (Arrington 1992) suggests that at any one time 23 percent of all viewers are "restless" grazers, practicing one of the new viewing styles of the 1990s (Walker 1992).

Limited Choice Theories: Cultivation and Demassification

As an RCD-activated audience makes more use of cable's diverse viewing environment, theoretical approaches such as cultivation analysis, which are based on assumptions of a limited and homogeneous symbolic environment, seem due for revision (Webster 1989a). RCDs may not increase the total amount of time spent viewing television, but their presence does increase the number of different sources viewed (Bryant and Rockwell, Chapter 6 of this volume). As such, they make the full variety of cable programming readily accessible to viewers. Exposure to a greater variety of entertainment and information sources may decrease both the cultivation and agenda-setting impact of television.

Cultivation theorists (Gerbner and Gross 1976; Signorielli and Morgan 1990) contend that television's "function is, in a word, enculturation"

(Gerbner and Gross 1976, 175). Heterogeneous representations in the symbolic world of television become the source of much information about society. Heavy television viewers develop perceptions of reality that are closer to the quantified reality uncovered in content analyses of network television than to the reality found in social statistics. Television is the only source of information many people have about a wide variety of subjects: "How many of us have ever been in an operating room, a criminal courtroom, a police station or jail, a corporate board room, or a movie studio? How much of what we know about such diverse spheres of activity, about how various kinds of people work and what they do—how much of our real world has been learned from fictional worlds?" (244).

Some cultivation critics (Bryant 1986; Webster 1989b) have argued that the increasing penetration of cable television and VCRs has weakened the major foundation of cultivation theory: the limited diversity of network television. Although network shares are still substantial, especially in prime time, the inroads made by cable television, independent stations, and VCRs are substantial and growing. The RCD offers no new sources of diversity, but it does facilitate the use of the available variety. Grazers flipping channels every few seconds are likely to encounter cable channels that they would never have sought out willfully. Many such encounters quickly end, but others bring new sights and insights to the viewer. The active grazer may learn about the courtroom from Court TV as well as from "Matlock," about the operating room from medical programming on Lifetime as well as from reruns of "St. Elsewhere," and about jail from "Cops," an HBO behind-the-scenes documentary, and "In the Heat of the Night." Cable television brought choice, but the RCD made it easier for viewers to be choosy.

Demassification

The escalating choice brought about by cable television and other new communication technologies, and greatly assisted by RCDs, is also seen by many scholars as leading to the demassification of media. Webster (1989b) argues that cable, satellites, and VCRs have three characteristics: programming is diverse, programming is correlated with channels, and channels are differentially available. These characteristics have lead to audience fragmentation and polarization. Similarly, Rogers (1986) asserts that audience segmentation in the mass media is one of the most important social impacts of the new communications technologies. Indeed, one industry critic (Donnelly 1986) sees new communications technology as fragmenting America, bringing on the "Confetti Era, when all events, ideas, and values are the same size and weight ... when ideas and experiences float down like cheap confetti" (182). A consequence of such fragmentation may be a reduction in the media's ability to set the public agenda.

METHODOLOGICAL ISSUES

Most previous research has used survey research to measure remote control use, grazing, commercial avoidance, and multiple program viewing. The difficulty of accurate recall of such quick and frequent behaviors is self-evident and common to studies of new telecommunications technologies (Webster 1989a). Few active grazers could recall accurately how many times they used a remote control during the previous hour of viewing, much less during the previous day. Thus, survey researchers have relied on relative scales ("never" to "very often"), rather than asking for specific frequencies of RCD use. Clearly, other methods of measurement should be explored. We concur with Williams, Rice, and Rogers's (1988, 13) call for a variety of approaches to the study of new media: "As for methodology, we take the position . . . that the new media researcher should understand and take advantage of alternative research designs, including use where appropriate of multiple research methods or 'triangulation.' "

To our knowledge, this is the first book-length volume of research on the RCD-use phenomena. We feel an obligation to present a series of "state of the art" studies that will enable the reader to see both the breadth and depth of the many scholarly approaches to the study of an important new technology. We invite you to "graze" (but not to "zap") these studies, which we hope will allow you to better understand the impact of RCDs on both mass communications research and the changing television industry. We are confident that you will find answers to some of your questions, and we are equally confident that you will formulate new and unanswered questions that will be the impetus for further thinking and research.

STRUCTURE OF THE VOLUME

Chapters 2 and 3 provide the historical context for the development and diffusion of the remote control device. Louise Benjamin provides a narrative history of the RCD based largely upon primary source materials, emphasizing the importance of Zenith in the development and promotion of the RCD. She also discusses the early experiments in radio RCDs, illustrating the surprisingly long-standing search for control of electronic media. Bruce Klopfenstein's study is a detailed examination of the diffusion of RCDs in an industrial context. His chapter presents data that enable us to contextualize RCDs as an integral part of a rapidly changing television industry.

Chapters 4 through 7 apply a variety of methodological tools to the question of how and how often individuals use the RCD. Nancy Cornwell and her colleagues provide detailed baseline data on RCD use. The researchers content analyzed 122 hours of videotaped home viewing, precisely recording grazing, multiple program use, and commercial avoidance (zapping and zipping). Their results raise questions about the accuracy of survey items measuring RCD use. Paul Traudt concentrates on the phenomenology of the RCD experience through interviews with and an analysis of the videotaped viewing episodes of a group of RCD users. He provides a finely detailed analysis of how individuals use the RCD in their everyday life. Jennings Bryant and Steven Rockwell report the results of an experimental study that demonstrates how variations in an RCD's capacity and in viewer gender and personality can affect both channel changing and program choice. They demonstrate how changes in the technology lead to critical shifts in the empowerment of RCD users. An experimental methodology is also employed in the study by Carrie Heeter, Kak Yoon, and James Sampson. These authors review the dynamic nature of the RCD technology, reminding us that the RCD of today is only a "dumb remote." They anticipate a world with "program viewing agents" that automatically scan the available channels, searching for programs to satisfy our video desires. Their experiment shows the impact that one RCD feature can have on RCD use.

As the concept of an active audience is key to the study of the RCD, Chapters 8 and 9 apply a uses and gratifications perspective as a means of following up previous RCD research (Bellamy and Walker 1990a; Walker and Bellamy 1991a). Jim Walker, Rob Bellamy, and Paul Traudt use a sample of adult users to present baseline information on the motivations for grazing behavior and as a means of seeing if there are differences in the motivations for adult RCD users as contrasted to college students. Lawrence Wenner and Maryann Dennehy expand upon this descriptive gratification research. Using a transactional model, they employ a hierarchical design to assess the relative influence of demographic, psychological, and technological variables on the "gratifications of grazing."

Chapters 10 through 12, similar to the studies of individual use in Part II, apply different methodological tools to the question of RCD use in group viewing situations. Kathy Krendl and her colleagues use a multiple-methods approach as a means of responding to the limitations of self-report measures and the lack of research on how children use new technologies (including the RCD). Their employment of trained observers to monitor actual family viewing patterns provides us with several interesting and important insights into "real life" televisual behavior. Gary Copeland and Karla Schweitzer employ survey research to study the relationship between family communication patterns and RCD use, finding that attributes of the family member who controls the RCD relate to differences in overall family functioning. One of the assumptions of most popular media accounts of RCD use is that men and women use the RCDs in different ways. Elizabeth Perse and Douglas Ferguson employ a survey research design as a means of testing these assumptions. In doing so, they integrate the varying theories that have been advanced to explain gender differences in society.

The increased power of the television user through the use of RCDs and other "new" technology is having a major impact on the structure, conduct, and performance of the television industry. Chapters 13 and 14 attempt to map and explain some of these changes. Susan Eastman and Jeffrey Neal-Lunsford (1) detail the changes in television programming and promotional strategy resulting from the widespread use of the RCD, and (2) present the results of a survey of television executives on how they envision the RCD affecting their operations. Eastman and Neal-Lunsford's finding that a sub-stantial number of local television executives do not appreciate or even recognize the impact of the RCD does not bode well for the future of the over-the-air, advertiser-supported television industry. Rob Bellamy's chapter is an attempt to contextualize the diffusion and impact of RCDs (and other technologies) on audience "empowerment" as part of a continuum of con-trol in the relationship between television providers and users. He explains how the new level of audience empowerment, while a "reality" in certain respects, also serves as an excuse for continuing the shift of the costs of television service to the user and the resultant disenfranchisement of large segments of the population.

Although several chapters provide critical views on the advent of the RCD, Chapters 15 and 16 are the explicit critical capstones of the volume. David Lavery employs a reading of one of his RCD-induced viewing episodes as the centerpiece of a discussion of the cultural aspects of what it means to be "remote." His examination of the mythic status of the RCD is a natural lead-in to Bruce Gronbeck's chapter. Gronbeck provides a fitting final perspective on the impact of RCDs and other "new" technologies by absorbing them into the myth of Persephone. He wisely cautions us to temper our excitement (i.e., our "technoromance") with the RCD by recalling the Western myths of technological change.

There you have it: a collection of studies and essays that employ historical methods (Chapters 2 and 3), empirically based recorded observations of viewing behavior (Chapter 4), a qualitative research paradigm (Chapters 5 and 10), experimental research methods (Chapters 6 and 7), survey research (Chapters 8, 9, 11, 12, and 13), and critical analyses (Chapters 14, 15, and 16) to the study of remote control devices. Graze and enjoy.

2

At the Touch of a Button: A Brief History of Remote Control Devices

Louise Benjamin

Once novelties, remote control devices (RCDs) have become a way of life: a means of easily accessing the vast array of video and audio services. They are considered integral components of any advanced audio or video system. By mid–1992, nearly 96 percent of all color television sets and all video-cassette recorders sold in the United States had remotes (*Industry Sales* 1992) and the consumer had begun using the "universal" remote, which links several units to one overall control device (Brown 1988; Fleischmann 1990; Sweeny 1989).

Remote controls and their convenient tuning capabilities have become so much a part of American life that users rarely think of them unless they happen to have thrown them out with the Sunday paper. Today's systems offer useful, simple, clear, and convenient commands. The desire for such control over programming has been a part of the American quest for ease and convenience in selecting entertainment and information sources ever since the early days of radio. Americans have long aspired to tune in favorite programs quickly and to avoid unwanted programming and commercials (Walker and Bellamy, Chapter 1 of this volume).

RADIO AND THE DESIRE FOR REMOTE CONTROL

The search for remote control began soon after radio's commercial inception in the 1920s. Consumers wanted control over a program's volume and in choosing the programming they wanted to listen to or avoid. Early devices, about the size of a two-pound box of chocolates, were developed in the late 1920s by Kolster to allow a listener some command over the radio from the comfort of an armchair (Tuning the radio 1930). Instead of getting up to change the station when the listener wanted to switch programs or when an announcer began delivering an ad for a particular product, the listener "merely pushes a button and immediately the unwanted station disappears and another one is immediately tuned in to the desired volume" (Tuning the radio 1930).

The majority of the early control devices worked through a small, slow-speed electric motor attached to a control cable running (usually under the rug) from the armchair to the set. The motor was geared to a condenser shaft and equipped with stops so that it turned only so far when any individual button on the control box was depressed (Tuning the radio 1930). Other models in the late 1920s and early 1930s consisted of small control boxes and speakers installed in various rooms. Flat ribbon cords under rugs connected the radio set system to several control positions, such as an armchair, the dining table, or the bedroom. From each control position an individual could turn the receiver on or off, switch as many as four loud-speakers on or off, and automatically tune to eight stations (Radio or record 1933).

These early devices had serious limitations. For instance, what happened when one wanted to go back to a station, or if the motor turned just a little too far either way? What happened if the station deviated slightly from its assigned wavelength? To help overcome these problems, devices were offered with two buttons, one to make the motor turn slightly to the left and the other to make it turn right. By the mid–1930s, these early remote controls provided visual alignment meters and tone controls so that stations could be tuned quickly and sound reproduction could suit the acoustics of any room (New methods 1934).

A 1937 RCA model lauded its ease of use and its refined, tasteful features. "Tune your radio electrically from your armchair," the introductory ad read. The model could "be attached to any RCA Victor radio with Electric Tuning at small cost. The compact control unit, in a Bakelite case, can be placed on the arm of your favorite easy chair or an endtable. Inconspicuous, ribbon-like electric cable connects [the] control box to [the] radio and lies flat, under the rug. [An] attractive cover conceals [the] buttons when not in use" (Sarnoff 1937).

Primitive as these designs were, they worked. But, often their costs added more to the price than people were willing to pay in the Depression years (Sarnoff 1937). In addition, the characterizations of "automatic tuning as being an invention in the same class as that produced by the man who developed an automatic hat lifter" helped prevent their rapid adoption (Tuning the radio 1930).

However, predictions in the 1930s agreed that RCDs were inevitable— someday. In fact, one 1933 article noted that the devices could be used "to distribute the sound parts of talking movies and television" as well as radio or phonograph music (Radio or record 1933). So, while the cost and awkwardness of the devices prevented their adoption in the 1930s, optimism ran high concerning their eventual use. The advent of World War II halted any developments on radio remote control until the late 1940s, and by then attention to in-home entertainment devices included television as well as radio.

TELEVISION REMOTE CONTROL

As television developed in the early 1950s, the search for remote control of both radio and television continued. One means of cutting undesired commercials out of radio music programs was devised. The gadget discriminated between speech and music so that when speech began, the device cut off the sound from the speaker. After the speech ended, the device automatically turned the sound back on. But, singing commercials and light opera caused the device to silence the signal (Kill that commercial! 1950), so other, more sophisticated devices were sought to control unwanted programming and commercials on both radio and television.

The "Blab-Off" soon followed. This hand-held device featured a 20-foot cord that was attached to a television loudspeaker. One click of the switch turned the sound off but left the picture on so the viewer could tell when the unwanted sound material, usually an ad, had ended. Another click of the switch brought the sound back on. Its inventor, an advertising executive, noted that the $2.98 Blab-Off allowed "the TV fan [to] select the advertising he wants to hear, and he can get away from the commercial he dislikes" (Walker 1953).

Such sound control mechanisms did not give viewers control over changing programs from a remote location. In 1952 authors of articles in *Popular Science* (Baldwin 1952) and *Radio & Television News* (Gottlieb 1952) sought to overcome this deficiency by instructing their hobbyist readers how to make a simple, mechanical remote control device for under ten dollars. Much like early radio tuners, these mechanisms used a small motor and three gears to tune the station-selector switch. Controls also allowed viewers to turn the set on and off, to control the volume, and to adjust the contrast. Such instructions may have been useful for the mechanically inclined, but the majority of set owners did not rush to make their own remote controls.

By 1955, set manufacturers were providing wired remote controls, both in-set and as attachments. With some, such as the "Remot-O-Matic," skill was needed to keep from stopping between channels or overshooting the desired channel (Remote controls 1956). It and others such as the "Tun-O-Magic" could turn a set on or off and switch channels from a remote location. The "Tun-O-Magic" consisted of a cylindrical control attached to a 20-foot cable. Channels were switched by pushing a button on the top of the unit, and a switch on the unit's side permitted the receiver to be turned on or off (Remote control 1955). However, a major problem with these RCDs was breakage or damage to the wire between the control unit and the set (Buchsbaum 1955). Similar problems existed with the Zenith "Lazy Bones," the first remote marketed by Zenith. The clumsiness of the wires outweighed their convenience (Adler 1992).

Other systems, such as Zenith's "Flash-Matic," sought to overcome the problems caused by the wires through the use of a series of photoelectric cells and light beams. In this system a beam of light aimed from a small, pistol-like flashlight hit one of the four corners of the television screen. After the beam was turned on, the light could be directed to the appropriate corner of the screen, so the viewer could perform a number of functions: turn the set on or off, rotate the tuner back or forth, and mute the sound, presumably during commercials or to talk to someone in the room. Lack of cables and the ability to use the control unit from anywhere in the room were advantages of this device (Remote Control 1955).

Drawbacks included sensitivity to ambient and incident light, which performed the remote functions when the viewer did not initiate them. A manual sensitivity control was designed to minimize this problem (Buchsbaum 1955), although it did not eliminate it. Another major disadvantage was that consumers had to remember which corner of the screen performed which function. The functions were not easy to recall, and people constantly complained that they hit the wrong corner—so the end result was not what they had intended (Adler 1992).

In response, another wireless system (which never made it past the drawing board) was conceived. The system incorporated a radio signal that was beamed to a receiver in the set. Although the radio waves worked well, the waves had the unfortunate side effect of controlling not only the owner's set but that of the neighbors as well (Johnson 1986). Because the technology at that time relied on vacuum tubes, not integrated circuits, it was impractical to construct different circuits or different codes for each set. Consequently, use of radio waves was an unrealistic solution to the "Flash-Matic's" problems (Adler 1992).

With Zenith's development of the "Space Command" in 1956, wireless remote control devices became practical. The "Space Command" operated through ultrasonic waves and was the brainchild of Zenith's Robert Adler. Adler was among a team of Zenith engineers and scientists who gathered in the office of the chief engineer in 1955 to receive the mandate of Zenith's founder and president, Eugene F. McDonald, to work on a dependable RCD that consumers would purchase. McDonald was adamant that unless viewers could somehow circumvent commercials, the ads would kill television (Adler 1992; Johnson 1986). Consequently, "the Commander," as he was known to his subordinates, charged his engineers with finding a workable device that fulfilled three criteria: It had to be wireless, hand-held, and have no extraneous energy source—neither battery nor electrical cord (Adler 1992).

The Zenith sales force was unyielding on this last point. In the mid–1950s batteries were used in only one instrument, the flashlight. No transistors or battery-operated toys existed, so people were not used to replacing batteries in gadgets. When the flashlight batteries died, people would replace them because they would see no light emission. But the Zenith sales people feared that because no one could see a remote control cease operation, once the battery died, the remote would be considered a piece of non-functioning junk. Sales reps feared that if the device was perceived as "junk," customers would abandon Zenith products. Consequently, the sales force wanted no remote control that relied on batteries (Adler 1992).

Faced with these challenges, the engineers began discussing ways to use sound to achieve McDonald's goals. Some did not like the idea of using loud noise emissions to initiate the functions; others thought it would be difficult to develop a mechanism that would use sounds that could not be duplicated by other household devices or produced by the television set itself. At this point in the meeting, Adler suggested that ultra high frequency (UHF) sound be used. UHF sounds were so high that neither people nor dogs could hear them, and they also would not penetrate walls as radio waves did (Adler 1992). After a "feverish" amount of work, Adler's research team was ready to show McDonald a prototype. After the demonstration the Commander exclaimed, "We've gotta have it. We've gotta have it." Then, according to Adler, "All hell broke loose." Everybody ended up working nights in order to get the device in general circulation (Johnson 1986).

In June 1956 the Commander's dream materialized and was in production. The entire unit, retailing for $399.95, was introduced as "Space Command Television." The model introduced a remote control with a simple, four-button operation: on-off, channel up, channel down, and a mute button that "shut off the sound of long, annoying commercials" (Johnson 1986). The control box consisted of four short aluminum-alloy rods of slightly different lengths, each adjusted to vibrate at a certain frequency. When a control button on the top of the box was pushed, a small hammer struck the end of the rod, producing the signal that activated the desired control on the set (Adler 1992; Remote control 1956). The signals were effective up to 40 feet from the set (Burgi 1988).

The company claimed that other ultrasonic waves would not affect the controls because they were sensitive only to a tone set at exactly the right frequency and lasting for a specified, electronically measured period of time, about two-tenths of one second (Adler 1992; Spracklen and Desmares 1956). However, this claim was not completely accurate. Jingling coins or keys or even the bouncing chain around a pet's neck triggered these ultrasonic devices (Adler 1992; Prentiss 1977). Despite these drawbacks, other manufacturers began trying to copy the ultrasound device and still others began making battery-operated devices (Adler 1992).

By Christmas 1956, both Admiral and Zenith were marketing television sets with RCDs. Admiral's wired unit could be attached to most sets. After initial adjustments were made, each time the automatic tuning device was activated it would advance in a clockwise direction, past non-operating channels, and stop when an operating channel was reached. The unit was activated either on the set or by a hand-operated wired remote control device. The switch had twelve positions and was mounted on a printed circuit board; each position corresponded to a VHF channel. Each of the circuits could be opened or closed to adjust for all of the channels. If a circuit was opened, the device would stop on that channel; closed, it would not (Sheneman 1956).

By the end of 1957, a variety of wired, wireless, hand-held or chair-side devices was on the market. All TV sets then being manufactured had some provision for remote control, and in the majority of sets the controls were wire-connected motor-relay devices. In tuning stations, most of these units used motor-turned tuner shafts that turned in one direction. If the set was on Channel 7 and the viewer wanted to turn to Channel 5, he or she would have to turn up through Channels 8, 9, 10, and so on. Mechanisms were still needed to turn the dial both ways (Buchsbaum 1957). In addition, for the larger wired devices, ways of connecting to multiple points in a house were promoted so viewers moving from room to room could have the sound follow them (Peters 1958).

While the 1960s brought some changes in remote control devices, it was not until the late 1970s that advances were made from the ultrasonic or wired principles (Klopfenstein, Chapter 3 of this volume). Complicating matters for remote control manufacturers during the late 1960s and early 1970s were the now-mandated in-set UHF tuners. When remote control devices were first manufactured, both they and the TV sets usually did not provide for the UHF spectrum. After Congress passed the All Channel Receiver Act in 1962, new devices were needed to tune in these stations.

One device, built by Jerrold Electronics of Hatboro, Pennsylvania, had a channel selector of twelve buttons, each corresponding to one of the twelve VHF channels. A press of a button automatically brought in that VHF signal. To view a UHF channel, the viewer hit a selector switch that changed the buttons to a UHF range of six channels—Channels 14 to 19, for instance. The viewer could then preset one of the six UHF channels permanently or fine-tune a channel each time the button was pressed. Generally, viewers chose the former option, because the Federal Communications Commission (FCC) usually allotted the UHF frequencies so that a certain geographical area had only one UHF channel. However, like many of the early RCDs, the Jerrold device lacked mobility. A 26-foot cable attached the selector to the set (A practical remote 1978). Improved, non-wired devices were still sought.

By the mid–1970s, infrared beams began to replace the ultrasonic wave as the triggering mechanism for remote control in a system developed by General Electric. The beams worked well because they relied on developing microchip technology and used digital codes that could provide as many functions as desired. Infrared beams made remote control much more reliable and were immune to outside interference. The viewer entered a channel number or a command to change volume on a keypad. A particular binary coded decimal (BCD) digital code was stored in an integrated circuit chip inside the remote control transmitter. By pushing the "enter" button, the viewer actuated three infrared LEDs (light emitting diodes), pulsating them on and off to duplicate the code. On the set, an infrared detector picked up the pulses of light, decoded them, and performed the keyed-in function (Adler 1992). Color, hue, brightness, and contrast could also be adjusted with this remote control (Prentiss 1977). In addition to these developments, by the mid–1970s one set, made by Heath, was programmable: The set automatically changed the stations to preselected programs (Free 1977).

With the advent of home VCRs in the late 1970s and early 1980s, remote control devices developed further. Early devices were usually attached to the VCR with wires and could be used to locate program material rapidly or to speed up commercial breaks when playing back off-the-air tapes. Timers and tuners allowed individuals to record in absentia. Most of the early recorders with RCDs were priced around $1,000 (Berger 1980).

VCR owners, of course, often use their machines to record programming for later viewing (i.e., time-shifting). In the later viewing, VCR owners were zipping through station breaks and advertising much of the time (Ainslie 1985). Advertisers reacted with alarm, and discussion focused on how to "zap-proof" a commercial. Suggestions ranged from blurring the distinctions between programming and ads to "cliff-hanging," a process in which a program (especially a live show) would announce a special contest winner or product "right after a word from the sponsor" (Ainslie 1985).

In the early 1980s, remote controls moved from TV and VCR use to other purposes. GE touted its "Homenet" command post, which allowed individuals to perform a variety of household tasks without moving from their easy chairs. With "Homenet," the remote control was linked to a computer-based home controller. It could change channels and list choices for chores on the screen. Lights could be turned off or on, doors could be locked, the oven turned on—all at the touch of a button (GE's bid 1983).

The remote-controlled home had been achieved. The TV set could be attached via remote control to a myriad of devices: stereo sound, VCRs, giant screens, cable, and satellite. The remote control often made it possible to switch from one to another easily (Banks 1984). By the end of the decade, devices were on the market that allowed individuals to control lights or room temperatures and to start their cars on a cold winter morn (Cole 1988; Sweeny 1989; Fleischmann 1990).

By 1987, wireless remote control devices were marketed for sets that had not originally carried remote control devices. Hand-held infrared remote control units allowed viewers to scan sequentially up and down through the channels or access a particular channel directly. Fine-tuning, volume control, and volume mute were also advantages of the devices. Costs for these control units were often high—as much as $400. So, it often made more sense for an individual to purchase a new set equipped with remote control for around $500 (Equipment reports 1987).

By the end of the 1980s, over 66 million households were equipped with remotes. An estimated 34 percent of viewers with remotes switched channels at least half the time when a commercial came on (Burgi 1988). Today, remote control operators graze freely within the video fields, zapping commercials and checking out other channels—a process that is not looked upon favorably by advertising executives, television programmers, and audience measurement firms. The changes in viewing habits brought about by the diffusion of RCDs are unlikely to abate, as RCDs have become a permanent part of the electronic media scene.

3

From Gadget to Necessity: The Diffusion of Remote Control Technology

Bruce C. Klopfenstein

Research inquiries related to the impact of new communication technologies tend to lag behind the initial diffusion of those same new technologies (Rogers 1986). Although television remote control devices (RCDs) have been available for more than thirty years, research on the uses and impacts of these devices on viewing behavior is far more recent.[1] The publication of this volume is testimony to the importance currently attributed to the RCD phenomenon.

The purpose of this chapter is to catalog the diffusion of the RCD in the United States. A television remote control is understood to be any device that allows the user to operate some or all of his/her television set's functions from channel selection to audio bass control without the viewer having to physically touch the set itself.

As simple as this research task might appear, statistics on the historical diffusion of remote controls have proved to be quite elusive. Television set remote controls went from an optional accessory with color TVs in the 1970s to an integral part of nearly all sets by the 1990s. Disaggregate data on the household presence of these remotes are not generally available. Television RCDs do not have their own unique standard industrial classification (SIC) code, a seven-digit number assigned by the U.S. Department of Commerce for tracking production and/or sales data. Television remote controls generally have been considered an accessory rather than a separately identified product.

Understanding the increase in the number of remotes is further complicated because their diffusion has been influenced by the growth of three parallel technologies: television receivers with remotes, videocassette recorders (VCRs) with remotes, and cable television with remotes. Aggregate data on estimated RCD penetration may reflect the presence of one or more of these remotes, each of which significantly contributed to the complete diffusion pattern.

DIFFUSION OF INNOVATIONS APPLIED TO THE RCD

One theoretical approach to understanding the reasons behind the widespread adoption of a new technology like the RCD is the diffusion of innovations perspective. A wealth of research in this field has identified four characteristics that generally are related positively to likelihood of innovation adoption: relative advantage (the degree to which an innovation is perceived as being better than what it displaces), compatibility (consistent with the adopter's values, past experiences, and needs), trialability (ability to "try out" before committing to adoption), and observability (visibility of the innovation benefits). The fifth innovation characteristic, complexity (perceived difficulty of use), is negatively related to adoption probability (Rogers 1983). The first television RCDs also may be thought of as a discontinuous innovation (Engle and Blackwell 1982) in that there was no analogous technology that they replaced. More recent wireless remote controls are continuous innovations in that they represent incremental improvements over previous wired remotes.

Perhaps implicit in the innovation attributes is another important one: cost. Cost (whether manufacturing cost or retail price) affects trialability, relative advantage, and compatibility. Price acceptability among potential adopters will influence the growth curve of a new communication technology (Carey and Moss 1985; Carey 1989). The historical growth of RCDs is presented in the general context of innovation attributes and cost.

Growth of Television Set Remote Controls

Zenith claims to be the inventor of the first successful wireless television remote control through the efforts of engineer Robert Adler. Zenith president Eugene McDonald reportedly feared losing television set sales to viewers who were put off by television commercials (Taylor 1992). This early remote used ultrasonic sound and was commercially available by 1957 in a TV console that sold for a list price of $395. Four functions were featured on the RCD: on-off, channel lower, channel higher, and sound mute (Johnson 1986; see Benjamin, Chapter 2 of this volume, for a more complete history of remote control technology).

An RCA executive contends that remote controls were originally marketed with expensive console television as a means of differentiating models and brands from one another (Donahue 1992). This brings up another issue in the diffusion of RCD technology: technology push versus demand pull. The notion that viewers want to control the TV sound to avoid commercial announcements is an example of expected demand pull from those potential adopters. Including the RCD as a method of product differentiation is an example of pushing the technology on the market with less explicit emphasis on adopter needs.

Television Digest, an authoritative industry newsletter, reported that the remote control was the most popular television accessory by 1960 (April 18, 1960, p. 15). This notoriety was short-lived. By 1962, no remote control diffusion bandwagon materialized. Although reliable data were not available, the percentage of sets sold with a remote control was estimated to be around 10 percent in 1961 and 9 percent in 1962 (April 9, 1962, p. 11).

Television Digest concluded that three factors were stopping any increase in the sale of sets with remotes. High price was identified as the biggest obstacle to RCD adoption. The additional set cost ranging from $40 to $100 was noted to be especially high in light of the simple remote control unit consumers could visibly see. The costly circuitry within the television set itself that worked with the remote was not seen. This is an example of the innovation attribute, observability, that is directly related to likelihood of adoption.

The second reason cited by *Television Digest* for the slowdown in remote diffusion was a decline of the expensive monochrome console segment of the television set business. Finally, there was a general lack of effort by distributors and dealers to sell remotes. The future of set remotes was predicted to be in portable sets that would often wind up in the bedroom (April 9, 1962, p. 11).[2]

Remote control penetration slowed in the early 1960s as consumers began to substitute color television sets for monochrome sets. The percentage of monochrome sets sold with remote declined between 1965 and 1968. Color sets with remotes were about $100 more expensive than comparable color sets without remotes in that same period. By early 1968, *Television Digest* (April 15, 1968, p. 7) reported that only 1 percent of monochrome sets had remotes while 6.3 percent of color sets did (numbers represent factory sales).

The earliest figures uncovered for sales of television sets with remote controls date back to 1965, and they represent color television factory sales. These data show that 1 in 20 color television sets included remote controls, and that percentage did not begin an upward trend until 1974 (see Table 3.1). Because the remote control added to the cost of the set, remotes were limited to the more expensive color sets that were available up to that time. By 1981, a high-end Zenith model cost $40 more with a remote than without one (*Television Digest,* June 1, 1981, p. 11).

These data cannot be directly translated into figures for household penetration of TV RCDs for two important reasons. First, these are factory sales data rather than consumer sales data. Second, raw sales data do not

Table 3.1
Color Television Factory Sales (Domestic and Import)

Year	Total	With Remote	% With Remote
1965	2,693,634	134,416	4.99
1966	5,011,816	267,132	5.33
1967	5,562,651	298,237	5.36
1968	5,971,992	335,713	5.62
1969	5,744,395	272,265	4.74
1970	4,729,222	209,623	4.43
1971	6,255,733	271,505	4.34
1972	7,825,192	458,202	5.86
1973	9,660,038	497,204	5.15
1974	8,015,820	552,352	6.89
1975	6,651,452	506,554	7.62
1976	7,893,784	796,881	10.10
1977	9,397,435	1,148,048	12.22
1978	10,497,004	1,611,782	15.35
1979	10,042,495	2,157,218	21.48
1980	11,459,413	3,131,758	27.33
1981	11,769,281	3,826,898	32.52
1982	11,673,195	4,180,351	35.81
1983	14,309,696	5,453,777	38.11
1984	16,266,307	7,105,279	43.68
1985	17,144,648	9,201,805	53.72
1986	18,767,958	11,031,050	58.78
1987	19,330,375	13,136,009	67.96
1988	20,216,355	15,258,360	75.48
1989	21,706,124	17,983,434	82.85
1990	18,658,103	16,577,065	88.85
1991	20,808,396	18,540,395	89.10
1992*	5,402,874	5,141,744	95.17

* Sales as of April, 1992.

Source: Electronics Industries Association (1992). *Electronic Market Data Book*. Washington, D.C.

reveal which households were adopting their first RCD. In other words, the cumulative number of households with a remote cannot be determined directly by sales statistics alone.

As seen in Table 3.1, more than half of *all* color television sets sold by 1985 had remote controls. By 1988, three out of four color sets sold came with a remote control, and that increased to 90 percent by 1990. With sales having plateaued at about 20 million units per year by 1990, an estimated 40 percent or 8 million were first color set purchases (Electronics industry association 1991). Given the data in Table 3.1, approximately 85 percent of these first color sets (6.8 million) would have had remotes in 1990.

It is difficult to know directly how these first adopters of color TVs would have affected the overall household penetration rates of remote controls. It seems reasonable to suggest that the last households to adopt color television would have also been among the last to subscribe to cable television or

Table 3.2
Television Stations on Air

Year	Total VHF & UHF	Annual Growth
1962	603	4.14%
1963	625	3.65%
1964	649	3.84%
1965	668	2.93%
1966	699	4.64%
1967	737	5.44%
1968	785	6.51%
1969	837	6.62%
1970	862	2.99%
1971	881	2.20%
1972	906	2.84%
1973	927	2.32%
1974	938	1.19%
1975	953	1.60%
1976	960	.73%
1977	972	1.25%
1978	982	1.03%
1979	998	1.63%
1980	1011	1.30%
1981	1038	2.67%
1982	1065	2.60%
1983	1106	3.85%
1984	1138	2.89%
1985	1197	5.18%
1986	1235	3.17%
1987	1290	4.45%
1988	1362	5.58%
1989	1403	3.01%
1990	1442	2.78%
1991	1459	1.18%
1992	1481	1.51%

Source: Adapted from *Television and Cable Factbook No. 60* (1992). Washington, D.C.:
Television Digest.

adopt a VCR. The probability of RCD presence in the home increased with the presence of either a VCR or cable television.

The utility of early remote controls was also limited by the number of broadcast television stations on the air. While volume controls might be useful, the utility of having a "channel changer" is clearly related to the number of channels available in a person's home. As of 1962, 563 stations were on the air, up from 511 five years earlier. By 1969, 672 stations were on the air, with the number increasing almost 50 percent in ten years to 992 stations. As seen in Table 3.2, however, the growth of stations on the air from 1974 to 1980 grew slowly on an annual basis. Today there are approximately 1,500 television stations on the air with another 200 already authorized (*Broadcasting & Cable Market Place*, 1992, p. E-110). Even in those households not subscribing to cable, the more broadcast channels

Table 3.3
Growth in Cable Television 1978–91

Year	Basic CATV Homes	CATV % TV HH	Systems	TV HH
1978	13,000,000	17.7%	3875	73,307,000
1979	14,100,000	19.0%	4150	73,901,000
1980	16,000,000	21.1%	4225	75,793,500
1981	18,300,000	23.7%	4375	77,251,800
1982	21,000,000	25.8%	4825	81,496,500
1983	25,000,000	30.0%	5600	83,462,600
1984	30,000,000	35.7%	6200	83,971,800
1985	37,900,000	43.9%	6668	86,400,000
1986	40,640,600	46.5%	7737	87,476,100
1987	43,529,660	49.2%	7836	88,420,260
1988	46,662,200	52.4%	8413	89,120,260
1989	50,699,000	55.6%	9010	91,192,205
1990	54,871,330	59.0%	9621	93,065,870
1991	55,786,390	60.6%	10,704	92,040,450

Sources: Electronics Industries Association (1992). *Electronic Market Data Book*. Washington, D.C.; Electronics Industries Association (1987). *Electronic Market Data Book*. Washington, D.C.

available to be viewed, the greater the relative advantage of the remote control over manual tuning.

Growth of Cable Television Remote Controls

Early cable television systems simply brought weak, over-the-air signals to subscribers, often using the actual frequency of the broadcast signal. Cable added to the number of channels available in the home. Thus, cable proliferation is another independent variable that added to the utility of the television RCD. When cable began to expand to include satellite-delivered programming in the latter part of the 1970s, cable down-converter boxes with remote controls began to diffuse. The number of channels again increased with the onset of satellite-delivered services beginning with HBO and television superstations like WTCG (now WTBS).

As seen in Table 3.3, the number of households subscribing to cable television grew from 13 million in 1978 to almost 56 million in 1991. Without question, the diffusion of cable television brought with it an increase in the household presence of cable converters and RCDs. Not all cable households had a remote control, however. No data on cable-only remote penetration were discovered in industry sourcebooks or via direct contacts with the Electronics Industries Association, the National Cable Television Association, and various individual consumer electronics manufacturers.

The increase in cable channel capacity by number of subscribers between

Table 3.4
Channel Capacity of Existing Cable Systems by Subscribers

Year	Channel Capacity			
	< 30	20-29	13-19	> 13
1983	49.56%	23.88%	4.31%	22.25%
1984	58.27%	21.43%	2.87%	17.43%
1985	65.49%	12.44%	2.31%	19.77%
1986	73.66%	16.30%	1.63%	8.41%
1987	78.29%	14.27%	1.31%	6.12%
1988	82.86%	11.86%	1.02%	4.26%
1989	88.24%	8.99%	0.62%	2.15%
1990	90.87%	7.41%	0.38%	1.35%
1991	93.36%	5.36%	0.31%	0.97%
1992	95.24%	3.86%	0.24%	0.66%

Sources: Adapted from Television & Cable Factbook, Nos. 51–60 (1983–92). Washington, D.C.: Television Digest.

1983 and 1992 is demonstrated in Table 3.4. The more cable channels in the home, the higher the probability of RCD presence for 3 reasons: (1) A cable converter (whether supplied by the cable operator or included in a "cable-ready" set) is needed to display more than Channels 2–13 (Weinstein 1986), and many converters came with a remote control; (2) households with a cable-ready television set also were more likely to have an RCD with that set; (3) an increase in the number of channels increased the need to change channels and, once again, the utility of the remote.

In technical terms, cable remotes did not change rapidly from the mid- to late 1980s. This is because manufacturers like General Instruments' Jerrold had to make them backward compatible with existing, older cable converter boxes already in use. More focus was given to ergonomic design than technological advancements (Dawson 1989).

Cable operators had significant economic incentives to promote converter box remote controls in the home. First, converter boxes generally were necessary for subscribers to get the additional basic cable channels progressively made available in the 1980s. Second, converter boxes were specifically necessary for subscribers to receive otherwise scrambled pay services including pay-per-view. Third, many cable operators charged a premium to subscribers with remotes. A typical RCD might cost the cable operator $6. With just a few months's revenues, the device would be paid off and the additional fees padded the operator's income (Dawson 1989).

As has been noted, cable-ready television sets came with downconverters built into the set. Offering remote controls with these sets especially made sense in that they were higher cost sets already and were sold with the expressed capability of being used with the larger number of channels offered

Table 3.5
Factory Sales of Cable Compatible Color Television Receivers, United States,
1981–87

```
--------------------------------------------------------------------
   Year            Cable Compatible Units         Cable Compatible
                   ------------------------          % of Total
                   With Remote      Total
--------------------------------------------------------------------
   1978                *           402,000                *
   1979                *           475,000                *
   1981                *         1,361,000                *
   1982                *         2,035,000                *
   1983                *         4,091,321                *
   1984                *         7,615,791                *
   1985            8,355,292    11,336,420            73.70%
   1986           11,100,569    12,005,415            92.46%
   1987           11,701,846    11,701,846           100.00%
   1988           10,748,210    10,748,210           100.00%
   1989            9,759,772     9,759,772           100.00%
   1990           10,118,839    10,118,839           100.00%
   1991           10,591,209    10,591,209           100.00%
   1992**          4,775,512     4,775,512           100.00%

   *Unknown
   **Sales as of April 1992.
--------------------------------------------------------------------
```

Source: Electronics Industries Association (1992). *Electronic Market Data Book*. Washington, D.C.

by cable television. By 1984, more than half of all color television sets sold were cable-ready (see Table 3.5).

As reported in Table 3.3, cable penetration in 1983 was estimated to be 30.0 percent of U.S. television households. Nearly 50 percent of those households had at least 30 cable channels available (Table 3.4). Thus, about 15 percent of households subscribed to a cable system with at least 30 channels available. The vast majority of these households would have had a converter box and remote, and/or a cable-ready television set with a remote. The Kagan newsletter has estimated addressable converter boxes as reported in Table 3.6. The total number of cable remotes, of course, is higher than this subset of cable households.

Not all cable subscribers had a cable RCD. Some obsolete cable systems did not offer them (although that number clearly diminished in the 1980s). Other cable subscribers may have opted not to lease them from operators who offered RCDs for an additional fee. The larger the number of channels, however, the greater the relative advantage of having a cable RCD. A reasonable estimate of the number of households with a cable RCD would seem to be the number of homes subscribing to cable systems with at least 30 channels. The assumption that all subscribers to such systems had a cable RCD inflates the actual figure for that segment of cable subscribers. That bias is offset by the assumption that no one subscribing to systems with 29

Table 3.6
Cable TV Addressable Converters in Service

| Date | Units in Place |

March 31, 1984	3,400,000
September 30, 1984	4,700,000
May 31, 1985	5,900,000
May 31, 1986	7,400,000
May 31, 1987	9,200,000
June 30, 1988	11,400,000
September 30, 1989	13,800,000
September 30, 1990	15,500,000
September 30, 1991	17,100,000

Source: National Cable Television Association Citation of Paul Kagan Associates' *Cable TV Technology Newsletter*.

channels or less had a remote. By 1992, virtually all cable subscribers had access to 30 or more channels (Table 3.4) and, therefore, a cable RCD.

Growth of VCR Remote Controls

Like that of cable television, the role VCRs played in the diffusion of RCDs into the home is both critical and complicated. The VCR remote allowed viewers to change channels while viewing whether or not a working TV set remote control device was present in the household. A 1988 report by the Gallup Organization called attention to this phenomenon (*Television Digest*, June 27, 1988, p. 14).

The diffusion of VCRs in the United States is reviewed by Klopfenstein (1989). Early VCRs introduced in the late 1970s were designed to receive standard broadcast channels and did not include wireless remote controls; some did have wired remotes. Following the example in television sets, VCR marketers saw remote controls as one way to differentiate high-end VCR models. It may further be argued that remote controls represented higher user utility to VCR users than television users for both programming and viewing purposes.

Understanding the role played by VCR diffusion in household RCD diffusion is complicated by limited data on VCR decks sold with remotes. The VCR, however, clearly played an important role in overall RCD diffusion. By 1987 when VCRs were at the peak of their U.S. diffusion, all VCR decks sold came with a remote (see Table 3.7). Of VCRs sold in 1985, 85 percent were purchased by first-time buyers (Zahradnik 1986). Given the data in Table 3.7, this suggests that about 7 million households bought their first VCR with a remote in 1985. Between 1985 and 1987, more than 31 million VCRs with remotes were sold.

Table 3.7
VCR Deck Penetration Growth

Year	With Remote	Total	EIA Estimated HH Penetration	Nielsen Estimated HH Penetration
1978	*	402,000	NA	.3%
1979	*	475,000	NA	.5%
1980	*	805,000	NA	1.1%
1981	*	1,361,000	NA	1.8%
1982	*	2,035,000	NA	3.1%
1983	*	4,091,321	NA	5.5%
1984	*	7,615,791	10%	10.6%
1985	8,355,292	11,336,420	NA	20.8%
1986	11,100,569	12,005,415	30%	36.0%
1987	11,701,846	11,701,846	40%	48.7%
1988	10,748,210	10,748,210	52%	58.0%
1989	9,759,772	9,759,772	61%	65.0%
1990	10,118,839	10,118,839	68%	NA
1991	10,591,209	10,591,209	74%	70.2%
1992**	4,775,512	4,775,512	77%	73.3%

*Unknown
**Sales as of April 1992.

Source: Electronics Industries Association (1992). *Electronic Market Data Book*. Washington, D.C.

OVERALL HOUSEHOLD PENETRATION OF REMOTES

Surprisingly little data are readily available on the cumulative growth of U.S. household RCD penetration. The data presented in the preceding sections indicated that the three feeder technologies for overall remote control penetration all were accelerating by about 1986. In that year, more than 11 million VCRs were sold with a remote (90 percent of all VCRs), a nearly identical number of TVs with remotes were sold (representing more than 60 percent of all TV sets sold in 1986), and cable television penetration reached 47 percent. An increasing percentage of television sets was also equipped with quartz-synthesized computer tuning, making direct (as opposed to sequential) selection of a wide variety of channels possible (Electronics Industries Association 1986).

A survey of 1,000 households by the Gallup Organization for the Electronics Industries Association found that RCD penetration had reached 63 percent by mid–1988. The results ironically revealed that single TV set households were more likely to have a remote control than multi-set households. The report also pointed out that the 63 percent figure might include some who use the VCR remote for television channel changing, apparently due to the way respondents were asked about remote presence (*Television Digest*, June 27, 1988, p. 14).

Nielsen has some incomplete data on household remote penetration. Niel-

Table 3.8
Nielsen and CONTAM Remote Control Penetration Estimates

Year	Nielsen Remote Penetration as of January 1*	CONTAM/SRI Remote Control Estimates**
1981		16%
1982		20%
1983		24%
1984		30%
1985	29%	38%
1986	42%	47%
1987	51%	57%
1988	66%	
1989	73%	
1990	77%	
1991	78%	
1992	84%	

*Source: A. C. Nielsen, 1986–89; Nielsen Media Research, estimated from *Electronic Media*, April 27, 1992, p. 28, and *Broadcasting*, May 11, 1992, p. 52.
**Source: Cohen (1987).

sen data are reported as of January 1 of the listed year.[3] As depicted in Table 3.8, the Nielsen data are more conservative than RCD penetration data reported from another source.[4] Research supported by the broadcasting industry showed higher household remote penetration than Nielsen's estimates as seen in Table 3.8. The CONTAM (Committee on Network Television Audience Measurement) data show progressively greater annual increases in household remote penetration beginning in 1983.

The period of most rapid overall RCD diffusion appears to have occurred between about 1984 and 1988. During that time, remote penetration doubled from about one-third of television households to two-thirds. This coincides with the rapid diffusion of VCRs. VCR penetration also grew from about 10 percent to over half of television households from 1984 to 1988. From Table 3.7 it can be seen that nearly all VCRs sold in this period came with remotes. Assuming that most of these were also first VCR adoptions in the household, the VCR accounted for about 50 million new RCDs in television households in the five-year period.

Cable penetration and system capacity grew more gradually during the period of rapid RCD diffusion. Combining data from Tables 3.3 and 3.4, it can be determined that cable subscribers with at least 30 channels grew from 20.8 percent of television households in 1984 to 43.4 percent in 1988. Assuming that most households with at least 30 channels had a converter and remote, cable would have added about 40 million new household RCDs in that period. By 1992, however, all cable households still represented only about 60 percent of all television households. Because total remote penetration exceeded 80 percent of television households, cable does not represent the most important factor in total RCD diffusion.

Sales of color television sets with remotes also surged in the mid–1980s. Data from Table 3.1 indicate that nearly 56 million color sets with remotes were sold between 1984 and 1988. Unlike the data for VCRs and cable, however, a significant portion of these color set sales undoubtedly were second and third sets in the household (see *Trends in Viewing*, 1988, p. 4). Thus, these figures would translate into some smaller number of households with their first remote. It is difficult to ascertain whether VCRs or color TVs were more responsible for bringing RCDs into the living room. Cable's role in RCD diffusion may have been most critical in increasing the channel selection utility of the RCD.

Extrapolation of even the conservative Nielsen data in Table 3.8 suggests that remote control penetration should be about 90 percent of television households in 1993. Remote control penetration should be near 100 percent of TV households by the year 2000, as nearly all color sets now sold include remote controls and the life expectancy of a color TV set is ten years (Lilienthal 1986). RCD presence in the future television household seems assured, and one RCD may be all that is required.

Birth of the Universal Remote

One disadvantage of a "free" marketplace is the potential lack of technological standards.[5] Producers are free to design their own systems without regard to what others may be doing. In the case of remote controls, various manufacturers use different frequencies for communication between the remote unit itself and the device being controlled (whether cable converter, VCR, TV set, or audio unit). The result can be a coffee table holding a different remote for each consumer electronics device in the living room.

Universal remotes are designed to be programmed by the user to work with the technical specifications used by any remote manufacturer. The first universal remotes required users to program them by, for example, lining up and aiming a device's specific remote into the universal remote. The universal remote then "learns" the other remote's functions button by button. New universal remotes come with various manufacturers' command codes already programmed in the universal remote's circuitry (Remote controls 1991). Consumer studies indicate that the motivation to purchase universal remotes actually did not come from clearing up coffee table clutter; they served most often as replacement or second remotes (Seavy 1992b). Although about 80 percent of universal remotes sold were as replacements for old or lost remotes, more expensive new television sets included universal remotes (Seavy 1992d).

Many early (mid–1980s) universal remotes were both expensive and complex, having a multitude of buttons and functions from which to choose.

A price breakthrough on universal remotes eventually took place. Priced around $129 suggested retail in the mid–1980s, universal remotes were available by 1992 for under $20 (Seavy 1992c). Household penetration of universal remotes is expected to continue increasing due to their functional utility (and possible relative advantage over having one remote instead of several) as well as their adoptability as replacement remotes (Seavy 1992a). Sales of universal remotes were projected to be as high as 9 million units in 1993 (Dalton 1992). The less expensive universal remotes available by 1992 were also simpler remotes in that they provided consumers with relatively few functions (e.g., power, channel selection, and volume selection) (Seavy 1992d).

The newest universal remotes reflect what promises to be a future trend in the near term. A universal remote introduced in late 1992 included a small liquid crystal display (LCD) window similar to that used on electronic calculators. The manufacturer claimed that the user would no longer need an instruction book to program the remote. Commands on the LCD would lead the user through setup instructions one step at a time. This unit initially carried a list price at the high end of the remote market ($129.95) (Universal to unveil 1992).

FUTURE REMOTE CONTROL TECHNOLOGIES

Remote control devices are now standard pieces of equipment for television sets, VCRs and much home audio equipment (Remote controls 1991). Remotes clearly have gone from an optional accessory to an integral controlling unit for increasingly complicated consumer electronics products. The remote has become the subject of considerable research and design efforts among product manufacturers. Yesterday's remote operated in a simple environment of viewing options limited in both program (software) availability and display (hardware) options. Tomorrow's remote promises simplicity in design and complexity in functions.

As noted by Heeter, Yoon, and Sampson in Chapter 7 of this volume, future remote controls will be both simpler and more intelligent. One truism in the advancement of circuit technology is that the capabilities of computer chips continue to *increase* while both size and cost continue to *decrease*. This trend is expected to continue into the next century, allowing further miniaturization of increasingly sophisticated devices including RCDs (Markoff 1991).

Palm-sized remotes are already a reality, and voice recognition remotes are on the way. A California company has planned to begin shipments of its VCR Voice Programmer, a remote control–like voice recognition device that operates all VCR functions and can control TV sets and cable converter boxes. Priced at under $150, the 31-word vocabulary device reportedly can learn to recognize up to four different voices from up to 40 feet away (Seavy 1992d).

Assuming engineers continue to advance voice recognition technology, the need for remote control units may diminish as users simply command the desired component with two-step commands: the first addressing the component and the second the actual command (e.g., "VCR, rewind"). Future remotes using radio frequency (RF) rather than infrared can control devices from outside the room in which those devices operate. RF remotes are already used with home satellite TV systems (Dalton 1992).

Intelligent remotes like Gemstar's VCR-Plus allow users to control their equipment more easily. Still newer technologies under development promise to automatically change channels during commercials while viewing or delete them when recording. A survey by Backer Spielvogel Bates found that the concept of this intelligent remote appealed to about half the adults polled, with 70 percent of the 18- to 24-year-old segment indicating a propensity to buy one (Technology projections 1992).

RCDs being used in other applications may hold the key to future RCD designs. At GTE's Cerritos, California, fiber-to-the-home trial, a remote control with a small joystick is used to control options on one service based upon compact-disc-interactive technology. The joystick is located near the top of the remote and is controlled by the user's thumb to select menu items overlaid on the television screen (Emberson 1992).

A new remote design with its roots in the aerospace industry is part of an advanced home information technology trial in the Cascades housing development in a Virginia suburb of Washington, D.C. Bell Atlantic has chosen Selectech's AirMouse as the interface for viewers to select video and information services from pull-down menus on their television screens. The remote has only one button and is used to activate a menu overlay on the television screen. The user points to a menu selection and presses the button to choose it. One application using this interface allows users to select movies-on-demand by categories such as actor or director (McMahon 1992). The technology was originally designed to allow a fighter jet pilot to aim his weapons by moving his head (Hindus 1992). If this system is adopted by households in the Bell Atlantic trial, it could be the first step toward an icon-based personal computer metaphor for television interaction.

Other telecommunications technologies will work with remotes to allow viewers to select television programs more easily. InSight Telecast provides program titles, start times, and descriptions to subscribing cable systems. The interface also allows viewers to record programs with one push of a button (The smart TV 1992; Zenith gets 1992). Users can search for programs by type, title, or channel (*Television Digest*, May 4, 1992, p. 16). Unlike the VCR Plus system, InSight is a subscription service that uses the vertical blanking interval (VBI) to send programming information (Jaccoma 1992).

The probable convergent trends in future remote technology are trans-parency and intelligence. Future control devices are likely to be voice ac-tivated. Speech synthesis may guide the user through otherwise complicated menu screens for selection of viewing and/or recording options. Interfaces incorporating artificial intelligence will be able to seek out programs re-quested by the user and to suggest others. Users will have the technological capability to command their television sets to search for programs by various personal interest categories (i.e., format or genre, actor, director, etc.) for viewing-on-demand. The future user demand for this capability is more in doubt than the technological capability for accomplishing it.

CONCLUSIONS

The television remote control device was introduced in the 1950s as an expensive add-on to high-end console televisions but was generally rejected by the majority of television purchasers into the 1960s. The early strategy for remotes seemed to be that of supply-side technology push rather than demand pull.

By the 1970s, a confluence of factors coalesced in the U.S. marketplace to set the stage for the rapid adoption and diffusion of the wireless remote control device. The invention of quartz-synthesized computer tuning, the dramatic increase in the channel capacity of cable systems (and converter box remotes followed by cable-ready television sets), and the rapid diffusion of VCRs (most of which came with remotes by 1985) made the remote part of the typical living room.

Why did the remote control diffuse into American households? Did the remote diffuse because of technology push, demand pull, or some combi-nation of the two? It could be posited that the only people who had an inarguable, demonstrable need for an RCD for their television viewing be-fore the 1970s were the debilitated. Given the unreliability of early remotes, it would seem that the gadget aspect may have been part of the early appeal.

Returning to the general innovation characteristics that are related to adoption, some hypothetical conclusions can be suggested and further in-vestigated in future research, including empirical tests where appropriate:

- *Relative advantage*: The previous way to control a television set was by manually manipulating control knobs on the set itself. The RCD certainly held a large relative advantage in this respect. In the case of VCRs, menu-driven programmability with remotes presumably held significant advantage over early VCR timers. As the price of remotes came down, the perceived relative advantage may have gone up.

- *Compatibility*: This variable is difficult to comment on in a post hoc fashion. To the extent that the remote is a discontinuous innovation, it is not compatible with the way viewing had been done prior to RCD availability. Watching two or more programs at once, for example, was possible primarily through the availability of the RCD. The role of compatibility in RCD adoption could be addressed through a review of the RCD research literature.

- *Trialability*: There may have been little risk in experimenting with an RCD. Those who opted not to use it could have ignored it at little cost. The risks associated with early, more expensive remotes were probably considerably higher than with later remotes that became standard accessories with color televisions and VCRs in the mid–1980s.

- *Observability*: The remote control is observable. Its presence and functions seem to be easily visible to others and easily communicated to other potential adopters. This could be tested through a survey of remote adopters.

- *Complexity*: The first remotes were quite simple, but complexity of operation increased with remote diffusion in the 1980s. The current trend with universal remotes is back toward simplicity.

Price is another important factor in communication technology adoption and diffusion (Carey 1989). Cost was a key factor in the early history of the RCD. The functional utility of the RCD grew with the increased availability of channels and the need to control the viewing environment (e.g., use of the VCR) even as the cost of RCD technology came down. In other words, a decline in the RCD cost-benefit ratio may have crossed the threshold for consumer adoption in the 1980s. Cost became largely irrelevant by 1990 as VCRs and television sets came complete with RCDs, and universal (replacement) remotes were priced at less than $20.

One dichotomous way of looking at the diffusion of new communication technologies is to examine the question of technology push versus demand pull. In the early history of the RCD, television set manufacturers pushed the wireless remote technology onto the marketplace even though it had initially been rejected. By the 1980s consumer demand may have begun pulling RCD technology, as device control became important due to increased cable channel availability and the existence of VCR programmability.

This chapter has been limited to an analysis of the available diffusion data on RCD-related products. A more definitive answer to the reasons for RCD diffusion could be found through examination of the RCD's innovation attributes. It is hoped that this narrative has offered additional knowledge about how the remote control device went from being an accessory in the past to a virtual necessity today.

NOTES

1. The study of broadcast channel switching behavior could have begun with car radios. Although some commercial research on this topic was completed, little if any scholarly research on this topic is known to exist in the literature.

2. This prediction proved to be prophetic. *Television Digest* (March 16, 1981,

12) reported that the percentage of console model televisions with remotes passed that of portable televisions for the first time in 1980.

3. Nielsen data derived from a chart in *Electronic Media* (April 27, 1992, 28) show a slight RCD penetration decline between 1986 and 1987. It appears that this figure is in error. *Broadcasting* (May 11, 1992, 52) reported a similar chart based upon Nielsen data with a logical increase in RCD penetration between 1986 and 1987. The data for 1987 reported here are in line with those found in the *Broadcasting* chart.

4. Klopfenstein (1989) found inconsistencies between Nielsen VCR penetration estimates and those of other bodies. The Nielsen VCR numbers were also more conservative than those of other sources.

5. Lack of standards was also a key problem in the case of cable-ready television sets. Because there was no cable industry standard pay-television scrambling system, set manufacturers could not include the decoder in their cable-ready sets. The result was that cable-ready televisions and VCRs with their RCDs could not be used with cable if pay channels were included, much to the chagrin of many cable-ready adoptors (*Television Digest*, October 5, 1981, 11).

Part II

Individual RCD Use

4

Measuring RCD Use: Method Matters

*Nancy C. Cornwell, Shu-Ling Everett,
Stephen E. Everett, Sandra Moriarty,
Joseph A. Russomanno, Michael Tracey,
and Robert Trager*

Although cable television created a vast new electronic landscape, it is the remote control device (RCD) that has given viewers the ability to graze upon this new vista at will. However, despite the proliferation of RCDs, there is scant information about their use. A major limitation of previous RCD research is that it has relied on self-report measures, usually from college students. The exploratory study described in this chapter will determine whether recording RCD use in subjects' natural viewing environments elicits different results from self-report and other data gathering techniques.

There is little doubt that cable television, video cassette recorders (VCRs), and RCDs have changed the viewing environment (Ainslie 1989; McQuail 1987; Sims 1982). RCDs have been connected with masculine identity and desire for power (Bing 1990; Brandt 1989; Hirschman 1987). Others see the RCD as a form of control and creative expression. Gilbert (1989) noted that using the remote control frees the viewer from traditional restraints, making the RCD a tool by which to control the media environment. Ainslie (1988) suggested that the RCD is not just a vote against commercials or boring programs but a form of entertainment itself. The ease of viewing more than one program at a time may enrich the viewing experience (Lavery, Chapter 15 of this volume). Thus, semiologist and novelist Umberto Eco may be only partially joking when he says, "with a remote control, I can make the television into a Picasso" (Stokes 1990, 40). However, others including columnist George Will (1990) have dismissed the RCD as a diversionary toy.

PATTERNS OF REMOTE CONTROL USE

Since its introduction in 1955 (Benjamin 1989), the RCD has entered almost 70 million households (Ainslie 1989; Gilbert 1989). As the popularity of RCDs has grown, use patterns have emerged that have been labeled "grazing," "cruising," "flipping," "multiple-program viewing," "zapping," and "zipping," among others. Some researchers believe that this chaotic use of media content is nothing new, since readers often flip through magazines and newspapers (Stipp 1989). Reviewing the data from a survey published in 1989 by *Channels* magazine, Stipp (1989) suggested that grazing may be concentrated in the first one to five minutes after a viewer begins watching and during a few commercials. According to Stipp, most people choose a program and watch it to its conclusion. Others suggest that a permanent change in viewing is imminent; people are less likely to watch programs from beginning to end (Moriarty 1991). Thus, stations and networks that respond to audience erosion with the wrong strategies, such as narrowcasting, may not survive (Selnow 1989).

Some patterns of RCD use among certain types of viewers have emerged from recent research. One early study of RCD use, relying on self-reported data, was undertaken by *Channels* magazine (Ainslie 1989). The study was based on telephone interviews with a national sample of 650 adults. The research revealed that in 1988, 75 percent of Americans had remote controls, 54 percent subscribed to cable television, and 46 percent had both cable television and a remote control device. Of those who had RCDs, 67 percent said they grazed frequently and another 13 percent said they grazed sometimes. Half the respondents who used the RCD frequently or sometimes said they changed channels during programs. People who had remote controls watched programs on a greater variety of channels (9.1 channels) than people who did not have remote controls (5.5 channels). Likewise, people who reported frequent remote control use watched more channels (10.1 channels) than people who rarely used their remote controls (6.4 channels). Forty-eight percent of the respondents said they enjoyed television less when they grazed; 41 percent said they enjoyed television the same or more when they grazed. When viewers switched from a program, almost half found a second choice program and continued to watch it. However 45 percent continued to switch throughout the program. The most common reasons for stopping on a channel while grazing were that (1) something caught the viewer's eye, or (2) the viewer saw something familiar. The study concluded that about 30 percent of the adult television viewing population could be considered heavy RCD users.

Heeter and Greenberg (1985b) studied RCD use in five surveys conducted over two years. More than 1,500 adults and 400 children were questioned. The studies showed that men were more likely than women to use RCDs (sometimes by a 2 to 1 margin), and young adults were more likely to use

RCDs than older adults.[1] No use differences were found due to income, education, marital status, household size, or number of children in the family.

Heeter and Greenberg (1988b), Greene (1988), and Ainslie (1988; 1989) also found that gender affected patterns of RCD use. According to Heeter (1988b), women were more likely than men to agree that other viewers often interrupted their viewing by changing channels. Men were more likely to change channels (1) when they first turn on the set, between programs, at commercials during a program, and during a program, (2) to see what else is on, (3) to avoid commercials, and (4) because of boredom. In addition, men were more likely than women to (1) watch more than one program at a time, (2) change channels and stop at the first program they liked, and (3) change channels out of numerical order.

COMMERCIAL AVOIDANCE AND RCD USE

Most research into RCD use has focused on whether viewers are attempting to avoid commercials. Yorke and Kitchen (1985) found that 66 percent of viewers eliminated some commercial breaks by pausing the VCR while recording programming or by fast-forwarding through commercials already recorded. Kaplan (1985) suggested that much more channel changing occurs during the several minute gap between programs than occurs during programs or commercials within programs. Such gaps can be filled with continuous form programming such as MTV, CNN, and ESPN. Heeter and Greenberg (1988a, 41–42) found that 50 percent of "the cable subscribers surveyed generally do not even consider changing channels until the program they originally selected has ended.... The other 50% use commercial breaks as an opportunity to examine other program options, and half of them (24% of subscribers) will even change in the midst of program content, exhibiting the weakest program orientation and greater activity level while viewing."

There is some disagreement about the impact of zapping (switching channels to avoid ads) and zipping (fast-forwarding over tape-recorded ads) on commercial effectiveness. Stout and Burda (1989) suggested that zipping did interfere with the viewer's ability to process information, affecting product, brand name, and ad content recall. However, Greene (1988) pointed out that switching channels or fast-forwarding a videotape requires a viewer's attention to remain on the television set, whereas attention was more likely to waiver or be absent in an environment in which grazing does not occur.

More recent studies using methodologies other than self-report have attempted to refine earlier descriptions of RCD use. One pilot study using observers placed in the subjects' viewing environment reported that channel changes occurred twice as often during commercial breaks than during a program (Moriarty 1991). Initially, these results seemed similar to the previous research that found commercial avoidance to be a main reason for grazing. However, Moriarty's work also found that only 20 of the 50 commercial breaks observed stimulated a channel change. During the other 30 breaks, viewers let the commercials run, but their attention was often diverted to other activities until the program resumed. Moriarty concluded that viewer disinterest has a greater impact on commercial viewing than RCD use. The results of this pilot study are important because they show the relative impact of the RCD during the commercial encounter.

Nevertheless, RCD use still is perceived as a problem by advertisers, and there has been no shortage of suggestions on how to discourage the behavior. Montgomery predicted, "[W]e may see a further blurring of the distinctions between commercials and programs" (Ainslie 1988, 61). Gross (1988) also suggested targeting strategies that aim at specialized audiences, and "broadcaster-assisted roadblocks" that would "frustrate the flipper as he finds commercial material at every turn of the dial" (p. 97). He also suggested a move toward shorter commercials (even less than 15 seconds) or longer (5, 10, and 30 minutes) "infomercials."[2] Kaplan (1985) outlined tactics to hold viewers, including closing epilogues and previews positioned after closing credits, action sequences before opening credits, commercials that are integrated into programs, and a move toward more entertaining commercials. Another suggestion is to schedule mid-program breaks, as they are "far more likely to produce better audience viewing, perception and recall" than end-of-program breaks (Yorke and Kitchen 1985, 24).

LIMITATIONS OF PREVIOUS METHODOLOGIES

Common weaknesses in RCD research are reliance on self-report measures (Ainslie 1989; Heeter and Greenberg 1985b; Heeter and Greenberg 1988b; Walker and Bellamy 1991a; Wenner and Dennehy 1990) and university students (Walker and Bellamy 1991a; Wenner and Dennehy 1990). With self-reports, respondents do not always accurately remember their behavior. Also, self-report data are not as detailed and, because of their structural limitations, can reduce to simple descriptions more complex forms of behavior.[3] An additional concern with self-report data, especially in studies involving possibly multifaceted patterns of behavior, is that respondents are required to recall past events and extract from their memories interpretations of activities that may have been shaded by more recent experiences.[4] This recall can be subject to confounding factors such as primacy and recency effects, which, for example, may (1) cause a subject to more clearly remember the way he or she used the RCD the evening before completing a self-report form than the way it was used in earlier periods (Hovland and Mandell 1957), or (2) cause events to be distorted, merged, or oversimplified when reported. For example, a viewer switching between two sports events during an evening might recall a considerable amount of RCD use if asked the next day about his or her remote control habits, but might not take into consideration that the RCD was rarely used during evenings when situation comedies were watched.

The diary, commonly used in advertising audience research, reveals the drawbacks of self-reporting as a method of gathering data. Friedman (1989) found the diary method particularly inadequate for measuring the viewing options of cabled households, especially late at night and during low-rated or brief viewing periods. Self-reporters confused less-viewed news and music channels with the more prominent ones. Children's viewing and viewing of pay services, low-rated channels, and services viewed briefly also were underreported. Although underreporting is significant for some channels, overreporting of total viewing is also a problem (Mandese 1988). There are reports of diaries overestimating viewing behavior by 30 percent (Bechtel, Achelpohl, and Akers 1972).

To compare self-reports with actual viewing, Anderson (1985) used cameras and diaries to record television viewing behavior. He found that in his experimental group, records of the time spent with the television (a general measure of television viewing) were fairly accurate. However, records of estimated time looking at the TV (times when the viewer was attending to the television) were less accurate. More significantly, the diaries of the control group (for whom there was no camera recording the viewing behavior) appeared to contain more inaccurate and ambiguous records than the group filmed with a camera. This suggests that the camera's presence may have encouraged subjects to supply more detail about their viewing in the diaries, which further illustrates the distortions possible with self-reporting methods.

Besides filming, other methods of viewing measurement refrain from self-reporting. Two studies used computer-generated data. In Heeter, D'Alessio, Greenberg, and McVoy's (1988) study, all monitoring was done by wiring random samples of cable subscriber households to a computer located in a cable system's headend. The computer stored the time of each change, channel changed to, and household identification number. Similarly, Williams, Rice, and Rogers (1988) used computer-automated data collection.

Two recent studies employed observers, placed in the homes of viewers with whom they were acquainted, who recorded the frequency of RCD use during 45-minute periods (Everett 1992; Moriarty 1991). The observers also noted the viewers' activities concurrent with television watching, such as ironing, folding laundry, or reading. Everett found in her preliminary study that the frequency of RCD use was higher than other studies had reported. Additionally, in the interviews after the field observations, participants underestimated their RCD behavior that had just been observed and recorded. Moriarty found that RCD use occurred on the average of once every three minutes.[5] These studies suggest that viewers using self-report methods generally underestimate their frequency of RCD use.

While it would seem that gathering data on RCD use by electronic means

(Heeter and Greenberg 1988b) or by direct observation (Everett 1992; Moriarty 1991) would solve the problems inherent in self-report methods, each of these two techniques has its own limitations. The electronic method does not allow researchers to determine which member of a viewing group is using the RCD, only that it has been used. Further, the circumstances under which the RCD is used are not recorded, such as conversations leading to RCD use or disagreements over its use. These concerns are alleviated with direct observation, but the presence of observers may alter the viewers' normal RCD use patterns. Additionally, observers may not be able to accurately record complex RCD uses, such as switching among several channels in a very short period of time.

ELECTRONIC RECORDING OF VIEWING

The form of inquiry used in this study—installing cameras and electronic recording devices in the participants' homes to monitor their television viewing patterns and behaviors—has the advantages of (1) removing the influence of an observer, and (2) allowing for longer observation periods without observer fatigue.[6] It also creates a record that may be analyzed further as required. Certainly, electronic recording devices create their own form of intrusion into the naturalistic setting, and they do not allow researchers to query subjects immediately on their interpretations of situations. Until this study, recording devices had not been used in RCD research but had been used for other types of television studies (Collett and Lamb 1986; Anderson, Field, Collins, Lorch, and Nathan 1985; Lull 1982, 1980a; Anderson, Allwitt, Lorch, and Levin 1979; Bechtel, Achelpohl, and Akers 1972; Allen 1965).

Allen (1965) used a time lapse film camera in homes over a two-year period to gather data on television viewing. The camera shot one frame every 15 seconds, taking in the viewing area and the television set. He found that there were many activities concurrent with television viewing and, thus, subjects were often inattentive to television programming. Bechtel et al. (1972) used real-time video cameras and microphones with a small group of families in Kansas City, Missouri. They distinguished between subjects who were merely in the same room as the television set and subjects who were actually watching the television set. They found that diaries generally overreported viewing but accurately recorded the presence in the room of a family member. Anderson et al. (1985) used time lapse video equipment in 99 homes in Massachusetts, studying each house for 10 days. Wide-angle lenses took in the entire viewing environment, including the television. An image was taken every 1.2 seconds with equipment designed to turn on and off with the television set. Anderson et al. found that viewers were engaging in an assortment of concurrent activities varying with age, sex, temporal variations, and the viewing environment itself. He found that the concurrent activities tended to be highly predictable within families and highly variable between families.

RESEARCH QUESTIONS

The primary focus of this pilot study was to determine if the methodologies used in much of the RCD research have elicited accurate data. Most studies to date have used self-report methods or have gathered information through the presence of an observer where television viewing was taking place. The former approach results in underreporting of actual RCD use, while the latter may inhibit channel changing. We argue that use of cameras, microphones, and video cassette recorders secured inside wooden boxes and placed in television viewing rooms will allow a more accurate measurement of RCD use.

Using this more precise technology, the study addressed four elementary but critical questions:

1. How frequently do viewers use the RCD, graze or flip from program to program, and engage in multiple-program viewing (watching two programs simultaneously)?
2. Do male viewers use the RCD more than female viewers?
3. Do viewers use the RCD more during commercials than during programs?
4. How much do the figures obtained in this study differ from the results of earlier studies of RCD use?

METHOD

Sample Selection

A list of randomly selected telephone numbers for both the city and county of Boulder, Colorado, was generated to screen prospective participants. Callers identified themselves as part of the University of Colorado's Center for Mass Media Research, stated that they were conducting a study of how people watch television, and that households that qualified would be paid a nominal amount for their participation. The purpose of the screening interview was to insure that participants had cable television service and a cable converter box or type of television set with an LED or on-screen display of channel numbers. The screening questionnaire also gathered demographic information about the household. If the household passed the technological requirements and indicated interest in participating in the study, its telephone number was forwarded to the research team, which then arranged a time for the recording equipment to be placed in the home. Attempts were made to select, from the qualified households, an array of family types to yield the widest range of family viewing situations. The following households participated in the study: (1) two female roommates, both students at the University of Colorado; (2) a single, middle-aged, human resources professional female; and her son, a recent college graduate; (3) a single male electrical engineer; (4) a doctor; her spouse, a human resources manager; and their infant child; (5) a male architect sharing a home with a male food products broker; (6) a sales representative and his spouse, a receptionist; (7) a single female dental hygienist; (8) a male who works in advertising and his spouse; (9) a newspaper editor; his spouse; and their children, two and five years of age; and (10) an electrical technician; his spouse, a weaver; and their four-year-old male twins and a nine-month-old girl.

Procedures

The equipment was placed in each home for six days.[7] The cameras and VCRs were housed in the two cabinets, to make the equipment less obtrusive and to reduce the possibility of the equipment being inadvertently knocked over or damaged.[8] The VCRs were programmed to record from 5 P.M. to 11 P.M. each day, with each household providing 36 hours of electronic observation. In each household the equipment was set up in the room most commonly used for television viewing. A researcher returned to the house daily to check the equipment and replace videotapes. Data were collected from the first day, since previous research had shown that an acclimation period was not necessary.[9] Shortly after the equipment was removed from a subject's home, the participants were asked (1) further questions regarding their reaction to the presence of the equipment, and (2) detailed questions about their use of the remote control device.

Coding

In spring 1992, two graduate students in journalism and mass communication were recruited as coders. They were trained by two members of the research team during six hours of practice coding. Coding began in March, as soon as the recording from the first sample family was available, and continued until May 1992, a few weeks after the last family's viewing was videotaped.

Operational Definitions

An *RCD use* was defined as each time an RCD was used to change a channel, mute sound, turn the TV on or off, and the like. Grazing or multiple-program viewing or consisted of multiple uses. *Grazing* was operationalized as moving sequentially through three or more channels and staying on any single channel no longer than five seconds. The entire series of sequential channel-changing was defined as one grazing behavior. *Multiple-program viewing* was defined as moving back and forth between two channels at least three times during a period of five minutes. Although it consisted of several RCD uses, the entire sequence of channel changes was considered as one multiple-program viewing behavior. *Zapping* was operationalized as switching from a commercial at any point prior to its final three seconds. *Zipping* was defined as fast-forwarding through commercials when viewing a recorded program.

RESULTS

Nine adult males, six adult females, and one female child (nine years of age), who used a remote control at least once during the observation period, provided the data for this study. There were several members of subject households who did not use an RCD during the taping period, and their viewing times are not included in the analysis.[10] Cameras recorded the television viewing area in participants' homes for a total of 336 hours.[11] Of that time, television sets were turned on for 122 hours and 19 minutes. The total number of RCD uses for all participants was 1,255, an average of one use per 4.8 viewing minutes. If the viewing time is eliminated for the one subject family that did not use an RCD at all, the RCD was used an average of once every 4.4 minutes when RCD users[12] were in the television viewing room.[13]

RCD use differed slightly for males and females. The adult males in this study used the RCD on average every 5.7 minutes.[14] The adult females used the RCD on average every 5.2 minutes. Children rarely used the RCD in this study. Only one child, a nine-year-old girl, was recorded using the RCD, and her use was infrequent.

The videotapes also provided information on four common RCD behaviors: multiple-program viewing, grazing, zapping, and zipping. Grazing and zapping were the most common behaviors; the former occurred 112 times (an average of once every 53.8 viewing minutes) and the latter occurred 99 times (an average of once every 11.2 minutes of time viewing commercials).

Multiple-program viewing and zipping were far less common behaviors; the former occurred only five times during the study, and that was primarily with one subject who moved between CNN Headline News and CNN. Only one household used the RCD to "zip" six different times through commercials on recorded material.

The results indicate that the rate of RCD use is related to the television content. When the frequencies were weighted[15] to account for higher proportion of program compared to commercial minutes per hour, the RCD was more likely to be used during a commercial than during a program.[16] On average, the RCD was used every 10.0 program minutes and every 8.7 commercial minutes.

DISCUSSION

The pilot study used videotape recordings, without an observer present, to determine if data gathered through this methodology differed from that generated in self-report or observer-recorded studies. One difficulty in making these comparisons is the subjective nature of defining RCD use frequency in self-report studies. In many previous RCD self-report studies (Ainslie 1988; Bellamy and Walker 1990a; Heeter and Greenberg 1985b, 1988b; Walker and Bellamy 1991a), there was no indication of how many RCD uses constituted "frequent," "sometimes," or "rare" use. The categories of a 1 to 5 scale ranged from "almost always" to "almost never"; those of a 1 to 4 scale ranged from "very often" to "not at all." Data gathered in this study—actual frequency of use—are more precise but yield results that are not comparable with the earlier studies.

Two other studies (Heeter and Baldwin 1988; Kaplan 1985), using electronically generated data, did report average RCD use per hour. However, it is impossible to determine from these data whether the RCD use was confined to a single individual or was the result of more than one person changing channels. Additionally, in the average RCD use per hour calculated from these electronically derived data, it is assumed (possibly incorrectly) that RCD users were watching television. If subjects were, in fact, not watching television during part of the recorded time, then the electronically derived average RCD use would be underreporting actual RCD use. Thus, Heeter and Greenberg (1988b) reported that active RCD users ("zappers") change channels 6.8 times per hour, which is half the 13.6 RCD uses per hour reported in this study.

The data gathered in this study are closer to the frequencies found in studies using human observational methods than to those in self-report research. Moriarty's (1991) and Everett's (1992) observers found RCD use occurring every 3.5 minutes and 2.5 minutes on average, respectively. The differences between the Moriarty and Everett results and the finding in this study of an average use of every 4.8 minutes may be explained by the methodological differences. Moriarty and Everett observed the subjects for a single evening. They did not consider any variations over several days in viewing and RCD use, as did this study. Although there was great variation of RCD use in individual viewing sessions in this study—as little as one use in a 2.5-hour viewing session to as many as 109 uses in a 3.5-hour viewing session—these variations were averaged over 122 hours of viewing.

Our research did not find the distinct gender differences reported in other studies. Ainslie (1989), for example, reported that males used a remote control to "flip" through channels more often than did females. Heeter and Greenberg (1988b) reported that males were twice as likely to use an RCD as were females. This study found that females used an RCD only slightly more frequently (every 5.2 minutes) than males (every 5.7 minutes).

However, one female participant who was the sole occupant of her house-hold had an extremely high frequency of RCD use (every 2.6 minutes). When her RCD use is removed from the analysis, the RCD use by females drops to once every 9.9 minutes on average. This difference indicates that there may be an interaction between gender and individual/group viewing. The present findings suggest that one person usually controls the remote in a household. In households that included adult males and females, most often (but not always) the main RCD user was an adult male. In male-female group viewing situations, males used the RCD 77 percent of the time and females used it 23 percent of the time.

Many earlier studies have reported that a common reason for RCD use was to avoid commercials (Ainslie 1989; Heeter and Greenberg 1988b). The data this study collected on videotape confirm that channel changing is more frequent during commercials (every 8.7 commercial minutes) than during programs (every 10.0 program minutes). However, this study showed that participants watched most of the commercials shown during their view-ing periods, changing channels on average once for every seventeen 30-second commercial spots viewed.

Follow-up interviews revealed that participants in this study had some awareness of the recording equipment when it initially was installed in a home, but it faded rapidly. All participants reported that the equipment's presence did not alter their amount of TV viewing, the types of programs viewed, or activities and conversations normally carried out while viewing television. Participants reported that their RCD use was "normal" through-out the study, except for one male who indicated that for the first day or two he used the RCD less than normal because he "didn't want to appear like he was exhibiting stereotypical male behavior flipping around the chan-nels."

LIMITATIONS AND FUTURE RESEARCH

The results of this study indicate that videotaped data gathered over extended viewing periods reveal very accurate and detailed information about RCD use that often is missed in self-report studies and that may not be recorded in the necessarily limited data-gathering time frame of human observational methodologies. The quality of videotaped data, however, is dependent upon the quality and sophistication of the cameras, microphones, videotape recorders, and other equipment used in such a study. For example, wide-angle lenses would allow recording of a wider area in television viewing rooms, making it less likely that subjects would be out of camera range while still watching television and using an RCD. Future research should distinguish the time of the participants' presence in the room from time actually attending to television programming. It is likely that the RCD use per minutes of viewing time will continue to rise as the data become more discriminating.

This study was conducted with a purposefully selected sample (cable subscribers, primarily adults, owners of television sets with on-screen read-outs when a channel is changed) in a college town and nearby large city. Future research using videotape to gather data on RCD use should employ a more representative sample. To do so will require sophisticated equipment, perhaps including the ability to record channel changes onto a computer disc directly from the television set. Whatever technology is needed and the commensurate expense, the videotaping method is superior to others used to date in reducing measurement error. The self-report method is particularly suspect. Despite the benefits of a large, random sample, self-report survey data may not be accurate.

NOTES

1. Greene (1988) also found that men use RCDs more than women, but the difference was small. When respondents were asked if they had used the RCD the previous evening, 54.8 percent of the men and 50.7 percent of the women answered affirmatively.

2. Patzer (1991) found that 15-second commercials were 20 percent less effective than 30-second commercials.

3. For example, respondents reacting to a question asking why they use an RCD may be given only a list of several choices in which to fit their responses (such as boredom, avoiding commercials, and so on), when their reasons may have been different or more complex than the choices presented.

4. Gathering data through naturalistic inquiry may, however, cause investigators to interpret events differently than they would if subjects completed a questionnaire.

5. Moriarty said that this was a very gross indicator of overall patterns because some respondents never changed channels during the session and others were constantly using an RCD.

6. In naturalistic inquiry, the researchers do not attempt to manipulate the research setting. Therefore there are no "predetermined constraints on [the] outcomes" and the goal is to "understand naturally occurring phenomena in their naturally occurring environment" (Patton 1990, 40–41). As a result, studies based on a naturalistic approach may provide insights not available from studies using self-report, whereby phenomena are often studied in isolation from their naturally occurring environment.

7. This was done to make the observation as unobtrusive as possible. Earlier studies employed similar techniques (Collett and Lamb 1986; Svennevig and Weinberg 1986; Anderson, Allwitt, Lorch, and Levin 1979; Bechtel, Achelpohl, and Akers 1972; Allen 1965).

8. Two wooden cabinets housed the cameras, microphones, and recording equipment. One cabinet was taller than the other so that the camera could be angled over furniture. The video equipment consisted of one Minolta Series C–3400 VHS-C camera, one Canon VM-E708 8mm video camera, and two Funai VHS SC 660

VCRs. One camera was focused on the viewing area to videotape the audience, the other on the television to videotape the screen and the channel display. Audio was recorded with two Sima Micro TeleMike unidirectional microphones, one attached to each camera.

9. For this study, acclimation refers to the amount of time necessary for subjects to become accustomed to the recording equipment placed in their homes. Previous studies that recorded television viewing behavior vary in their concern with an acclimation period (Everett 1992; Anderson 1991; Moriarty 1991; Alexander, Ryan, and Munoz 1984; Lull 1982; Bechtel, Achelpohl, and Akers 1972; Allen 1965).

10. It was not possible to determine from the video tapes whether an individual who did not use a remote control during an evening of watching television (1) had the opportunity to use the RCD but chose not to, or (2) was not given the opportunity to do so. This study, then, can be seen as an analysis of individuals who are remote control users, as shown by their actual use.

11. The cameras recorded six hours per night over a six-night period in each home, for a total of 360 possible hours. On four nights, technical difficulties prevented successful recording, for a loss of 24 hours.

12. RCD users did not include participants (often children) who never used an RCD during the study, and these participants' viewing times were not included in the calculations.

13. The total minutes of viewing when males and females viewed together were only counted once. Therefore, this average cannot be compared to the separate averages for males and females.

14. This frequency was calculated by dividing the time the subjects were present in a viewing room by their number of RCD uses.

15. The difference in minutes per hour devoted to commercials and programming was calculated as follows: The number of minutes per hour devoted to commercials during prime time for (1) cable services is 11.2, (2) network affiliates is 9.12, and (3) independent stations is 11.21. See Lipman (1992). These figures were averaged to 11.02 minutes per hour, creating a ratio of programming to commercials of 49:11.

16. For this calculation, grazing was counted as one use.

5

Surveillance and Cluster Viewing: Foraging through the RCD Experience

Paul J. Traudt

The early hand-held remote control device (RCD) with pressure-resistant buttons emanating odd-sounding mechanical tones has evolved to a compliant, silent, battery-energized companion with functions few of us maximize. The RCD has forever changed the way we communicate with video receivers; when combined with the multi-channel capabilities afforded by cable television, it forges a formidable obstacle in terms of traditional methods of audience measurement.

Patterns of televiewer consumption have been greatly affected by widespread adoption of the RCD. The context for reception of programming content is radically changed from that of just a few years ago. Televiewing requires less and less of the up-and-down physical activity required of earlier television receivers. Few of us position ourselves in front of the television receiver as we did just a few seasons back, content to mark time in half- or full hour periods.

Why have we now accommodated the RCD so readily? What are the characteristics of this accommodation? How does the device contribute to our televiewing experience? This chapter provides answers to these questions, drawing from a theoretical perspective within the broad bandwidth of audience-centered mass communication theory and research. The particular approach has been labeled and mislabeled as many things. The most prominent of these labels is *interpretive research in mass communication,* where "[Proponents] view meaning as a product of the interaction between media texts and the multiple, at times contradictory, interpretive strategies employed by audience members" (Carragee 1990, 87).

Within this hermeneutic perspective, knowledge and meaning are seen as ongoing processual adjustments between internal states and external communication sources, including mass media sources. Research in this area, employing a range of premises and methods, attempts to distill both the processes and texts of this meaning construction.

This chapter examines the RCD experience within the interpretive framework of phenomenology. The examination includes three steps. Step one briefly reviews the basic philosophical tenets of phenomenology and selected contemporary extensions. Step two isolates the context of television experience suitable for phenomenological study with extensions to the RCD. Step three provides an empirical phenomenology of the RCD experience based on qualitative data collected from a convenience sample of RCD users.

PHENOMENOLOGY

Phenomenology is the study of the lived experience of persons (Nelson 1989, 389). A number of contemporary derivatives have evolved from the philosophical traditions established in Husserl's phenomenology of the mind (Husserl 1931). These derivatives all emanate from a theoretical position regarding the nature of human understanding: the shape of consciousness and experience. This philosophy has been extended to social research in order to provide insight into processes of meaning construction and social interchange.

With phenomenology, understanding is generally seen as a cyclic process. At one moment is our experience in the lived world—what our senses encounter in the world. In another moment is what our senses tell us about the world—our knowledge claims about that world. Phenomenology has identified the two components of this lived experience as *intentionality* and *reflexivity*: "If intentionality secures a view of everyday life, reflexivity provides a means for understanding the knowledge claims derived from that view as part of the very scene being observed. The individual displays... knowledge claims within the meaning structures rendered visible. In doing so, the experienced world becomes meaningful" (Traudt, Anderson, and Meyer 1987, 302).

Intentionality and reflexivity can be seen as the two principal and interactive components of consciousness: exerted experience about the world. The two share in supporting the repository of conscious knowledge.

Phenomenology and the Television Experience

Little in communication research serves as edifice having direct descendence from Husserl's philosophy of phenomenology. Some attention has been given to phenomenology for the study of interpersonal communication processes (Pilotta 1982), including an examination of how telephony filters these processes (Ihde 1982). Nelson (1989) adapted Merleau-Ponty's existential-semiotic phenomenology to the study of television and human behavior, with the purpose of examining a collection of televisual signs and experiences as articulated by subjects. Her analysis of extended-interview data suggested that televiewers "wrap the body in a pleasurable lethargy, thus imposing a temporary respite upon the continual intentional drive that projects it into things and toward others. . . . To experience television is to 'bracket' the body and its contingency from the space where they are visible for others to the place where others are visible for them" (Nelson 1989, 395).

Nelson suggested that it is conceivable that television provides not only a form of experience that informs us about ourselves and others, but that in the act of televiewing persons achieve an experiential position somewhere in between. Through televiewing, persons find some compromise between the efforts required during acts of intentionality in order to provide more temporal control of those reflexive moments of sensemaking.

Humans use technologies as hermeneutic tools within the process of communication. Television, of course, is such a tool: "We consume television not just in our relationship to the content of its transmissions, but also in our relationship to it as technology, as an object to be placed in our domestic environment and articulated into our private and public culture" (Silverstone 1989, 80).

For phenomenology, our relationship to television goes further than representing hardware located in various locations—in both private and public settings. As Silverstone suggested, television technology is also taken up as part of our experience of the world and in so doing tells us something about that world.

RCDs and the Television Experience

The RCD, along with the multi-channel capacity afforded by cable television, alters this form of experience. Flexibility in user-end programming management heightens the potential. The cultural signifiers in popular cultural content, including those of televisual content, are important to break down, codify, and assign cultural and political values, but the simple adoption of the RCD in the majority of televiewing contexts is equally if not more compelling because of a real shift in the redistribution of programming power. It is now easier, by means of the RCD, to monitor ever-flowing events across channels. Because of this so-called *grazing*, a term with its roots in a bygone television era characterized by homogeneous programming choices (and a term that glosses over an extremely personalized human process), televiewing patterns have come to represent something akin to modern-day radio consumption—with characteristic scanning of the wavelength for suitable material. The televiewer's increasing empowerment has greatly altered the viewing experience. RCD manipulation allows the televiewer to fine-tune directed experience in the world—in this case, the world provided via television. Central to the current investigation is an examination of this experience as practiced and explained by those who use RCDs in their daily televiewing regimens.

A PHENOMENOLOGY OF THE RCD EXPERIENCE

Method

It is the domain of phenomenological inquiry to study the lived experience. A phenomenology of the RCD experience requires two types of data. The first type are real-time videotaped recordings of televiewing and RCD activity—the RCD users' own recording of their video bread-crumb trail. These recordings provide (1) a sample from the individual's repertoire of televiewing episodes, and (2) a visual and auditory record of programming sampled by the RCD user. Viewed phenomenologically, the videotaped record corresponds to aspects of intentionality—how and what it was that individuals chose to encounter when initiating a viewing episode with RCD in hand.

In addition, the videotape recordings provide a point of entry for gathering a second type of data—the examination of reflexivity as exercised by the individual in making sense of and deriving knowledge claims about the RCD experience. These same videotapes provide not only a record of RCD manipulation, they also provide the focus for open-ended interviews with participants who can observe and reflect upon their previously recorded televiewing patterns.

Questions for these audiotaped interviews were organized into an agenda comprising four sections. The first section explored televiewer proxemics. Subjects provided a verbal mapping of their televiewing setting, the electronic components constituting their entertainment center, and their typical location within this setting when engaged in televiewing activities. Section two explored the physical characteristics and communication functions of subjects' RCDs. This section also examined subjects' knowledge and use of channels and programming afforded by cable television in their geographic area. The third section explored general perceptions of RCD use. Questioning probed the subjects' styles of RCD use, utilizing a compare-and-contrast method of inquiry suggested by Spradley (1979). The technique allowed the researcher and the subject to isolate and differentiate various domains of RCD usage. A fourth and final section of questioning occurred during a co-viewing period between the researcher and the subject. Here the subject was asked to relive and describe experiences as they were summoned during repeated exposures to the videotaped recording of previous RCD activity.

Sample

A convenience sample was used for this research. Prospects were generated from a list of individuals known to the researcher. Prospects were screened using a sequential series of questions: (1) Do you have one or more remote control devices? (2) Is there a time when only you would be using an RCD to watch television? (3) Do you have a video-cassette recorder (VCR)? (4) Can your VCR record the output of your RCD activity?

Twelve prospects were screened. Three were dismissed from participation because their televiewing activity was not characterized by regular RCD usage. Four prospects were unable to participate because of VCR incapacity to record the output of RCD activity. This limitation in technical capability proved to be frustrating in the generation of qualified individuals. Five subjects participated in the study. Debates concerning sample size in media research are well known, particularly those between researchers who invoke qualitative methods in order to study human behavior and those who incorporate the tools of social science. Though small, the current sample was seen as more than adequate given the in-depth nature of inquiry and the lack of prior phenomenological research examining the RCD experience.

Participants ranged in age from 22 to 42 years. Four were male and one was female. Three were students known to the researcher from classroom experiences, but none had studied mass communication theory in general or remote control research in specific. The two other participants were off-campus acquaintances known only through limited social contact.

Participants were provided a two-hour VHS videocassette and instructed to record the output from one of their viewing episodes. These tapes were then returned to the researcher for preliminary examination. All videotapes were advanced at least one-half hour during this preliminary phase. This was done in recognition of the potential for participants' initial awareness that RCD activity was being preserved on videotape. Later footage had greater potential in recording more naturalistic rhythms in RCD activity. All videotaped RCD events were in excess of one and one-half hours. Three of the five videotapes represented a full two hours of recorded RCD activity. Two of the three represented segments of much longer televiewing periods.

Follow-up interview sessions, incorporating the previously established agenda for questioning, were then scheduled. Follow-up interviews were audiotaped. The videocassette recording of a subject's RCD activity served as stimulus material during the final part of open-ended interviewing.

In general, follow-up interviews lasted for one hour. Transcriptions from audiotapes were generated and logged according to a scheme developed by Nelson (1989, 401). The scheme included a unique number assigned to each subject, identification of the A or B side of the audiocassette, and the digital counter number. For example, the data citation "5A391" indicates a transcription item from subject five, side A of the audiocassette, at digital marker 391.

Analysis

The data generated from these procedures were submitted to phenomenological analysis. The goal of phenomenology is to reduce experience to its invariant features, a process that isolates experience to a taxonomy of universals. For phenomenologists, this method can incorporate the three interrelated processes of *epoché* (description), phenomenological *reduction*, and phenomenological *interpretation* (Lanigan 1988, 7–11). In the reduction process, "the method is to determine which parts of the description [compiled previously] are essential and which are not ... which parts of the experience are truly part of our consciousness and which parts are merely assumed" (Lanigan 1988, 10). It is this stage of phenomenological reduction that isolates experienced phenomena to those essential and nonessential signifiers. Essential features are isolated and examined for their intrinsic value to the experience as a whole. For Nelson, "descriptions obtained from the interviews are thematized ... [where] converging points in speech can be located ... abstracting relevant words and phrases that function as existential signifiers" (1989, 390).

INTENTIONALITY: ENGAGING TELEVISION'S TECHNOLOGIES

The tools afforded subjects for engaging television included a combination of one or more RCDs for communicating with monitor, VCR, and cable television components. None of the five subjects possessed a cable-ready VCR or television receiver. As a result, all subjects used the RCD provided by their local cable franchise in order to communicate with a cable-converter box. Two of the five subjects also used this remote to manipulate an A/B switch housed in the same box. Use of a television-monitor RCD was limited to controlling volume during televiewing and, in a few instances, to manipulating power to the television monitor. None of the five subjects used video cassette player/recorder RCDs for televiewing.

Isolating Importance of Primary RCD Functions

Subjects were asked to identify the most important features of their primary RCD. Responses served to isolate one of the first steps taken by individuals in order to engage television. The most basic of these was the manipulation of one or more buttons to move up or down from an existing channel. References to these buttons reflected differences in RCD manufacturer labeling. The following responses were offered to a question concerning important RCD features: "An up arrow and a down arrow" (2A176). "Uh... the plus and minus. I'm a plus-minus guy... plus, plus, plus all the way up to... just keep plussin' plus, plus, plus" (3A190). "Mostly the plus and minus" (4A104).

Four of the five subjects used RCDs that also contained more sophisticated functions for communicating channel manipulation. As later analysis will demonstrate, use of these functions varied according to viewing context. In terms of effort, the simplest of these functions was use of a "Recall" or "Last Channel" button located on the RCD. These features were also included in the subject's accounting for important RCD features. "I have to program.... If by chance there's two [channels] that I want to watch I may program them in... take the recall button and just flip back and forth from them" (3A188). "Yes, the last channel [button].... If I'm gonna be flipping between two channels, that last channel button is very useful to me" (5A190). Two of the subjects lamented the lack of more sophisticated communication options experienced with cable-system RCDs provided at previous residences. "This particular device is not programmable.... In the past when they've been programmable I was more in the habit of sweeping through... the subset of channels I normally view" (5A195). "On the last remote you could do that so you would have, like, six or eight channels that you tend to watch a lot programmed in so you can flip through and see what was on" (1A174).

Four of the five subjects used RCDs containing a numeric keypad for direct entry of specific channels. However, only one subject used this mode of communication with regularity. "I will normally punch through the numbers, but if I feel particularly lazy I'll start up at CNN, 34 on my particular cable, and sweep downwards" (5A205).

RCD Location During Use

The physical location of the primary RCD remained, for these subjects, in one of two places: either within hand's reach or held in a preferred hand during televiewing. "It would be my right hand. I'm right-handed. It's just easier for me to operate" (2A271). "I would be clenching it in my [right] hand... the first finger for the last channel [button] and then the second finger for the channel up channel down button" (5A302).

One subject's primary RCD was malfunctioning, but minor obstacles were overcome in order to change channels: "Left hand. That's because that's where I get the best angle. It used to be the right hand when it [RCD] was normal. Now that it's screwed up, it's usually down low and the left hand ...I can't get my right hand down low enough [given subject's favorite position while televiewing] to get it to work" (3A821).

Encountering Channels: Knowledge About the Spectrum

Subjects' knowledge about channel availabilities provides an important link for phenomenological analysis. The RCD technologies available to subjects, combined with channel availabilities, form the basis for reflexive understanding and knowledge claims about the RCD experience. In essence, these factors combine to afford subjects methods by which to use RCDs during televiewing. Subjects were asked to describe the channels on their cable system. The responses were lengthy, reflecting considerable knowledge on the part of the subjects concerning location of channels within the spectrum. The pattern of each subject's description provides keys to the analysis of consequent methods of RCD use explored in later sections of this chapter.

Most subjects chose to describe channels on their cable system using sequential ordering from low to high. For example:

Okay...I got the basic networks and, plus [W]PGH and FOX. Channel 5 is HBO, 8 TBS, WOR, C-SPAN, which alternates with the Meadows Racing Network. Uh ...[W]QEX, [W]QED, Showtime, Discovery Channel, ESPN, TNT, USA, Lifetime, uh...a lotta home shopping...um...MTV, Nickelodeon, CBN, CNN, TNT, VH–1, and KBL. (3A255)

Okay...we have a...our premium channels are Encore, which is a movie channel. We have the Movie Channel and Cinemax.... Also included on the cable tier that we have is both CNN and CNN Headline News, MTV, ESPN, KBL, which is a local sports network, um...all the affiliates in Pittsburgh...KDKA, [W]PXI, [W]TAE, [W]PGH and [W]PTT...also PCB 40 I'm pretty sure is covered in that. ...Uh, C-SPAN One and Two is carried. There's a community access channel for the City of Pittsburgh. I'm trying to think, there's um...there's several that are text-only things like subscriber information, uh, things like that. Uh...Lifetime, Discovery, um CBN, uh, the Nashville Network is also carried. Oh, Nickelodeon also ...and...USA. I'm pretty sure...those are the bulk. I know there's some more but those are the ones I most recognize...the majority of those I know their channel number. (2A261)

Subjects exhibited varied degrees of sophistication in their knowledge of the channel spectrum. Most related this knowledge in linear form, describing channels as they moved from lower to higher ends of the cable spectrum. Most also associated channel numbers with channels more frequently viewed. Channels less often viewed fall into a form of spectrum void: Subjects know their general location but are less familiar with specific channel number assignments. In addition, subjects whose cable system incorporated A/B switching showed little difficulty in mastering the additional layer of cable-system organization and consequent paths for pursuing desirable programming:

Local PBS channel, NBC, then at thirteen you get either another PBS channel or ESPN. Fourteen is either American Movie Classics or Channel 4, which is ABC.

Fifteen is Encore. Sixteen is the Movie Channel. Seventeen is the weather pattern thing. Eighteen is Cinemax and TNT. Nineteen is court TV. Twenty is USA cable. Up to 25 is A&E. Twenty-six is WOR. Twenty-seven is TBS. Twenty-eight's MTV. Twenty-nine is Lifetime. Thirty is Nickelodeon. Thirty-two is the Discovery Channel and twenty-seven is also the Learning Channel...'cuz of the A/B switch....And then thirty-three is CNN and thirty-four is Headline News. (1A422)

Free-flowing descriptions of cable-channel structure established the subject's road map for consequent RCD use. With the ontology of the RCD televiewing environment having been established—the identification of viewer setting, RCD functions, and knowledge of cable channels—the analysis can turn to how it is that subjects use these tools.

REFLEXIVITY: KNOWLEDGE CLAIMS OF EVERYDAY RCD USE

Subjects were asked a series of questions concerning RCD usage. An initial query, "Can you tell me about remote controls and your use of television?" laid the base for far-ranging discussion. Subjects' responses, though reflecting different programming preferences, uniformly involved descriptions about RCD activity. These included descriptions about methods of RCD use, patterns of channel switching, and preferences for certain programming texts. Responses were explored in an attempt to identify all methods, patterns, and uses. Then, subjects and researcher reviewed a portion of the previously videotaped record of RCD activity at least three times, with the researcher pausing here and there to ask questions and allow for subject embellishment. The combined elements of this phase shifted phenomenological analysis from an initial phase (description) to the identification of phenomena central to the RCD experience (reduction). Three invariant features of the RCD experiences emerged for these viewers. In general terms, the features characterize the televiewing patterns of subjects when using the RCD.

Surveillance of the Video Landscape

All subjects related events in which they use the RCD to surveil programming on all available channels. Surveillance occurs most predictably at the onset of a televiewing episode but can also occur within segments of viewing characterized by longer time periods spent with one or more cluster channels (discussed in a later section). Surveillance also occurs when subjects observed production cues in program content foretelling the end of a program or program sequence. The expressed, motivational antecedents behind surveillance show a common pattern:

Okay ... I'm lookin' for something that's catching my eye. I'll just hold the plus channel and I just go right through all the ... every channel until I see something. ... I say, "Okay, let's stay here for a couple of seconds to see what's going on." And then I'll decide, well, this isn't what I thought it was, or this isn't good enough, or this is getting boring, or mushy, or whatever, and then I'll go to find a new channel. (3A300)

Well, I guess to browse. When you don't know what you want to watch and you're just, kinda, trying to find something to watch. That would be it. (4A144)

Surveillance does not always lead to discovery of one or more preferred channels. The pattern can repeat itself many times: "Ah ... just went right back around. That's [Channel] 5. And I've sampled these about, maybe I've sampled everything about a dozen times" (3B043). "You just kind of page ... just scan through those and there's nothing, but I will ... very often sit there for five minutes just going ... just scrolling through all the channels" (1A326). "I watch bits and pieces, take whatever's there and then go look, ya know, almost foraging for programming" (2A300).

The rhythm to surveillance is rapid-fire. Subjects will roll through channels and decide to stay or move on in about the time it takes to repeatedly depress a change or recall button on the RCD. The precision of such frequencies cannot be explored in this analysis, but the following interview data, incorporating sound recorded from videotaped RCD activity, afford an impression. Channel switching is noted as part of the transcription by the notation <S>:

<S> <S> <S> Okay, so looks like I went eight, nine, ten. Commercial was on eight, eight, nine, ten. <S> Jumped to fifteen. <S> <S> Seen that. <S> I went back to that sleep thing, it looked like something I wanted. <S> Can't stand that. <S> Can't stand that. I can tell exactly what I'm doing here [in reference to recorded images]. I'm doing the same thing that I'd be doin' now, flip this, boring. (3B195)

<S> And that's the weather channel. <S> And then the home-shopping network. <S> <S> <S> <S> <S> Those are just going two, three, four, five, six. <S> That's eight, <S> that's 53, it's running "Hogan's Heroes" at this hour of day. <S> PBS. <S> Preview Channel. <S> Channel 11, NBC. (1B327)

Surveillance includes attention to the video tributaries afforded by multichannel systems. Surveillance, as noted by subjects using terms such as "browsing," "paging," "scrolling," "scanning," and "foraging," requires constant attention to the video monitor. This ongoing process of spectrum monitoring has been previously documented in the literature on RCD "zapping" (Heeter and Greenberg 1988b, 71). The present study revealed that subjects used surveillance to isolate a limited number of programming possibilities requiring less-constant monitoring of all available channels—cluster viewing.

"Clusters"

The pattern of surveillance often evolves to a second invariate characteristic of RCD usage. All subjects expressed certain program preferences—combinations of genres such as soap operas, movies, or sports. Surveillance behavior matches program preferences with current channel opportunities:

There are channels that I'm more likely to stop at more frequently with, again, MTV and CNN Headline News being the two dominant channels, with Discovery, ESPN and, then, depending on the time of day, Nickelodeon also. (2A336)

I know that I'm gonna catch SportsChannel, I'm gonna catch stuff...as I'm interested in that. Um...there may be a good movie on HBO. At 2:30 at night...there's only four channels...four or five channels where I might find something good. (3A405)

I've probably already gone through a process of scrolling, so I will have identified a couple of programs that I may be interested in....It won't be that I'll hit one channel and stay there. Usually I will probably flick through a few...weigh'em out ...and decide on the one or two that I'm most interested in. (5A391)

Having surveiled the available video landscape, RCD users fall upon a narrowed choice of channels suitable for ongoing monitoring. "I use the term cluster because I...rarely do I just sit there and watch something straight through" (1B255). Monitoring within the cluster was performed, for four out of five subjects, by using the up/down arrow or plus/minus keys on their RCD. At times, the road map within the program cluster for this surveillance includes twists and turns:

<S> This looks like I hit thirteen. Now it's another A/B situation....I'm probably trying to see if...the Pirates are there and I'll probably change immediately after this. <S> Oh, no, <S> <S> I've rolled up one to CNN Headline News. Then I rolled back down to CNN. <S> Now I'm trying to see what's on Discovery, which was previously that ad[vertisement]. (5B273)

Though surveillance produces a cluster of channel offerings, there are occasions for monitoring channels outside of the cluster:

I really never know what to expect when I'm looking through channels. So I keep looking until I find something I like and I go with that for a while and if I lose interest or I'm just...kinda say, "What else might be out here..." and I'll go look again and I'll flip through more. Um...even if I am interested by something...if I have the remote in my hand the chances of my moving onto something else are far greater. (2A311)

A substantial portion of subjects' RCD activity incorporated surveillance evolving to cluster viewing. This behavior was most often associated with televiewing episodes in which the subject was intent on televiewing in general, without regard for specific programs or awareness of programming schedules. Subjects would often position themselves in the viewing area intent on sampling whatever television had to offer at that time and would use the RCD to reduce program choices to a cluster. Subjects were aware, for example, that afternoon program schedules afforded possible cluster selections between soap operas, movies, or syndicated programming. The cluster composite was dependent on the content available at any given time.

Within-Cluster Televiewing

This pattern was typified by limited surveillance but with RCD activity geared to closely monitor the events on two or three channels contained within a cluster. Other research has identified these phenomena as "channel repertoires" (Heeter 1988a, 16). In general, longer time is spent viewing segments of programming within the cluster. Movement within the cluster can be initiated by observing one of many cues, including the end of a program or program sequence on one channel, the onset of commercials, or the user's desire to monitor developments in narrative among other programming within the cluster. Here, subjects were more likely to incorporate recall rather than up/down or plus/minus functions available with their RCD.

On soap operas there are a couple of characters or story lines that I'm interested in, but not the whole thing. These two characters [in reference to on-screen characters from "Days of Our Lives"] I rather like.... I hate that woman, that character.... <S> That's Channel two, CBS, "The Bold and the Beautiful." (1B110)

Some televised sporting events are prime candidates for within-cluster viewing. "I guess to switch back and forth ... if you're trying to watch two things at once ... it would probably be like sporting events.... There's a commercial on ... see how that game's doing" (4A155). One subject provided a descriptive account of the rules of engagement corresponding with such activity:

Okay, Penguin game ... uh, offsides call ... whistle stops. I hit the button and go to the other channel. Bearing ... keep in mind that I want to get back to the Pens game and I know that it's gonna be a couple of seconds then I want to get back on the Pens. I watch the baseball, I may watch one or two pitches.... I may watch it until there's a foul tip and then, just when there's another penalty or another whistle or some kind of stoppage in play, ... I'll get right off. (3B306)

Data indicated two types of within-cluster viewing. Some clusters were aggregated during RCD activity when subjects felt compelled to begin a televiewing episode without regard to time or programming availability.

These episodes often began with considerable surveillance of all channels afforded by the cable system in order to review programming as prospects for the cluster. The formulation of other clusters correlated with planned viewing events wherein subjects could anticipate certain programming, on certain channels, at certain times. Here there was less initial surveillance, if any at all. For both types of clusters, subjects would return to surveillance or develop new clusters upon the termination of one or more programs within the original cluster.

PHENOMENOLOGICAL INTERPRETATION

RCD users experience television, take it into intentionality, within a framework built from internal states and external conditions. The internal components of this process can include the individual's history with television—the evolution of personal and social functions served by television matched with an evolving repository of program and genre preferences. The external conditions of this experience are defined by the technologies of remote control devices and programming delivery systems. These technologies define the parameters of what the user can view and when, and the methods of manipulating exposure to programming. RCD functions and cable television systems define the operational structures of everyday televiewing. They are not silent or invisible. They establish the initial geography of an RCD user's consequent foraging and scanning. Viewed phenomenologically, these technologies define the parameters of intentionality for the RCD experience. Logically, a 100-plus cable-channel system provides the potential for a broader range of user experience than a system affording only 35 channels. Expanded channel opportunities would also create the potential for an extended hierarchy of program clusters.

Another component of external conditions influencing the RCD experience resides in the perceived technical limitations of the RCD and video delivery system. For the current study, subjects were limited to a style of channel changing dictated by the hardware relationship between a cable-converter box and a narrow range of functions afforded by the RCD, notably "up," "down," "last channel," and "recall" features. These conditions presented obstacles to the user's ease of initiating and maintaining surveillance and cluster viewing activities.

In addition, the structure for engaging televiewing fare remained within the domain of the hierarchy of programming offered by the individual cable system. The user's venture into more personalized styles was limited to binary decision making with additional extensions. The user would move from a current program being viewed to the one previously selected (one binary move), but multi-step manipulation was required to form clusters of more than two channels for any viewing period. These steps included some combination of previous channel commands and direct entry of specific channel numbers.

Within these technical limits, RCD users bent the technologies to best match personal and evolving televiewing behaviors. In exercising the intentional mode, RCD users developed logical schemes for enhancing the television experience. They created patterns of programming consumption characterized by unique and differentiated manipulations within the structure afforded by these technologies. The patterns were unique as fingerprints but classifiable through a basic ontology of tempos determined by user predisposition and programming availability. Within this framework, televiewing ebbs and flows from pure surveillance to clustered channel arrangements.

The RCD redefines physical exertion in the televisual experience to a sequence of one-handed manipulations. All five subjects exhibited physical gestures when relating RCD activity during interviewing. They would extend a preferred hand toward a monitor in the interviewer's office and use a favorite finger to depress imaginary buttons. Some would even pick up one or more stray RCDs on top of the interviewer's desk. They did this automatically. Few were aware of doing this as they provided accounts of their previously videotaped actions. The observable effect demonstrated the RCD user's intentional patterns of engaging television's offerings and at the same time reflected his or her reflexive claims about the RCD experience.

The RCD users in this study took advantage of available channel-changing technologies to accelerate the televiewing experience to personal and optimum levels. The intentional actions embodied in surveillance behaviors—leading to the more refined actions of within-cluster televiewing—caused reflexive claims about the world of television to be repeatedly tested. These claims are many; they include a sophisticated understanding of television's (1) temporal rules for structuring presentations, (2) production values and transitional cues, (3) narrative structures and genres, and (4) methods of program scheduling and technical aspects of distribution. Such knowledge claims about the RCD experience are practiced to a high degree to heighten the user's experiences during any given televiewing period. The world, as depicted by television, is sampled on an ongoing basis. Reflexively, the RCD user in this study demonstrated keen understanding of what television has to offer and how to best manipulate the offerings to personal ends.

The effect observed in the current study is different from that documented by Nelson in her study of televiewers—presumably non-RCD users—who were seen to bracket themselves from the "continual intentional drive" (Nelson 1989, 295). Subjects observed in this study positioned themselves with regard to television in a much different way. Intentionality, for RCD users, is usually embraced, enhanced, and maximized in the ongoing search for elevating the televiewing experience to optimum conditions.

Beyond the current findings, there is potential for future work in this area. A phenomenology of televiewing and emerging video technologies incorporating this type of methodology affords subjects the rare opportunity to reflect on previously recorded behaviors. Clearly, using the RCD was easier than talking about it at the time of actual use, but subjects enthusiastically talked about it when viewing their recorded actions.

The characteristics of televiewing surrounding the RCD experience, those of surveillance and cluster viewing, should be investigated further. One could investigate narrative structures and genre preferences on the part of individual RCD users so as to develop an extended typology of viewing clusters. Such investigation might reveal trends in the composite meanings derived from television programming as they represent part of the user's experiential framework.

Of additional interest would be the examination of how styles of RCD use are evident when subjects encounter cable systems characterized by more and more channels, and technologies affording more and more freedom in terms of RCD style. With widespread fiber optics and video compression on the horizon, RCD usage has the potential to provide truly unobstructed methods of televiewing, accelerating even further the reflexive claims that individuals display about the video experience.

6

Remote Control Devices in Television Program Selection: Experimental Evidence

Jennings Bryant and Steven C. Rockwell

If a nationwide poll was to be conducted to determine whether "man's best friend" is the dog or the remote control device (RCD), one of the long-held truisms of Western society might have to be redefined. After all, how many of us are willing to spend hours rummaging through the sofa pillows and cushions to find the dog, and how many of us are willing to disrupt domestic tranquillity with a power struggle over who gets to hold the dog? Yet, all over America, such activities go on nightly for the sake of commanding the RCD.

The remote control device has quietly evolved from a simple accessory to a potent and nearly necessary component in the modern audiovisual experience. Early remote controls, or "clickers," simply utilized a high-pitched tone to allow the user to change television channels from a distance. Other functions such as power, volume, contrast, and the like were accessible only on the set itself. However, design advances in remote controls have greatly enhanced their potency and utility. One author has argued that since the remote is often the only part of the equipment that is ever touched, it seems far more powerful than the object it controls (Rothstein 1990b).

As is common with technologists, Rothstein attributed the power to the device rather than to its human users. However, we would argue that the more critical shifts in empowerment that result from the development and improvement of remote control technologies are social changes arising from significant alterations in an extremely common form of human behavior: watching television. Evidence is accumulating that remote controls are little things that mean a lot to the televiewing process.

The focus of this chapter is to take an experimental research perspective on the impact of remote control devices on viewers' *selective exposure* to and style of consumption of various types of television programming. Several of these research questions have been asked in surveys of remote control use (e.g., Copeland 1989) or in descriptive studies of archival viewing data (e.g., Davis and Walker 1990; Walker 1988), but few have been addressed through experimental methods. Other questions we consider or suggest have yet to be addressed by systematic research.

Through the utilization of experimental methodologies in conjunction with modern data acquisition techniques, certain variables, such as frequency of channel changing, can be gauged extremely accurately. It would be difficult to achieve this accuracy in studies utilizing survey methodologies because the respondents are highly unlikely to accurately recall how many times they changed channels in a given viewing situation. Experimental research also allows rigid control over certain variables such as the level of functionality of the remote or the characteristics of programs from which to choose.

The chief drawback to experimental studies is this: For all they can offer in terms of control of certain variables, many lack a high degree of external validity, largely because of the propensity of experimental researchers to rely on "convenience samples." However, by providing a close approximation of the home viewing environment in the experimental setting and by employing random or quota sampling techniques, we increase the chances of gathering data that approximate at-home activity. This allows for an increase in both the generalizability and the ecological validity of the research. Furthermore, by combining the results of these experimental studies with the results of more qualitative methodologies, we can begin to gain more accurate insight into the role of RCDs in the televiewing experience.

Selective exposure theory contends that viewers make program choice decisions based on mood and arousal states (Zillmann and Bryant 1985a). These decisions take place outside the viewer's conscious decision-making process and offer the individual a means of regulating excitement and arousal. Although evidence in support of the selective exposure phenomenon is plentiful (e.g., Bryant and Zillmann 1984; Wakshlag, Vial, and Tamborini 1983; Zillmann, Hezel, and Medoff 1980), little work has been conducted in how the RCD might change individuals' selection patterns. Given the increased number of choices that cable or satellite systems offer today's televiewer, the ability for an individual to sample from competing media fare in order to select appropriate materials becomes increasingly important. Furthermore, when a viewer is armed with an RCD, the selection process becomes more complex than simply choosing one program from the universe of available options. Typically, the user is able to utilize the remote control to maximize gratification both between different programs (e.g., easily selecting among competing options) and within programs (e.g., adjusting the volume). Most critical for the preponderance of viewers, no longer do commercials have to cause interruptions to the viewer; another choice can be made simply and effortlessly. Of course, the individual would have to comprehend some level of each program sampled in order for it to exert any benefit, but given the formulaic structure of much of television today, this might not be as difficult as it appears.

In this chapter we quantitatively examine some of the changes in television use that take place when viewers are empowered through technological enhancements. More specifically, we focus on the *interplay* between (1) technical features of remote control devices, and (2) attributes of the television user that affect selective exposure to and consumption of various genres of television messages.

The attributes of the viewer have already been examined in surveys and quasi-experiments. For example, in a survey of RCD users, Walker and Bellamy (1992) found that both education and age were related to respondents' reported gratifications from using RCDs. Weaver (1992) reported a correspondence between personality type and media preferences. Findings such as these suggest that individual difference variables may indeed contribute to differences in RCD use.

However, differences in the levels of functionality of the RCD have not received much scholarly attention. Isolating this functionality variable would enable us to gauge specific attributes of the RCD that might affect viewer behavior. As best we can determine, only a single experiment has addressed this question empirically.

THE EXPERIMENT

Bryant and Rockwell (1990) attempted to approximate the conditions of enhanced empowerment the typical television viewer might experience with increased technological advances to his or her remote control device. To accomplish this while maintaining experimental control, 40 adult male and 40 adult female research participants from Evansville, Indiana, were given the opportunity to individually watch or not watch television. Participants were able to select from among nine television offerings as well as books and magazines plainly visible in the media room.

Variations in Remote Controls

Viewing took place in a comfortably furnished media room. The only factor that varied in the viewing situation was the nature of the remote control device made available to the participant. With some versions of the remote, the viewer could manage some or all of the functions of the television without leaving an extremely comfortable easy chair in which he or she was seated. (1) In a control condition, no remote control was made available to research participants. They had to get up from the chair and cross the room to turn the set on or off, change channels, adjust the volume, and so forth.

Figure 6.1
Remote Control Features

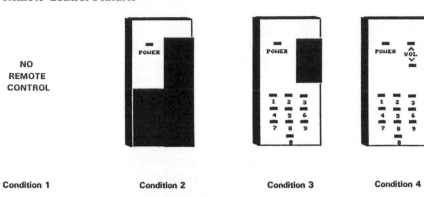

NO
REMOTE
CONTROL

Condition 1   Condition 2   Condition 3   Condition 4

(2) For the other experimental conditions, three versions of the remote control device were prepared through mechanical alterations to the remote control hardware. As can be seen in Figure 6.1, in Condition 2 the only feature the remote control offered was a button to control the selection of "power off" or "power on." Obviously this offered minimal practical utility to the viewer, who either had to physically get up and change the channel or watch whatever channel was tuned in at the time. (3) The second variation in the remote control, labeled Condition 3 in Figure 6.1, incorporated the power off/power on feature plus a set of ten buttons by which the viewer could access any of the channels remotely, that is, it provided a remote channel-changing capacity. This was perceived a priori to be the enhancement of greatest use to the research participants, because with this addition most of the features required for typical selective exposure decisions were at their fingertips. (4) The final variation in the remote control, labeled Condition 4 in Figure 6.1, incorporated all the features from Condition 3 as well as two volume-control buttons: "volume up" and "volume down." The volume levels between the nine programs fed by the VCRs (discussed later) varied somewhat, especially when commercials were included in the 30-minute programs (commercials were located in four of the nine selections). Pretests had shown that the audio variations between programs were similar to those of a typical cable system. With the addition of the volume control, the participants were provided with most of the features available to control program selection and reception quality in the home viewing environment without leaving their favorite chair.

The remote control was placed on a table next to the research participant, who was able to watch television in private and without interruption as desired during a 30-minute (1800-second) waiting period. A varied selection of magazines and "best seller" fiction and nonfiction books was close at hand and was offered to the participant by the experimenter. The experimenter showed the participant how to operate the remote control (or the TV set, in the no-remote-control condition), scanned through the programming available, and offered the participant the use of the television as well as magazines or books during the half-hour waiting period prior to the start of the experiment. The experimenter also indicated that the participant's time obligation would not exceed the one-hour commitment promised earlier, and he reminded the participant that he or she would be paid $7 promptly at the end of the hour.

Selection of Programming Content

In order to provide viewers with programming choices, the twenty-five-inch, color, stereo television set located in the media room was fed by nine one-half-inch VHS videocassette recorders located in an adjacent room, unbeknownst to viewers, who thought they were watching a closed-circuit commercial cable system. At any time during the 30-minute viewing period, research participants were free to choose between (1) any of three *entertainment* programs (e.g., "Cheers"), (2) any of three *educational* programs (e.g., "Nova"), or (c) any of three *informational* programs (e.g., the "MacNeil-Lehrer News Hour"). The order of the channels to which each of the nine programs was assigned was rotated according to a random procedure after each viewing session. By providing research participants with several viewing options, the experiment gained ecological validity with the typical home viewing environment. The participants' viewing selections, as well as their choices not to turn the set on or to turn the set off, were recorded by means of a 20-channel Esterline Angus event recorder located next to the VCRs. The procedure, but not the apparatus, is similar to that of Nielsen's audimeter metering devices.

In this study, the following research questions were posed: (1) Will the technological features of remote controls alter the overall amount of television that people watch? (2) Will the technological features of remote controls alter the frequency with which viewers change channels? (3) Will the technological features of remote controls alter the diversity of the type of programming selected by viewers? (4) Will the technological features of remote controls alter the variety of shows selected within particular programming types? It should be noted that the potential impact of the technologies has been highlighted because, as stated earlier, we are interested in the *interplay* of remote control technologies and human factors; this allowed us to contrast the impact of the human and machine dimensions of our investigation. Two so-called human factors were also incorporated into the design: a personality variable and an organismic variable.

Locus of Control

In examining machine-control features, an optimal way to explore the interplay between technologies and human factors is to incorporate a personality factor concerned with the degree to which individuals believe they are in control of their own behavior and fate versus feeling that their behavior and fate are controlled by external forces. Therefore, Rotter's (1966; 1982) notions of internal-external locus of control were incorporated into the research design.

Five weeks prior to our main experiment, Rotter's 23-item I-E scale, complete with his six recommended filler items, was utilized to identify a pool of potential adult research participants who would be widely differentiated in internal-external locus of control. Sixty-two participants were found who scored high in external control (i.e., they reported thinking they were controlled by events external to themselves) and 57 were found who scored high in internal control (i.e., they thought they were in charge of their own behavior and fate). For the main experiment, we tested 40 research participants from the internal-control population and 40 from the external-control group. T-tests on the pretests had indicated a significant difference on the I-E scale. A posttest following the main experiment confirmed the required differentiation.

Gender

The organismic or demographic factor incorporated into the design was participant gender. The reason for including this factor is quite simple. Prior research had found gender to be a major factor in remote control use within family viewing contexts. For example, Copeland's survey found that (1) male adults usually control the remote, and (2) "control of the remote is linked with program selection" (1989, 10). Morley's multi-method British study of family television reported: "Masculine power is evident in a number of the families as the ultimate determinant on occasions of conflict over viewing choices. More crudely, it is even more apparent in the case of those families who have an automatic control device" (1986, 148). By incorporating gender into the present design, we hoped to be able to determine whether or not such cultural factors generalize beyond the family viewing context and make a difference in individual viewing settings.

Design and Method

This study utilized a 4 × 2 × 2 factorial design. One technological and two human factors served as independent variables. Program selection was the primary dependent measure.

In terms of method, the study was quite simple. Once the research par-

Figure 6.2
Frequencies of Channel Switching by Remote Control Features

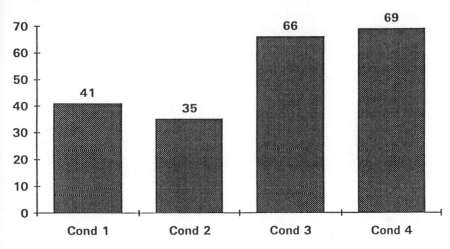

ticipant was seated in a comfortable chair, he or she was informed that there would be a 30-minute wait during which he or she could relax. The participant had an option of watching television, reading, or doing nothing during the waiting period. Any television consumption during this period was recorded unobtrusively. After 30 minutes, the experimenter ushered the participant into another room where he or she took part in a 30-minute unrelated investigation. Following the completion of the study, all research participants were debriefed by telephone.

RESULTS

The data were subjected to statistical analysis: the interval-level data by analysis of variance tests with Newman-Keuls's subsequent comparisons, the nominal (in this case, frequency) data by chi-square tests. The results, listed after each research question, follow.

Will the technological features of remote controls alter the overall amount of television people watch? No. We did not find that to be the case in this study. However, most of the research participants watched television most of the time, creating a ceiling effect. In fact, during the 1800-second time interval during which viewing was assessed, the mean duration of time the television was on was 1670.9 seconds, or nearly 28 minutes of the 30-minute waiting period. No main effects were found for either of the two human factors.

Will the technological features of remote controls alter the frequency with which viewers change channels? Yes (see Figure 6.2). Viewers without remote controls (Condition 1) changed channels a total of 41 times, slightly but not significantly more than the 35 times those with remotes limited to the on/off button changed channels (Condition 2). In marked contrast, viewers who could sit in their easy chairs and use remote control devices changed channels 66 different times, exhibiting significantly different viewing behavior from participants in Conditions 1 or 2. Having volume control on the remote did not affect viewing behavior significantly. Participants in the latter condition changed channels a total of 69 times. (The overall chi-square value was 18.69, $df = 3$, $p < .001$.)

The locus-of-control factor also yielded main effects for frequency of channel changing [chi-square(1) = 9.98, $p < .01$]. Participants high in internal control changed channels a total of 128 times; those high in external control changed channels a total of 83 times. Clearly those participants who perceived themselves to be in control psychologically exerted more control of their television viewing environment.

Gender differences were minimal on the measure of channel changing. In fact, women changed channels slightly more often overall (109 times) than men did (102 times). Obviously one cannot make too much of findings that support the null hypothesis, but we have reason to suspect that women's previously observed propensity to use remote controls less than men do in the home-and-family environment is a function of perceived social roles that do not appear to extend to an individual viewing environment.

Will the technological features of remote controls alter the diversity of type of programming selected by viewers? To answer this question, the frequencies with which each viewer switched between types of programming—that is, tuned from an entertaining program to an educational or informative show or the like—were computed. The overall chi-square value across the technological factor of remote control features failed to yield acceptable levels of significance [chi-square(3) = 3.56]. Nonetheless, the pattern of frequencies does indicate that there is a tendency for viewers to switch between types of programming when their remote controls allow them to do so more easily. The cumulative frequency-by-condition totals are (1) 27, (2) 27, (3) 36, (4) 39. Neither locus of control nor gender approached significance on this measure.

Will the technological features of remote controls alter the variety of shows selected within the same programming type? To help answer this research question, we computed the frequency of how often each viewer changed the channel to a different show within the same programming type he or she had been watching (e.g., entertainment 1 to entertainment 3, or information 3 to information 2). The analysis for type of remote control was significant [chi-square(3) = 10.52, $p < .05$]. Those participants without remote controls or with a remote control with only an on/off power control changed to another show of the same programming type a total of 35 times. Participants in the other two conditions changed channels but stayed within programming type a total of 57 times (see Figure 6.3).

Figure 6.3
Frequencies of Channel Switching to the Same Type of Programming by Remote
Control Features

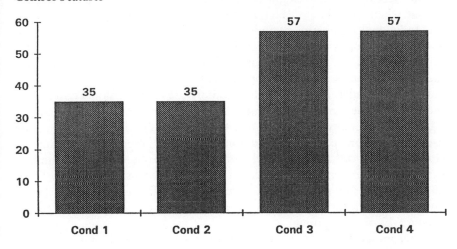

The chi-square analysis for the locus of control factor also yielded significance [chi-square(1) = 4.90, $p < .05$]. Those participants high in internal locus of control changed shows within programming type 107 times; those high in external control changed channels 77 times. No gender differences emerged in these data.

DISCUSSION AND CONCLUSIONS

What conclusions can be drawn from these results? What insights can these findings offer to those who would construct theory in the area of remote control usage, or, more generally, about audience behavior?

First, results indicate something about the nature of today's audience. For more than a decade, communication scholars have discussed and researched the notion of audience activity. The present findings indicate that it is very important to differentiate between *cognitive* and *physical* activity in constructing theories of the modern audience. No evidence was found that viewers who were deprived of the ability to change channels remotely were cognitively more passive than their peers whose remote controls allowed them to change channels without physical exertion. Yet the physical energy required to get up and change channels posed enough of a barrier to electronically "handicapped" viewers that they changed channels almost 50 percent less than their more electronically empowered peers.

One thing is certain: The participants in this study were not as cognitively passive as they were physically passive. When electronic aids were given, substantial evidence of cognitive activity was exhibited. Participants readily and frequently changed channels to suit their needs.

The second thing that might be learned about today's users of television is that when some human factors are considered, little things do mean a lot. Individual differences as indexed by a single score on a 23-item personality inventory yielded strong differences at times. In this instance, "*feeling* in control" was tantamount to "*being* in control," in terms of manipulating one's media environment.

Consider gender. Prior research on family use of the remote control may indicate that the number of X and Y chromosomes in one's DNA makes a significant difference. However, our findings suggest that issues of media use involve more complicated factors than that. Apparently only in the context of a *social world* of well-defined, subjectively interpreted, and ritualized roles are gender differences in remote control use manifested. These findings suggest that vastly more complicated audience models will be required if veridicality is a goal of our theories (see Perse and Ferguson, Chapter 12 of this volume).

Other implications for theory construction come from looking more directly at the *technological* factor—the availability of remote control devices and their features. Here it is also clear that little things mean a lot. In a deterministic perspective, our refined theoretical models must assert that remote control technologies create subtle differences that can have monumental impact on television viewing behavior.

In a humanistic perspective, our models have to reflect the fact that tool changes provide empowerment that permits audience members to control their media choices more economically and therefore more completely. When so-called convenience foods or convenience appliances (e.g., TV dinners or microwave ovens) came into vogue, a large proportion of consumers began employing these labor-saving devices to alter their lifestyles. In the case of remote controls, subtle shifts in one dimension of our lives—the way we watch television—may render obsolete and ultimately extinct today's television industries if they cannot or will not evolve with the times (see Bellamy, Chapter 14 of this volume).

Finally, the findings suggest that we will have to dramatically alter our "media effects" or "media impact" models. Several shifts appear to be in order. For example, when selective exposure models are refined to accommodate the gains in selectivity facilitated by remote control use and are superimposed onto so-called massive-exposure media effects models, assumptions regarding diversity in program selectivity will become secondary to assumptions regarding shifts in interest and attention between different examples of the same type of programming fare. This has critical implications for issues of habituation, periodization of attention, vigilance, and information acquisition, among others. It also has practical implications for the need to create more attractive and attention-gripping programs and commercials, not just during the opening segments but throughout. Undoubtedly we will have to change our formats to meet the challenges of an increasingly active audience.

Related to selectivity is the notion of the message diet of the media user. Current media systems offer the television viewer a multitude of viewing options. With the help of the remote control, it becomes effortless for the viewer to "graze" among a variety of offerings. What diet plan will viewers follow? Will they take advantage of the diversity of fare and choose media messages judiciously, selecting from the "three basic programming groups" (information, education, entertainment), or will they binge on "sweets"? As the abundance of programming choices continues to swell, issues such as diet become crucial in terms of media typologies.

A third factor to consider in attempting to redefine media effects or media impact models is that of interactivity. Whereas most of today's RCDs offer interactivity *across* programs, multimedia systems such as Philips CD-I (Compact Disc-Interactive) utilize a simple remote control to allow for interactive decisions and branching *among* individual programs. With the advent of multimedia systems such as CD-I and broadband delivery systems that allow for the home delivery of full motion, interactive programming, the RCD will permit users to engage in all sorts of preprogrammed interactions. Whether we will want to select the personalities or physical characteristics of our soap opera heroes or choose the denouement and resolution of our dramas are empirical issues for which we do not yet have satisfactory answers. Perhaps more important in considering the role of the RCD is this: Given a group viewing environment, upon whom will the task of making the interactive decisions fall? Again, the alterations in communication behavior that will occur in the interactive media environment are largely unknown but might be expected to result in qualitatively different sorts of media use.

A fourth dimension that needs to be examined is often referred to as system *agency*. "Agency" refers to the "degrees of control that an individual possesses in relation to a device" (Westrum 1991, 217). The term can be used to refer to individual differences among media users such as those discussed earlier in this chapter. However, here we use "agency" to refer to the potential for system control provided by the medium to the user; that is, the potential of the medium for user empowerment. In traditional mass-mediated communication, the potential for a high degree of agency is extremely low. Certainly, users can choose to use or not to use the system, but flexibility within the system's operational parameters is very limited. In contrast, the more advanced interactive systems will be designed to be personalized (see Heeter, Yoon, and Sampson, Chapter 7 of this volume). They will be easily customized to fit the needs and tastes of individual users. User decisions will be made a priori (e.g., the consumer will be able to preprogram her or his daily newscast) or spontaneously (e.g., the user will be able to select from among various plot options). The current degree of user control offered by devices such as the RCD has led many to use the term "sovereign consumer" (e.g., Bryant 1989) to refer to modern media users, who, unlike media consumers of the recent past, have rather abundant media choices. But use of the term may be premature. Perhaps the metaphor should be reserved for future media consumers in the era of intelligent, interactive networks. They will have access to virtually unlimited information, education, and entertainment "on demand."

Although it is important to consider these four elements in redefining our models, they are intended to be illustrative, not exhaustive. Nonetheless, they indicate just how different from current orthodoxy tomorrow's information systems will be in terms of unleashing human potential.

We must not stop with the research presented in this chapter and other chapters in this volume. As technological advances continue at a phenomenal rate, we must continue research that can keep us informed of changes in viewer behavior resulting from these advances. In the study discussed in this chapter, the RCD was, at its most functional, extremely limited when compared with many of the RCDs that are presently part of an audiovisual system. Increasingly, we are witnessing an escalation in the number of appliances controlled by and the functionality of remote controls. We may soon be faced with "overkill," or too much complexity in the RCD, which could inhibit remote use altogether. How much is enough?

In order to better gauge the optimal level of control needed by the user of an RCD, experimental studies in realistic viewing environments must be conducted that critically examine variables of RCD functionality. The manufacturers of electronic appliances should pay careful attention to the findings of such studies and incorporate their information into product design.

Another topic that to date has been addressed only with qualitative methodologies is how family units interact in the televiewing environment with the presence of an RCD. As a result of advances in interactive technologies, the power of the controller of the RCD will reach an all-time high. How will family members share this power? How will they reach decisions in making choices within television programs? Before we can begin to address these types of questions we must better understand how family members utilize current technologies. Informative research could be conducted by carefully examining how family members interact in a viewing situation. Comparing these findings with those garnered from more qualitative means could provide a better picture of the "power struggle" resulting from the presence of an RCD.

To reach these ends while controlling for extraneous variables and maintaining a high degree of ecological validity (problems discussed earlier that limit experimental research), some communication research establishments are beginning to utilize simulated environments. Many are commercial research firms, but some are universities. For example, some labs are being established that allow for the manipulation and control of stimulus materials; they are being equipped with automated, unobtrusive data-gathering equipment in a realistic setting. By offering a testing environment as well as both unobtrusive and nonintrusive data assessment, these labs will go far in helping to loosen the shackles that bind experimental research.

The results reported in this chapter suggest that RCDs provide a certain level of empowerment for the viewer over his or her media options. As technological advances continue to increase the level of empowerment, it is crucial that we attempt to more fully explore the implications of these increases for our existing understanding of media behavior. We must critically examine and redefine our approaches to understanding media behavior in light of the changes that new technologies bring to the media arena.

7

Future Zap: Next Generation Smart Remotes

*Carrie Heeter, Kak Yoon,
and James Sampson*

Television remote control devices are likely to undergo dramatic changes in the near future, so much so that they will be substantially different from the RCDs that are the focus of this book. Soon, we will call these old-fashioned handheld devices, which merely allow viewers to turn the set on and off, change channels, and adjust sound, "dumb remotes." Next generation remotes will incorporate microprocessors, mass storage capabilities, the ability to send and receive data, and, perhaps, the ability to communicate with viewers through voice recognition and speech synthesis. There will be "smart remotes" that know what is on each channel all the time; expert systems that know what each viewer likes and provide automated selection services to help viewers maximize their viewing enjoyment; and "personalizable channel selection agents" that inhabit brands of smart remotes and work interactively with viewers to facilitate their viewing goals.

REMOTE CONTROL TECHNOLOGY OF THE FUTURE

Some of the attributes of radically different RCDs are already being exhibited as prototypes. Apple Computer has been demonstrating its new voice recognition–speech synthesis technologies (Sculley 1992). For the prototype, Apple programmed an "invisible agent" named Casper, which listens for commands and acts on them. The user must address the agent by name, so it knows when it is being spoken to. As part of the demonstration, the human said, "Casper, program my VCR." A VCR control panel showed up on the Macintosh screen. "Casper, record channel 7 from 9 P.M. to 11 P.M. next Wednesday." On the screen, the appropriate values appeared in the fields for record time and date. Apple claims that voice recognition and speech synthesis will eventually be standard components of the Macintosh operating system. Voice Powered Technology recently announced a VCR voice programmer that can be programmed to recognize several different voices (VPT Offers 1992). Viewers will be able to use speech to input start and stop recording times, channel changes, and most other TV and VCR controls. The unit is expected to retail for $150.

The most relevant impact of industry directions on remote controls is that there will be a substantial increase in powerful electronic devices (both specialized and multipurpose) with built-in microprocessors located near or connected to television sets. We believe it is very reasonable to expect viewing services to emerge that take advantage of these technologies to link existing and new technologies to television schedules, VCRs, and remote controls.

There are many technological possibilities for bringing schedule information to the agent device. All telecast channels have a vertical blanking interval containing space unused for the broadcast signal, which can carry digital information to decoder boxes. The VBI is used in England and elsewhere for teletext services that display pages of text and graphics on the television screen (Tydeman, Lipinski, Adler, Nyhan, and Zwimpfer 1982). In a matter of seconds, an agent device could scan the VBI of a program guide (or other) channel that is carrying data about the broadcast schedule and instantly know the day or week's telecast schedule. There are many other options: encoding the signal into a 1–2 second burst as part of normal broadcast, using a bar code reader over television guide bar codes, or inserting a magnetized card containing digital information once a week.

RCDs of the future will be linked to sophisticated channel selection agents that will know a viewer's preferences and what programs are available. Viewers will need to teach their "program viewing agent" what kind of shows they like, both long-term preferences and moment-to-moment whims. The agent will learn a lot by observing its viewer's program choice and channel-changing behavior over time, continuously improving its ability to suggest appropriate alternatives at the right moments. The agent will also "know" the telecast schedule of all available channels. It will suggest desirable viewing options and warn viewers when something comes on a different channel that might interest them more than the one they are watching.

Some program viewing agents would be anthropomorphized, with a human or animal being that interacts with the viewers. The agent would have a name, like Casper or Seeker or Fred. Seeker would have noticed that the viewer is interested in science documentaries, any news about science, and new episodes of "Star Trek, The Next Generation." Seeker would also know which movies, weekly series, and sporting events the viewer would like to consider when they come on. When commercials appear, some viewers will want Seeker to automatically switch to the next best program option and return at the precise moment when original program content resumes. If a commercial comes on that the viewer has not seen about a product type that the viewer is considering purchasing, perhaps programming would be interrupted. For a reduction in cable fees, viewers might be able to subscribe to a targeted commercial service that exposes them to a certain number and type of commercials each viewing day.

With the integration of computers and television, it becomes easy to digitize frames of video. A new sport/hobby might be TV photography, grabbing special moments as they happen. Because you can store your family photos and captured TV moments on computer, Seeker could cover dull viewing periods with personal programming comprised of audio from the home CD collection and video images of loved ones intermixed with great moments from the home video photographer's TV viewing past. The viewer could tell Seeker to save a particular frame or motion sequence in a program on a personal computer, for future use. During any particular viewing period, Seeker could be programmed to inform the viewer via speech, an on-screen message, or picture-in-picture image about other worthwhile programs that are starting, or to switch automatically for 10 seconds when a new program starts up. The possibilities abound.

Gratifications from the Next Generation of RCDs

Uses and gratifications research on RCDs has identified a small set of reasons why people change channels: selective avoidance, annoying others, finding out what's on, getting more from TV, avoiding commercials, accessing music videos and TV news (Ainslie 1989; Walker and Bellamy 1991a; Walker, Bellamy, and Traudt, Chapter 8 of this volume). Wenner and Dennehy (1990) discuss RCD in terms of communication-work (a tool for getting something done) or communication-play (artistic expression in the form of creating one's own television through selection). Walker and Bellamy (1991b) conclude from their study that RCD use is more often a diversionary activity than an expressionistic one.

These studies examine RCDs as they are configured today. An interesting question for the kinds of future RCDs described in this chapter is whether viewers would choose to take advantage of agent services. In part this question tests the veracity of gratifications a user claims to be seeking with RCDs. If an agent could optimize a viewer's stated channel-changing goals better than the viewer can, who would choose to use that agent and who would not? Are those the real gratifications sought, or are there different, more subtle gratifications that channel changing provides? Wenner and Dennehy (1990) suggest that zappers have a desire for control or sensation seeking. Walker and Bellamy (1991a) wonder whether channel changing frees viewers from the constraints of television programming or simply lets them engage in a physical activity.

There will likely be purists who insist on changing channels by hand, much like the expert chef who bakes from scratch rather than stooping to use a commercial cake mix. We are not aware of RCD studies that have asked viewers to rate their skill at zapping or to estimate how good they are at getting the most out of what TV has to offer on any given night. How significant is the sense of achievement at missing the entire commercial break and getting back at the exact moment the program resumes? To what extent does it feel like winning a treasure hunt to chance across a fascinating program? Is watching more than one program at a time a pleasant challenge? Perhaps RCDs have turned passive TV viewing into a game of skill.[1]

Viewers who have expressionistic goals can work with agents that offer expressionistic tools. The Amiga Toaster is an example of a personal computer acting as a sophisticated switcher with hundreds of fancy fades, wipes, and special effects to transition between scenes. Rather than just zapping, viewers might someday be able to move from scene to scene adding weird or elegant special effects, or to zap to a rhythm. For viewers who really want to direct their own television programs, advanced interactive television services such as ACTV are experimenting with ways of allowing viewers to select among several simulcast channels, each carrying the same event from a different camera angle. Currently, Le Groupe Videotron in Montreal is using ACTV with a subscriber base of 180,000 (Analysis: Interactive 1992). They offer hockey over four channels, where Channel 1 is a camera that always follows the local hero, Channel 2 always follows the arch-rival player on the other team, Channel 3 is a 10-second delay of the main camera for continuous instant replays, and Channel 4 is the regular program. This service also carries multi-channel interactive news: During each segment of the evening, newscast viewers can select among six different news options.

Awareness of some of the possibilities may help researchers conceptualize RCD use and television viewing. For example, it may suggest more sophisticated uses and gratifications for RCD use now or in the future. Technology trends suggest that television will someday be able to fulfill a wider range of viewing goals and facilitate a wider range of selection strategies.

THE IMPACT OF RCD FUNCTIONS

As RCDs, personal viewing agents, and VCRs evolve, their functionality and design will have long-term impacts on viewing behavior, extending the kinds of changes we have seen with the introduction of RCDs and VCRs. Minor changes in RCD technology may also affect viewing styles, albeit on a lesser scale than the eventual extreme technology changes described here. As example of a minor change in RCD technology, consider the "digital" VCRs and television sets that were introduced around 1988 by Panasonic and many other consumer electronic venders. These systems came with RCDs that enabled viewers to push a button to display miniature still frames of many channels simultaneously. These RCDs were intended as a channel-changing tool. Viewers could see still pictures of nine channels at a time (in the order they appeared in the channel lineup) and make viewing decisions on the basis of those freeze frames.

We suggest that this change in RCD design will have an impact on TV viewing styles. The science of human factors is grounded in the proposition that the design of a tool affects how that tool is used. The proposition has been demonstrated in study after study in a wide range of applications. Here are just three examples from software interface design:

1. in a comparison of paging through a document one screen at a time versus scrolling, paging was preferred by experienced users and resulted in better performance on sorting tasks (Schwartz, Beldie, and Pastoor 1983);
2. menus with fewer than ten items minimized search time in menu retrieval systems (Lee and MaGregor 1985);
3. a touch screen resulted in better accuracy for low resolution than high resolution tasks (Berringer and Peterson 1985).

Each of these studies used preference and performance as outcome measures. In the case of RCDs, performance could be measured by viewers' success in becoming aware of everything that was on, in their success in finding the best program for them at a particular time, or in their success at avoiding commercials.

In the early days of cable RCD, some of the units were pushbutton controls with 12 buttons in a row and a 3-position switch to select among the 3 sets of 12 channel choices. According to a study by Heeter and Greenberg (1988a), approximately 52 percent of cable viewers with that type of RCD reported that they changed channels in numeric order, moving from Channel 2 on up to Channel 36, stopping at the first program that looked good. On this system, it is difficult to keep track of channel number. In pretests asking cable viewers to identify call letters of each channel on their cable system by channel number, we noticed almost all respondents counting and using their fingers to press buttons on an imaginary 12-button box to figure out channel numbers for the spatial positions they normally used to select the channels. We switched from a numerical list to a spatial diagram that paralleled the 12 × 3 positions of the box, to better fit the viewers' mental model of channel position. Newer remote control devices offer a numeric keypad, which requires viewers to know the exact channel numbers they want to watch. There is also the option of moving up or down one channel at a time, most likely encouraging viewers to move to adjacent channels (Heeter 1988a). Although these types of differences were discussed and observed, they have not been formally studied.

The purpose of the study reported here is to investigate how one type of RCD enhancement, the digital multi-channel scan and display function, might affect television viewing and channel-changing behavior. The 9-Picture scan and display feature provides an alternative mode of orienting search (becoming aware of what is on) (Heeter 1988a). With 9-Picture scan, options available to viewers now include:

1. FLIP: moving up or down some or all channels in numerical order by pushing the up/down arrow keys;
2. DIRECT JUMP: entering a specific two-digit channel number to move to that channel;
3. 9-PICTURE: displaying nine still pictures at a time, beginning with the first nine, then the second nine, then the third nine channels and so on, interrupting at any point to enter a specific channel number.

One can postulate different effects of using each of these methods on viewing processes and outcomes, such as search behavior, amount of channel changing, exposure to and avoidance of commercials, breadth of channel repertoire, and optimization of viewing goals.

For viewers who use the FLIP method of channel changing, channels adjacent to favorite channels stand to benefit from incidental exposure due to flipping up or down the channels in numerical order. "Wastelands," or groups of consecutive locked-out pay channels, text-only community channels, or other channels of absolutely no interest to a viewer may discourage up and down flipping into that region, restricting the viewer to a particular region of the channel lineup that has a reasonable concentration of good possibilities and potentially missing additional channels of interest that appear beyond the wasteland. Flipping is easy and requires little mental or physical effort, encouraging a lot of channel changing.

The DIRECT JUMP method, on the other hand, takes considerable mental and physical effort. The viewer must enter two digits, remembering first which two digits to select. Incidental exposure to channels the viewer does not already watch is likely to be minimal. Because switching is such an effort, it is likely to happen less often.

9-PICTURE channel changing almost certainly biases channel exposure in favor of the first nine channels. To get to the last nine channels, the viewer must always watch all of the preceding sets of nine channels first. To the extent the viewer can interpret a still frame as being a commercial, 9-Picture provides the viewer with a means for avoiding commercials. On the other hand, exposure to that still frame from the commercial may provide at least part of the intended impact, by causing the viewer to look closely enough at the still image to perceive, for example, that it is the closeup of a Burger King hamburger, even if the viewer chooses not to go to that channel to watch the commercial. It is possible that 9-Picture RCD will help viewers maximize their viewing goals by providing a more systematic method for scanning all of what is on.

The present study is an exploratory look at possible impacts of 9-Picture scanning. It was conducted with a small sample and was intended more to consider whether this line of inquiry might be fruitful than to offer concrete answers about the effects of forced use of a channel selection method (9-Picture) with limited penetration in U.S. households. The point of the current study is not to claim that 9-Picture scanning capabilities will someday be commonplace. However, if we find interesting effects from 9-Picture scanning, it should encourage researchers to begin directing systematic attention to design and function features of future RCDs.

In this study, only FLIP and 9-PICTURE modes are compared. Two of the authors were graduate students in advertising at the time of the study. They were very interested in potential impacts of RCD design on commercial exposure and commercial recall. The first author was interested in the effects of RCD design on flipping and channel search behaviors.

METHOD

The study used a balanced experimental design (Campbell and Stanley 1966) that insured exposure of all subjects to both the 9-Picture scan/display and more traditional channel flip viewing mode. Differences between individuals were thus controlled for by exposing all subjects to both conditions. Twenty subjects were scheduled to watch a regular 36-channel cable system in a living room setting, one at a time, for an hour. The research was conducted Monday through Friday, from either 7 to 8 P.M. or 8:30 to 9:30 P.M. The subjects were volunteer students from an introductory telecommunication class.

Each participant was instructed to use both "channel up-and-down" button (flip mode) and "9-Picture" button (9-Picture mode) on the remote control for 30 minutes each, following brief training sessions on the new channel-changing method. The order of using the two different channel-changing modes was alternated such that if the flip mode was used first on the first day of the experiment, the next day during the same time period the 9-Picture mode was used first.

The subjects were left alone in the room to watch television. They were instructed to freely change channels as they would normally do. But when they were assigned to the 9-Picture mode they were asked to use only the 9-Picture button to choose a program that appealed to them most. After half an hour of television viewing using the scheduled channel-changing method, subjects were asked to complete a questionnaire that addressed (1) commercial recall, (2) program recall, and (3) evaluation of the channel-changing system. They then watched television for another 30 minutes, using the other viewing choice mode.

Each subject's viewing was videotaped. Coding was conducted by a team of three trained graduate and undergraduate students in advertising. They used a Betamax VCR with a real-time counter to translate each half-hour videotape of viewership into a viewing log spreadsheet. The spreadsheet was then used to calculate time totals and the time totals were merged with the self-report data set.

First, the log listed each consecutive "chunk" of viewing behavior, in order, with its duration. A chunk was a continuous period of one of the following three types of behavior: FLIP TIME, a period of channel flipping that avoids staying on any single channel for as long as 30 seconds; PROGRAM TIME, a period of watching a program uninterrupted by either commercials or channel flipping; and COMMERCIAL TIME, a period of watching commercials and/or program announcements for at least 30 seconds without changing channels.

Alongside the time log, coders identified the name of the program (consulting TV Guide if they were not familiar with the program) and the name of each product advertised in each commercial that appeared for at least 10 seconds. Thus, COMMERCIAL EXPOSURE included a count of any commercial viewed for 10 seconds or more, while COMMERCIAL TIME only included time for commercials or parts of commercials that were themselves part of a 30-second or longer commercial block uninterrupted by channel changes or program content. The reason for this duality is that the main focus of the time measures was channel-changing behavior, while commercial exposure addressed the issue of changes in advertising impact. The total number of different programs and commercials that viewers watched was counted.

For the 9-Picture mode videotapes, the amount of flip time was, by design, minimal. Viewers were asked to use the 9-Picture method when they wanted to change channels. Instead, the flip time category was replaced by a 9-Picture time category, which counted the amount of time viewers spent using the 9-Picture scan mode to look at still frames of channels. We also coded the number of different periods in which viewers used the 9-Picture function (separated by periods of program or commercial time). Some viewers might use the 9-Picture mode once at the beginning of the half hour and once at the end, for a total of two 9-Picture mode periods; others might do so frequently throughout the half hour. We counted how far into the channel lineup viewers went each time they used the 9-Picture mode before jumping to another channel. (Viewers always had to start with still pictures of Channels 2 to 10. They could then choose to continue on to see Channels 11 to 20, then on to 21 to 30, and finally 31 to 36.) By counting the number of times they went all the way to the second, third, and fourth banks of channels, we can infer long-term impact on viewership of channels at the end of the channel lineup if viewers were to rely on this method of choosing channels. In the interest of commercial exposure, we counted the number of small still images in the 9-Picture mode that were obviously commercials, showing either company logos, product closeups, or 800 numbers.

Table 7.1
9-Picture versus Flip Mode Viewing Data

	Flip Mode	9-Picture Mode	p
Number of Programs Watched	3.5	3.5	1.00
Number of Programs Recalled	2.3	2.8	.14
Number of Commercials Watched	8.4	8.2	.40
Number of Commercials Recalled	2.5	2.8	.24
Commercial Time	129	131	.47
Non-Program Time	320	373	.09
Total Number of Commercials	10.9	17.8	.02
Program and Commercial Recall	4.8	5.6	.13
Time/Commercial	13.8	16.1	.17
Time/Program	511	446	.25

The subjects answered attitudinal and behavioral self-report questions to measure enjoyment, ease of use, and perceived behavioral impacts after each half hour of viewing. They were also asked to respond to open-ended questions with suggestions to improve the device.

RESULTS

Table 7.1 presents results of the analysis of videotaped viewing behavior. Commercial and program times were not significantly different. Subjects watched an average of 3.5 different programs for 30 seconds or more during a half hour of viewing in both flip and 9-Picture viewing conditions. They watched an average of 8.4 commercials for 129 seconds in the flip mode and 8.2 commercials for 131 seconds in the 9-Picture mode.

A slight tendency was suggested for greater recall of commercials and programs when watching in the 9-Picture mode than in the flip mode. Specifically, subjects recalled 2.3 programs watching in the flip mode compared to 2.8 in the 9-Picture mode, and 2.5 commercials in the flip mode compared to 2.8 in the 9-Picture mode. T-test comparisons yield a significance of .14 for program recall and .13 for program and commercial recall.

Using a significance level of .10 because of the small sample size, we found that two significant differences emerged in viewing patterns. When watching in the 9-Picture mode, subjects spent an average of 373 seconds watching in short fragments (flip time), watching commercials, or using the 9-Picture mode, compared to 320 seconds in the flip mode ($p = .09$). Using the 9-Picture mode takes time, and that time comes out of time spent watching programs in other viewing modes. Perhaps more mental energy is exerted

Table 7.2
Attitudes about Flip and 9-Picture Modes

Question	9-Picture	Flip
How easy was it to change channels?		
SOMEWHAT or VERY EASY	60%	70%
SOMEWHAT or VERY DIFFICULT	35%	15%
How enjoyable was it to change channels?		
SOMEWHAT or VERY ENJOYABLE	35%	35%
NEUTRAL	25%	35%
UNPLEASANT or VERY UNPLEASANT	40%	35%
How often would you use this at home?		
OFTEN or VERY OFTEN	30%	65%
SOMETIMES	40%	25%
RARELY or NEVER	30%	10%
How often did you change channels?		
CHANGED MORE	25%	35%
THE SAME	25%	40%
CHANGED LESS	50%	25%
Was it easier or harder to find programs you like?		
EASIER	30%	45%
NOT DIFFERENT	40%	30%
HARDER	30%	25%
Were you more or less likely to watch commercials?		
MORE	10%	20%
THE SAME	25%	30%
LESS	65%	50%

Note: Each question was asked of subjects twice: once after they watched for half an hour using the 9-picture mode and once after half an hour of flipping.

in making program choices; perhaps viewers are better informed about the full range of options.

Although overall number of commercials watched was not different between the two modes, if one counts exposure to still images that are obviously commercials, viewers were exposed to portions of significantly more commercials in the 9-Picture mode (17.8) than in the flip mode (10.9). Forced flipping and 9-Picture channel-changing modes were both perceived as decreasing the number of commercials viewers watched. At least half the subjects reported that they were *less* likely to watch commercials in both conditions, compared to direct entry of a channel number (see Table 7.2).

Data on the number of times subjects used 9-Picture scans to look at each sequential set of nine channels show a dramatic drop in frequency for each subsequent set of nine channels. On average during their half hour of viewing, subjects accessed stills from Channels 2–10 6.85 times, Channels 11–20 3.7 times, Channels 21–30 2.2 times, and Channels 31–36 .65 times (Table 7.1). The 9-Picture technology clearly biases viewing in favor of the first set of channels. Constraints of the content analysis precluded coding of what channels subjects actually watched or flipped through, but in terms of exposure to program options through 9-Picture scans, the results are dramatic in the predicted direction.

Table 7.2 compares self-reported behaviors and attitudes across the two viewing modes. The only significant difference was that subjects were more likely to report that they would use the flip viewing mode "often or very often" at home (65%) than that they would use the 9-Picture mode (30%). Fully 60 to 70 percent thought both methods were "somewhat or very easy" to use. About one-third felt each method was "somewhat or very enjoyable."

Eighty-five percent said they would like to be able to control which channels the 9-Pictures display. Thirty percent would like to be able to add sound to one channel. Two-fifths of the subjects were satisfied to have 9 to 10 frames scanned and displayed at one time; 15 percent wanted to see only one channel at a time, always; the remaining 45 percent were split between wanting 2 or 3 or 4 or 6 simultaneous screens. Forty percent would pay no additional money to have this feature. Thirty-five percent would pay more than $15 beyond the cost of a normal VCR to have the 9-Picture mode feature.

In their open-ended suggestions, all but two subjects recommended improvements that would enhance their enjoyment of the 9-Picture mode. With these improvements, subjects would be much more interested in having the technology at home. More than half volunteered that the display time was too slow. Many wanted fewer screens, motion, or sound. Many wanted to be able to assign which channels would appear. Most interesting, six subjects suggested innovative improvements of two kinds. One was to have program titles appear superimposed over the still frames to help orient viewers. The other was to blank out or label commercials, to help the viewer avoid them. Both of these are features that viewing agents might someday perform.

DISCUSSION

Using a small sample, this exploratory study has shown that even a comparatively trivial technological feature appears to have the potential to change viewing behavior. In an experimental setting for subjects' first exposure to the multi-channel scan and display feature, some initial impacts were observed. Viewing when forced to use the 9-Picture mode method to change channels resulted in less time overall spent with program content and exposure to more different commercials because of the added possibility of encountering still frames of commercials in the 9-Picture mode display.

Many subjects suggested changes that would alleviate both those impacts. They wanted to speed up the display function so they would not have to wait for all nine still images to appear. They also wanted to blank out or label commercials encountered in the 9-Picture mode display. Several wanted to have program titles superimposed over the still images. Many suggested using fewer than nine frames to make them easier to see. And they wanted to be able to control which channels were scanned and displayed. Each of these suggestions would enhance the potential of 9-Picture mode to inform viewers quickly and efficiently of what was available. The participants in the study expressed definite interest in a new, improved 9-Picture scan device.

What do we hope the academic research community will do in response to the RCD predictions and exploratory research presented in this chapter? We have three suggestions. First, keep an eye on RCD developments as they occur, considering how the design might affect behavior. Conduct laboratory or small sample studies of emerging features like VCR Plus and the forthcoming VCR Voice Programmer. Second, anticipate developments by studying experimental RCD designs. Third, use the knowledge base of audience behavior and participate in the development and testing of new RCD services with the companies that are creating next generation RCDs.

Next generation RCD design will benefit from a comprehensive understanding of the higher level functions of TV viewing. A machine that is smart enough to understand human speech will not have to continue the practice of referring to channels by number. At a minimum, viewers will be able to refer to call letters, like CBS or HBO. Slightly more sophisticated would be commands such as "scan movies;" "scan sports;" "scan news;" "scan my favorite channels;" "show me programs and commercials featuring kids my own age, ethnicity, and gender." Higher level requests could be programmed. Imagine coming home and saying "relax me," "amuse me," "teach me," or "arouse me" to the TV set. For parents who want their children to develop critical viewing skills, a parental guidance data service could sell RCD agents that engage the children in question-and-answer discussions about the program they just watched, helping them recognize stereotypes, talking about the consequences of violence, and so on. Today's remote control device is a temporary technology. The future belongs to "smart" remotes.

NOTE

1. Future RCD agents probably will need to be designed to involve the viewer, to let them feel in control. The agent and the viewer will be on a joint mission to maximize the viewer's viewing pleasure. If the sport of zapping is important, perhaps the agent will keep score, timing how well the viewer did at skipping commercials and comparing it to yesterday's record. Perhaps the joint mission concept is more

important than the sport, and the agent will use a starship metaphor. The agent/ navigator will interrupt a program by saying "Captain, your favorite movie will be broadcast on an obscure Australian satellite channel in T minus 2 minutes—what should we do?" (Answer: "Use it for commercial break filler, Hal, but keep a steady course on the program we are watching now. Let me check it every ten minutes.")

Part III

Antecedents of Remote Control Use: Gratifications and Psychological Dimensions

8

Gratifications Derived from Remote Control Devices: A Survey of Adult RCD Use

James R. Walker, Robert V. Bellamy, Jr., and Paul J. Traudt

One of the major challenges for uses and gratifications research is the identification of original uses of new media (Williams, Phillips, and Lum 1985). This search has been a primary consideration in several previous studies of new technology (Levy 1980a; Levy 1980b; Rubin and Bantz 1987). The intrinsic nature of remote control devices (RCDs) suggests that the uses and gratifications approach is particularly well suited to studies of RCD use. RCDs require active participation from their users if the viewer is to derive full benefit from the television receiver and cable system and/or VCR connected to it. Uncovering the motivations for viewer involvement is an important issue in uses and gratifications research. In addition, the widespread diffusion of the RCD may alter the relationship between viewers and their televisions by enabling them to become "more active participants in selecting media content" (Heeter and Greenberg 1988a, 5). Ultimately, this more active participation in content selection will affect the economic structure and behavior of media industries (Becker and Schoenbach 1989; Bellamy and Walker 1990b; Palmgreen, Wenner, and Rosengren 1985). Finally, it is crucial to identify differences between gratifications sought and obtained by using RCDs and those associated with more traditional media use, because the uses and gratifications associated with new technologies may not fit existing typologies of media use (Palmgreen, Wenner, and Rosengren 1985).

GRATIFICATIONS OF RCD USE

Although the rationale for identifying the motivations for RCD use is compelling, only a few studies have attempted to do so. A national survey of RCD use conducted by *Channels* magazine (Ainslie 1989) reported the percentage of the respondents giving each of the following reasons for channel changing during programs: get bored with the program they're watching (29.4%), want to make sure they're not missing a better program (28.4%), want to avoid commercials (22.7%), want to keep track of more than one program at a time (10.8%), and want all the information they can get (4.1%). Clearly, the search for something better was the dominant motivation: Over 57 percent of the respondents wanted to avoid boredom or to make sure they were watching the best available option. Commercial avoidance was also a major reason for channel hopping.

Although it benefitted from a national sample, the *Channels* survey examined only a narrow range of reasons for RCD use during a program, ignoring gratifications that might have emerged from more probing, open-ended questioning. The study was also marred by a low response rate; only 18.5 percent of the 3,519 households contacted yielded a completed questionnaire. Even more significantly, the researchers' single question forced respondents to choose among reasons rather than evaluate each motivation for channel changing independently.

Less restrictive studies of undergraduate respondents (Walker and Bellamy 1991a; Wenner and Dennehy, Chapter 9 of this volume) have identified six to seven gratifications for remote control use. Walker and Bellamy used open-ended questions to generate a list of 47 six-point Likert items. Responses to these 47 gratification items from 455 undergraduates were factor analyzed, yielding seven factors. In descending order of mean gratification score, the gratifications were (1) finding out what's on television; (2) avoiding commercials; (3) accessing music videos; (4) getting more from television; (5) selectively avoiding unpleasant stimuli, including politicians, political advertisements, news reporters, and "people you don't agree with"; (6) accessing television news; and (7) annoying others. Four of the gratifications reflect a desire to get more from television (finding out what's on, getting more variety in general, and accessing more music videos and news in particular). Two gratifications reveal a desire to elude the less appealing content (avoiding commercials and unpleasant stimuli), and one gratification indicates the desire to use the RCD as a source of social control (annoying others).

Regression analyses were used to assess the relationships between each of these factors and several variables of media use (RCD use, VCR exposure, cable exposure, television exposure) and demography (gender, age, race, household income). All seven gratification factors were positively related to the amount of remote control use, while only one factor, selective avoidance, was positively related to television exposure and VCR exposure. Cable exposure was positively related to accessing music videos and accessing television news. Among the demographic variables, age was negatively related to getting more from television, accessing music videos, and annoying others. Males were more likely than females to use the RCD to get more from television, access news, and annoy others. Whites were more likely than non-whites to use RCDs to avoid commercials and get more from television.

Walker and Bellamy (1991b) also examined the relationship between RCD use and the general viewing gratifications, including cognitive, personal identity, and diversion/escape gratifications. In this study, RCD use was positively but weakly related to the use of television for diversion/escape gratification, suggesting that RCD use is more likely to be stimulated by a desire for more and better escapist entertainment than for information or personal identification. In a similar vein, Perse (1990) found a negative relationship between channel changing (facilitated by remote controls) and attention to television. Perse also found that a ritualistic viewing motive in combination with lower levels of television affinity (1) was related to more distracting activities, and (2) increased channel changing. Channel changing appeared to signal lower involvement in program viewing. She concluded that "higher levels of channel changing may be a way of avoiding programs that are not fulfilling gratifications" (691).

QUESTIONS ADDRESSED

Although initial studies of RCD use (Walker and Bellamy 1991a; Wenner and Dennehy, Chapter 9 of this volume) identified seven RCD gratifications and examined their relationship to RCD use and demographic variables, these studies were limited to undergraduate respondents. As Walker and Bellamy have noted, the use of these respondents may have reduced the importance of demographic variables in explaining RCD use and increased the importance of certain gratifications, such as the use of RCDs to access music videos and to annoy other viewers. The total amount of RCD use may also have been inflated by the use of mostly younger viewers. They suggest that "future research needs to focus on a population of greater diversity." As such, we used a more representative adult sample drawn from the population of a major metropolitan area. The study addressed three questions examined in earlier research:

1. What are the gratifications of RCD use and what are their relative importance?
2. To what degree are the gratifications identified in this study related to RCD use?
3. To what degree are the gratifications identified in this study related to media exposure (television, cable, VCR)?

Stepwise multiple regression analysis was use to evaluate the strength of the relationship between RCD gratifications and RCD use, media exposure, and demographic variables, which have been linked to RCD use in prior research (Ainslie 1989; Heeter and Greenberg 1985a; Walker and Bellamy 1991a; Yorke and Kitchen 1985).

METHOD

Samples and Procedures

A sample of 751 households was randomly selected from the residential listings in the most recent metropolitan telephone directory in Pittsburgh, Pennsylvania, a city with a 51-channel cable system. To lower the refusal rate, an introductory letter was mailed to each household, before telephone contact, explaining the nature of the study. Once the household was contacted, alternating requests were made for the youngest and oldest males and females over age eighteen (Frey 1983, 83). Of the sample of 751 households, 41.9 percent ($N = 315$) completed the survey, 21 percent (158) refused to participate, 30.8 percent (231) could not be contacted in four attempts (including disconnected numbers and business phones), and 6.3 percent (47) were not interviewed because they had either no television or no experience using RCDs. The respondents were 63.2 percent female, 94.3 percent white, and 92.7 percent had at least one television equipped with a remote control device. The respondents had a mean age of 46.6 years and a mean of 13.9 years of education. The median annual household income was between $30,000 and $45,000.

Trained graduate and undergraduate students conducted telephone interviews, which lasted approximately 10 minutes. Interviews were conducted in March 1990. Missing data for each variable (7 percent of respondents for household income and less than 1 percent of respondents for all other variables) were set to either the variable median or, for five-point Likert items, to 3 (neither agree nor disagree).

Predictor Variables

RCD Use. Five items were used to measure RCD use. Items 1 to 3 had four possible responses: (1) never, (2) seldom, (3) often, (4) very often. Items 1 to 3 were as follows: During a typical hour of TV viewing, how often do you change the channel ($M = 3.03, SD = 1.13$)? When you watch television, how often do you use the remote control to flip from channel to channel ($M = 3.47, SD = 1.32$)? When you watch television, how often do you use the remote control to switch channels so you can follow more than one program at a time ($M = 2.41, SD = 1.40$)? To answer Items 4 and 5, respondents gave percentages on a scale of 0 to 100. Items 4 and 5 were as follows: Some people like to use the remote control to flip from channel to channel. What percentage of the time you spend watching television is spent flipping from channel to channel ($M = 20.17, SD = 25.37$)? Some people like to watch two or more programs at the same time using a remote control. What percentage of the time you spend watching television is spent watching two or more programs at the same time ($M = 10.23$, $SD = 17.74$)? An index of RCD use was made by summing each respondent's z-scores for the five items ($M = 0.00$, $SD = .76$, alpha $= .82$).

Media Exposure Variables. Television exposure ($M = 3.31$, $SD = 2.15$) was measured by summing two proportionally weighted items: one measuring the number of hours watched during a typical weekday ($M = 3.11$, $SD = 2.37$) and one measuring the number of hours watched during a typical weekend day ($M = 3.82$, $SD = 2.85$). Cable exposure was measured using one open-ended item: What percentage of the time you spend watching television is spent watching cable channels ($M = 35.24$, $SD = 29.08$)? VCR exposure was measured using one open-ended item: What percentage of the time you spend watching television is spent watching a VCR ($M = 15.82$, $SD = 18.80$)?

Demographic Variables. Demographic variables included sex, race, age, household size (number of individuals living in the household), education, and household income. Seven income categories were used: below $15,000; $15,001 to $30,000; $30,001 to $45,000; $45,001 to $60,000; $60,001 to $75,000; $75,001 to $90,000; and over $90,000 per year.

Criterion Variables

The 24 RCD gratification items use in this study (see Table 8.1) were drawn from 47 items used in earlier research (Walker and Bellamy 1991a; Wenner and Dennehy, 1990). Since a telephone interview was employed, it was necessary to reduce the length of the interview by eliminating redundant items and items that did not load on any factors in earlier research. Also, because the earlier research used only undergraduates as a source of gratification items, a small sample ($N = 20$) of adults in the survey city were asked open-ended questions to elicit new gratifications for RCD use. Only one new item emerged from these responses: I like to use the remote control because it helps control what programs my family watches. A five-point Likert scale (1 = strongly disagree; 2 = disagree; 3 = neither agree nor disagree; 4 = agree; 5 = strongly agree) was used for each RCD item. Using a factor analysis, these 24 items were reduced to seven distinct RCD gratifications.

RESULTS

Means for the 24 RCD gratification items are presented in Table 8.1. Gratification items with the highest means include the use of RCDs for convenient channel changing, finding out what's on TV, obtaining more control over the television networks, avoiding objectionable parts of newscasts and other programs, and avoiding commercials. Gratification items with moderate

Table 8.1
Factor Loadings and Means: RCD Gratification Items

I like to use the remote control because I (it):

M		F1	F2	F3	F4	F5	F6	F7
	F1 = Selective Avoidance							
3.01	can change channels when some politician that I don't like comes on	.85	.15	.07	.12	.07	.05	.06
2.98	avoid people on TV that I don't agree with	.79	.14	.09	.14	.10	.02	.10
2.83	can change channels when some news reporter I don't like comes on	.74	.14	.10	.08	.18	.08	.04
2.96	can change channels when political ads that I don't agree with come on	.72	.21	.12	.08	.05	.07	.01
3.30	can change channels when some news story that I don't like comes on	.56	−.18	.00	.05	.16	.23	.42
	F2 = Getting More from Television							
2.96	makes television more interesting	.18	.71	−.03	.11	.09	.25	.05
3.03	get more out of watching TV	.15	.70	−.15	.20	.09	.04	.19
2.70	lets me make my own unique program by watching bits and pieces of many different shows	.12	.60	.32	−.05	.13	.30	.09
3.31	gives me more control over the TV networks	.27	.44	.27	.19	.05	.03	.18
	F3 = Annoying Others							
1.85	can annoy my friends with it	.09	.07	.77	−.02	.20	.07	−.04
2.08	can annoy members of my family	.14	.01	.76	.07	.12	.17	.01
2.52	makes it possible to control what others in the room are watching	.16	.00	.56	.43	−.03	−.29	.10
	F4 = Controlling Family Viewing/ Accessing Television News							
3.06	helps me control what programs my family watches	.11	.01	.21	.67	.02	.01	.10
2.96	get to see more news	.08	.35	−.08	.64	.30	.10	.04
3.16	can catch the news almost any time	.10	.24	−.13	.62	.28	.30	−.05
3.29	helps me avoid the objectionable parts of a program	.33	.04	.10	.50	−.28	.09	.05
	F5 = Accessing Music Videos							
2.27	can see more music videos	.24	.18	.18	.15	.81	−.01	.04
2.35	can catch videos of the top recording stars almost anytime	.20	.15	.23	.13	.78	.10	.07
	F6 = Avoiding Commercials							
3.34	helps me avoid TV commercials	.05	.15	.07	.17	.01	.84	.03
3.29	don't have to watch as many commercials	.21	.21	.09	.05	.06	.81	.20
	F7 = Finding Out What's on Television							
3.69	I can see what's on all of the other stations	.07	.32	.18	.12	.07	.11	.68
4.31	can change channels without getting up	.10	.10	−.22	.13	−.09	.11	.67
2.94	makes it easier to be a couch potato when that's what I want	.02	−.04	.07	−.25	.45	.04	.53
3.43	can find out what's on without looking at the TV listings in the paper or the TV Guide	.13	.47	.15	.06	.09	−.07	.52

Note: Underlined items loaded on a specific factor.

means include the use of RCDs to avoid specific individuals or political advertisements, get more out of watching television, catch more news, and control family viewing. Gratification items with the lowest means concern the use of RCDs to watch more music videos or to annoy other viewers.

The results of the factor analysis of the RCD gratification items are also presented in Table 8.1. The analysis used principal components analysis, a varimax rotation, and a minimum eigenvalue of one. Items were assigned to a particular factor if their strongest loading was on that factor, the loading was above .4, and the loading was at least .2 stronger on that factor than on any other factor. The factor analysis produced a seven-factor solution, which accounted for 63.1 percent of the variance.

Factor 1 (selective avoidance) included five items related to the avoidance of unpleasant stimuli, including politicians, political advertisements, "people you don't agree with," news reporters, and news stories. Factor 2 (getting more from television) included three items focusing on the capacity of RCDs to make viewing more interesting, get more out television, and build your own unique program. Factor 3 (annoying others) included two items focusing on the use of RCDs to annoy other viewers, including both friends and family. Factor 4 (controlling family viewing/accessing television news) included one item illustrating the use of RCDs in controlling what family members view and two items showing that RCDs make it easier to access newscasts. Factor 5 (accessing music videos) included two items focusing on the use of RCDs to see more music videos. Factor 6 (avoiding commercials) included two items specifying the importance of RCDs in commercial zapping. Finally, factor 7 (finding out what's on television) included items highlighting the use of RCDs to scan the available viewing options conveniently.

The items loading on each factor were multiplied by their loadings and then averaged to produce each of seven RCD gratification variables:[1] selective avoidance ($M = 3.02$, $SD = .87$, alpha $= .83$); getting more from television ($M = 2.90$, $SD = .88$, alpha $= .68$); annoying others ($M = 1.97$, $SD = .83$, alpha $= .71$); controlling family viewing/accessing television news ($M = 3.06$, $SD = .85$, alpha $= .65$); accessing music videos ($M = 2.31$, $SD = 1.02$, alpha $= .84$); avoiding commercials ($M = 3.31$, $SD = 1.12$, alpha $= .79$); and finding out what's on television ($M = 4.00$, $SD = .81$, alpha $= .49$).

The results of the seven stepwise multiple regression analyses used to assess the strength of the relationship between ten predictor variables (RCD use, television exposure, cable exposure, VCR exposure, sex, age, household size, education, race, and household income) and each of the gratifications variables are presented in Table 8.2. For six of the seven RCD gratifications, RCD use was the strongest predictor. The only exception was the accessing music videos gratification, where education had a slightly stronger relationship. In general, the demographic variables of education and age were significant predictors of the RCD gratifications. Education was negatively

Table 8.2
Stepwise Regression Analyses of the Seven RCD Gratifications

	Incremental r	Incremental R^2	Total R^2	Total Beta
1. Selective Avoidance				
RCD Use	.26	.07	.07	.26
Education	-.24	.05	.12	-.23
Sex (1=male, 2=female)	.06	.01	.13	.11
2. Getting More from TV				
RCD Use	.49	.24	.24	.49
Age	.13	.05	.29	.21
3. Annoying Others				
RCD Use	.21	.04	.04	.21
Education	-.12	.02	.06	-.12
Age	-.12	.02	.08	-.14
4. Controlling Family Viewing/ Accessing Television News				
RCD Use	.26	.07	.07	.26
Age	.13	.02	.09	.17
Education	-.17	.02	.11	-.12
Race(1=Non-White,2=White)	-.09	.01	.12	-.12
5. Accessing Music Videos				
Education	-.22	.05	.05	-.22
RCD Use	.20	.04	.09	.19
Age	-.11	.02	.11	-.17
Race	-.13	.02	.13	-.15
6. Avoiding Commercials				
RCD Use	.34	.12	.12	.34
7. Finding Out What's on TV				
RCD Use	.40	.16	.16	.40

Note: Only predictor variables with significant ($p < .05$) R^2s and Betas are included. The Beta, incremental R^2, and total R^2 figures given here are for the step at which the predictor variable was entered in the stepwise regression.

related to four gratifications (selective avoidance, annoying others, controlling family viewing/accessing television news, accessing music videos); age was negatively related to two gratifications (annoying others and accessing music videos) and positively related to two gratifications (getting more from television and controlling family viewing/accessing television news). Race was negatively related to two gratifications: controlling family viewing/accessing television news and accessing music videos. None of the media exposure variables—cable exposure, VCR exposure, or television exposure—was related to any of the RCD gratifications.

DISCUSSION

The major purpose of this study was to isolate the gratifications obtained by adults from the use of remote control devices. Six of the gratifications identified here (selective avoidance, getting more out of television, accessing music videos, annoying others, avoiding commercials, finding out what's on television) are very similar to those identified in studies of undergraduates (Walker and Bellamy 1991a; Wenner and Dennehy, Chapter 9 of this volume). One primary difference was found. The accessing news gratification that emerged in prior research was combined with the use of RCDs to control family viewing in this study.

Despite the similarity in gratifications identified, there were major differences between this and earlier studies in the relationships between demographic variables and RCD gratifications. Earlier studies found few relationships between demographic variables and RCD use, but in this study education and age were both significantly related to four gratifications, and race (although only 5.7 percent of the sample was non-white) was related to two gratifications. The use of undergraduate samples in earlier studies seems to have reduced the influence of demographic variables in accounting for differences among the RCD gratifications.

In addition, an especially substantial finding of earlier research (Walker and Bellamy 1991a; Wenner and Dennehy 1990) was the gratification for the selective avoidance of unpleasant stimuli, including politicians, political advertisements, news reporters, and others. This factor also emerged in our study. Selective exposure/avoidance are concepts of long-standing significance in mass communication research (Zillmann and Bryant 1985b), supporting limited effects models of media impact (Klapper 1960). Although it is not the strongest motivation for RCD use, selective avoidance is a distinct gratification and is significantly related to RCD use.

Equally significant was the finding that two of the item loadings on the selective avoidance factor reflected a desire to avoid political information, including political advertising. This result is supported by other studies (Walker and Bellamy 1991a; Wenner and Dennehy, Chapter 9 of this volume). Since exposure to mediated political information is related to the acquisition of political knowledge (Atkin, Galloway, and Nayman 1976; Becker and Dunwoody 1982; Culbertson and Stempel 1986; Patterson and McClure 1976), the political avoidance behavior of heavy RCD users may increase levels of political ignorance. This prospect is cause for concern in an era of rampant cynicism and declining political efficacy.

The emergence of a separate commercial avoidance factor was not unexpected but carries weighty consequence. Both industry and academic research have documented the role of RCDs in "zapping" television advertisements (Heeter and Greenberg 1985a; Yorke and Kitchen 1985). In this study, two of the higher ranking gratification items concerned commercial avoidance; of the seven gratifications identified, avoiding commercials was the third most strongly related to RCD use. Clearly, the viewers surveyed here perceive that their remote control device is a useful weapon in the battle against aggravating advertising. RCDs appear to free television's "captive" audience and undermine advertising support for television. Broadcast/cable advertisers must now face viewers who can quickly zap advertisements that offend or bore them. Advertisers may increasingly turn to other, more cost-effective media, while the electronic media seek new forms of financial support from pay-per-view, video rentals, and retransmission fees (see Bellamy, Chapter 14 of this volume).

In 1986, columnist Russell Baker (Ainslie 1989) pondered, "what is cable TV for if you don't keep changing the channels?" The results of this study show a clear link between cable television and RCD gratifications and use. Both the gratification to find out what's on television and to get more from television were significantly and moderately correlated with RCD use. In addition, RCD use was significantly related to accessing two kinds of cable content: music videos and news. Both music videos and continuous cable news services (e.g., CNN) provide short segments that conveniently allow the grazer to avoid commercials or boring segments of other programs. RCDs appear to be a facet of technology that increases the value of some of the specialized services offered on cable television, as well as the value of the variety of programming offered by cable.

The gratification to annoy others was clearly the weakest ($M = 1.97$) of the seven factors that emerged. In addition, of the seven gratifications, annoying others was the second most weakly related to RCD use. The emergence of these annoyance items as a factor, coupled with the low levels of this kind of RCD use, hint that respondents are aware of this kind of viewing behavior but generally do not perceive that they inflict it on others. Viewers appear to know that grazing must be a private affair or others will be offended.

The purpose of this study of adult viewers in one city was to identify the gratifications obtained from RCD use. Although it is important, identification of the gratifications of grazing in adult audiences is only an early step in answering important questions about the impact of new media such as RCDs. Although the results presented here support the view of the audience as an active participant in devising a personal media (television) menu, we do not know much about the more basic needs satisfied by RCDs and other new technologies. Research should explore explicit links between social and psychological theories of human motivation and the use of new media technologies (McGuire 1974; Wenner and Dennehy, Chapter 9 of this volume).

NOTE

1. To allow direct comparisons among criterion variables, the unweighted (not multiplied by factor loadings) items for each factor were used to calculate the mean and standard deviation of each gratification variable.

9

Is the Remote Control Device a Toy or Tool? Exploring the Need for Activation, Desire for Control, and Technological Affinity in the Dynamic of RCD Use

Lawrence A. Wenner and Maryann O'Reilly Dennehy

> The remote used to be an accessory to a television or audio system—
> its satellite, not its center. Now the reverse is true. The remote is often
> the only part of the equipment that is ever touched. It can seem far
> more powerful than the object it controls.
>
> Rothstein 1990a, B–1

The consumer electronics marketplace is a constantly changing parade of new products aimed at acculturating and meeting the needs of potential users. Communications-related products such as videocassette recorders, CD players, personal stereos, programmable stereo receivers, "smart" telephones and answering machines, home computers, video games, as well as the increasingly bigger and more refined television sets have come to dominate this marketplace. Some of these may be thought of as primarily "tool" technologies (Rogers 1986) that allow the user to gain control over the communications environment, and others may be thought of as "toy" technologies that allow the user to play or "graze" (Gilbert 1989) in the "field" of communications. An increasingly common feature of these products has been the ability to use the tool or toy from afar, to access the product from across the room using a remote control device (RCD) or from another location by telephone.

As more of these products have been adopted into the home, the television set in the corner of the living room has given way to the concept of the home entertainment center. Some consumers follow the lead of manufacturers who package integrated systems by attempting to construct a coherent communications environment from mismatched pieces. It is significant that one of the most recent "new" consumer electronics products is a second-generation "programmable" remote control device that promises to match many of the mismatched pieces of communication technology and to clear the coffee table line-up of remote controls for televisions, VCRs, stereos, CD players, and the like (Rothstein 1990a).

Indeed, with RCDs in some 70 million U.S. households (Ainslie 1989; Gilbert 1989) and with the RCD becoming more central in tying together pieces of our communication environment, it is striking how little we know about how or why people use the device. We know, with the expanded channel choices afforded by cable television and the coming of the VCR into the home, that consumers are increasingly "zapping," "zipping," and "grazing" (Ainslie 1988). We "zap" when we avoid commercials or programming by rapidly changing channels or "pause" the VCR during recording. We "zip" by fast-forwarding videotape through unwanted material. We "graze" by both zapping and zipping when we use the RCD to rapidly sample the viewing environment (Gilbert 1989). With these practices causing much consternation in a commercial television industry grappling with the loss of a once "guaranteed" captive audience, much of the limited research on the RCD has focused on its role in avoiding commercials (Bollier 1989; Heeter and Greenberg 1985b; Yorke & Kitchen 1985), its impact on a declining network audience share (Selnow 1989; Stipp 1989), and its role in curbing program inheritance effects (Walker 1988).

Recently, the RCD has begun to be considered more centrally within the fold of theoretical development concerning new media, rather than merely being viewed as peripheral to understanding cable (Grotta and Newsom 1982; Sparkes 1983) and VCRs (Boyd, Straubhaar, and Lent 1989; Greenberg and Heeter 1987; Levy 1987; Levy and Gunter 1988; Rubin and Bantz 1987). In Heeter and Greenberg's (1985b) snapshot study of "zapping," they find that people use RCDs, in order of importance, "to see what else is on," "to avoid commercials," "because they're bored," "for variety," and "to watch multiple shows." In a more systematic treatment, Bellamy and Walker (1990a) outline seven dominant gratifications associated with RCD use: selective avoidance, annoying others, finding out what's on, getting more from TV, avoiding commercials, accessing music videos, and accessing TV news. Their study tests a transactional model (cf. Wenner 1982; 1983; 1985; 1986) to examine different kinds of RCD use. Their findings show consistently that affinity for television, habitual media exposure, and RCD gratifications make important contributions to explaining the frequency of overall RCD use as well as its use for grazing and multiple program viewing.

This study builds on Bellamy and Walker's (1990a) findings and further explores the underpinnings of RCD use. Critical consideration of the RCD has drawn two distinct pictures. In the first view (Gilbert 1989), the RCD is considered a "tool" to control and construct a personally pleasing television environment. The tool's use may even range to artistic expression—as semiologist Umberto Eco suggests, as a paintbrush to "make the television into a Picasso" (Stokes 1990, 40). Even with such artful purpose, this view of the RCD focuses on the "control" aspects of the device as a means to do something more precisely or to get something done, uses that achieve what Stephenson (1967) has called "communication-work."

In the second view (Will 1990), the RCD is considered a "toy" that is merely a catalyst for grazing. In Stephenson's (1967) terms, this use characterizes "communication-play." Here, rather than being concerned explicitly with control as a terminal goal, RCD use is seen as ritualistic, subjective play, aiming to find pleasure in the process of exploring the communication environment. As Walker and Bellamy (1991a; Bellamy and Walker 1990a) have suggested, this embraces a "Roman circuses" view that sees RCD use as a playful physical activity (button-pushing) that subversively reinforces television's power by further diverting "couch potatoes" from political action.

In seeking to understand the variant uses of RCDs, this study addresses a frequent shortcoming in media gratifications research. In their review of the perspective, Palmgreen, Wenner, and Rosengren (1985) have observed that the psychological origins of media gratifications are frequently overlooked, even though they are touted as foundational to the gratifications process. Here, the psychological bases for "tool" versus "toy" use of the RCD are explored.

Taking the RCD seriously as a tool technology suggests examination of how much the control attributes of the device drive its use. Do people who use the remote control more or differently have different basic needs for control in their lives? Certainly, locus and desirability of control drive responses to a variety of situations (Burger and Cooper 1979; Burger and Arkin 1980; Rotter 1966). Burger and Cooper (1979, 383) describe people with high desire for control as "assertive, decisive, and active," with a preference "to avoid unpleasant situations or failure by manipulating events to ensure desired outcomes." It has been found that people with high desire for control have stronger reactions to aversive noise and have a stronger belief in personal control over chance outcomes (Burger and Cooper 1979; Burger and Arkin 1980). Such findings suggest that people with a high desire for control will be more likely to use the RCD as a tool to control their communications environment.

On the other hand, the view of the RCD as toy technology suggests an alternative activation theory model underlying psychological motives for RCD use. Two concepts, novelty seeking (Pearson 1970; 1971) and sensation seeking (Zuckerman, Kolin, Price, and Zoob 1964; Zuckerman 1971; 1974) are frequently seen in activation theory explanations of media use and effect (cf. Donohew, Sypher, and Higgins 1988). Although the two concepts have some areas of overlap (cf. Lawrence 1990), Pearson's novelty-seeking scale focuses more on the need for variety in stimulation, whereas Zuckerman's sensation-seeking scale focuses more on the intensity of stimulation (cf. Zuckerman 1974). Because research has shown that optimum levels of both variety and intensity of stimulation are related to patterns of media exposure, gratification, and enjoyment (cf. Donohew, Sypher, and Higgins 1988), both measures are used to explore RCD use for grazing the television environment. The collective research on these motives suggests that people with high levels of need for variety and intensity of stimulation will use RCDs more frequently to graze or explore television than to control it.

The various uses of the RCD may be viewed as incorporating elements of both play and work. However, using the device to avoid commercials or mute the sound would seem to be mostly purposeful or "controlling" work. On the other hand, using RCDs to graze or view more than one program at a time may be less purposeful and more playful. Some uses of the RCD seem to explicitly mix play and work. Using RCDs to scan the channels when first turning on the set could be viewed as gaining control over the alternatives or playing in the TV environment. Even a propensity to dominate control of the RCD in a group viewing situation mixes elements of control and play. The user may dominate the RCD to rigidly control content or be the play leader in a "game" of television viewing.

Beyond these psychological motives, how much someone uses the RCD in a certain way may be influenced by underlying feelings toward media. As mentioned earlier, Bellamy and Walker (1990a) find significant correlations between affinity for television and total RCD use, as well as RCD use for grazing and multiple program viewing. We may draw as well from research on computer anxiety (sometimes called "cyberphobia"), suggesting that underlying feelings about technology affect how and how much the technology will be used (cf. Rice 1984). Thus, the amount and type of RCD use may be affected by underlying affinities toward or phobias over using technological devices.

By adding these considerations to Bellamy and Walker's (1990a) foundational approach to understanding RCD activity, this study seeks to answer three research questions: (1) What are the primary motivations underlying RCD gratifications? (2) What explanatory roles do desirability of control, novelty seeking, sensation seeking, television affinity, and technological affinity play in understanding RCD gratifications and RCD activity? (3) How do demographic, psychological, media affinity, media situation, television gratification, and RCD gratification variables compete in a transactional explanation of RCD activity?

The first question seeks to provide re-test validation to the gratifications that Bellamy and Walker (1990a) find to be associated with RCD use. The second question prompts an uncluttered look at how different kinds of affect may differentiate RCD gratifications and activities. The last question permits examination of the strength of the affective variables in a larger system constructed to explain RCD activity. The transactional model that is tested follows Wenner's (1985) hierarchical approach, which systematically controls for the ordered effects of general background variables (e.g., social and psychological variables), general foreground variables (e.g., underlying media affinities), media reference background variables (e.g., habitual media exposure and viewing context), and media reference foreground variables (e.g., gratifications associated with television viewing and RCD use) on dependent levels of RCD activity.[1]

METHOD

Research (Rogers 1986; Rogers and Shoemaker 1971) suggests that the characteristic age, income, and level of education of undergraduate students cause them to become early adopters and heavy users of new technology. Thus, for the purposes of exploring the determinants of varying kinds of RCD activity, a student population was judged appropriate. The respondents were 219 students enrolled in a variety of undergraduate courses at the University of San Francisco, an urban, private university. The sample was 62.6 percent female and 62.6 percent white, with a mean age of 20.7 years and a median annual household income of $60,000 to $75,000. Eighty-five percent of the sample had television sets equipped with remote control devices at their summer or permanent residence. Missing data for each variable (5.5 percent of respondents for household income and less than 3 percent for all other variables) were set to the variable median.

Measurement

Following the logic of Wenner's (1982; 1983; 1985; 1986) transactional model of the media gratification process, the variables used in this study are clustered into a progressive hierarchy of six categories (demographic, psychological, media affinity, media situation, television gratification, and RCD gratification) of independent measures and one category of dependent measures (RCD activity).

General Background: Demographic Variables. Five demographic items are included in these analyses. Gender (male/female), race (white/non-white), and citizenship (U.S./non-U.S.) were dummy-coded. A household population variable measured the number of people (including the respondent) living in the normal (or summer) residence for the students. Household income was measured through categorical estimates (<$15K; $15K–$30K; $30K–45K; $45K–60K; $60K–75K; $75K–90K; >$90K).

General Background: Psychological Variables. The psychological basis for differential remote control use was explored by measuring three variables. The 20 items in Burger and Cooper's (1979) Desirability of Control

Scale (using seven-point Likert scale items) provided a summed variable (alpha = .79) tapping the general level of the motivation to control events in one's life. Lawrence's (1990) recently validated seven-point Likert scale versions of Pearson's (1970; 1971) Novelty Seeking Scale and Zuckerman's (Zuckerman, Kolin, Price, and Zoob 1964; Zuckerman 1971; 1974) Sensation Seeking Scale provided truncated measures of these two affective concepts. Twenty items were summed to produce a novelty seeking score (alpha = .86). Twelve items were summed to produce a sensation seeking score (alpha = .61).

General Foreground: Media Affinity Variables. Two variables were measured to examine how existing media affinities affect remote control use. Following Rubin (1981; Rubin and Rubin 1982), a media-specific index of television affinity (alpha = .71) was constructed by summing 5 seven-point Likert items. A broader measure of affinity for using "appliances and consumer electronics that have a variety of technical features" was developed for this study. Measuring affect, learning, and use of such products, 18 seven-point Likert items were summed to produce a technological affinity index (alpha = .87).[2]

Media Reference Background: Media Situation Variables. Five variables measured media availability and habits. The degree of diversity in the respondent's television environment was measured by an estimate of the number of different channels available on the television set that was "normally watched" ($M = 25.3$, $SD = 18.2$). Television exposure was measured by summing two proportionally weighted items measuring the number of hours watched on a typical weekday ($M = 3.2$, $SD = 2.1$) and typical weekend day ($M = 3.4$, $SD = 2.1$). Cable television viewing was measured using an open-ended estimate of the percentage of viewing time that was spent watching cable channels ($M = 34.4$, $SD = 31.2$). A similar open-ended question assessed the percentage of viewing time that was spent watching alone ($M = 37.2$, $SD = 29.6$). The likelihood of consulting *TV Guide* or program listings in the newspaper "when you get ready to watch television" was measured on a five-point scale of "never" to "very often" ($M = 2.7$, $SD = 1.2$).

Media Reference Foreground: Television Gratifications. Twenty items tapping commonly observed television gratifications as outlined by Blumler (1979) were measured using seven-point Likert items. The sum of seven items formed a cognitive gratification index (alpha = .83); another seven items summed to form a personal identity gratification index (alpha = .84); and six items summed to form a diversion/escape gratification index (alpha = .80).

Media Reference Foreground: Remote Control Gratifications. Building on the work of Bellamy and Walker (1990a), remote control gratification items were distributed among fourteen categories:

1. maintaining control over the television environment
2. avoiding commercial advertising
3. playing with the controls (or buttons)
4. looking for news or information
5. taking a music video break
6. staying put on a sofa or chair
7. annoying other viewers
8. seeing only the good parts of programs
9. avoiding certain personalities or issues
10. avoiding boredom
11. scanning to see what is on
12. getting the most out of television/cable/VCR
13. avoiding objectionable/obnoxious programming
14. muting or adjusting the sound

The degree of agreement with fifty-six statements distributed across these categories was measured using a seven-point Likert scale.[3] As will be outlined in the results section, the fifty-six items were reduced through factor analysis to six underlying RCD gratifications (see Table 9.1).

Dependent Variables: Remote Control Activity. In the subsequent analyses, remote control activity variables are considered as dependent measures that may be explained by desirability of control, novelty seeking, and sensation seeking in combination with other independent measures. The degree and quality of RCD activity was measured in a variety of ways, yielding the following seven variables:

(1) Remote control dominance ($M = 43.3$, $SD = 31.4$) measured the proportion of remote control changes made by the respondent when viewing a remote controlled television set with other people.

(2) Entry scanning ($M = 4.1$, $SD = .9$) measured (on a five-point scale of "never" to "very often") the likelihood of the respondent "to run through the channels to see what is on" when the television set is first turned on.

(3) Commercial avoidance ($M = 3.7$, $SD = 1.3$) measured (on the same five-point scale) how often the remote control was used "to switch channels so you can avoid commercials."

(4) Muting was measured through a summed index (alpha $= .59$) of the z-scores for

   (a) muting frequency ($M = 2.1$, $SD = 1.0$), which measured (on a five-point scale) how often respondents muted the sound during a typical hour of viewing, and

   (b) muting percentage ($M = 11.0$, $SD = 20.1$), which was based on estimates

Table 9.1
Factor Analysis: Remote Control Gratifications

Loading	M	SD	I like to use the remote control because . . .
			Factor 1: Selective Avoidance
.77	3.2	1.82	I can change channels when some news reporter that I don't like comes on.
.77	3.1	1.83	I can change channels when some politician that I don't like comes on.
.74	3.1	1.88	I can change channels when political ads come on.
.73	3.2	1.88	I can change channels when some news story that I don't like comes on.
.72	3.4	1.92	I can avoid obnoxious things I don't think belong on television.
.65	3.1	1.83	I can avoid people I don't agree with.
.64	3.1	1.90	it helps me avoid the objectionable parts of a program.
.63	3.4	1.82	I can change channels when some actor that I don't like comes on.
.57	3.0	1.86	I can change channels when political ads that I don't agree with come on.
			Factor 2: Aggressive Play
.80	2.3	1.83	it's fun to tease other people watching the same TV set.
.76	2.2	1.74	I can annoy my friends with it.
.75	2.4	1.88	I can annoy members of my family with it.
.75	2.5	1.95	it gives me something to do with my hands while I'm watching TV.
.70	2.5	1.74	I enjoy playing with the buttons.
			Factor 3: Commercial Avoidance
.77	4.8	1.94	I don't have to watch as many commercials.
.77	4.9	1.91	it helps me avoid TV commercials.
.66	5.3	1.63	I can see what's on all of the other stations.
.61	4.2	1.84	I can avoid the dull parts of a program.
			Factor 4: Music Scanning
.72	4.5	2.09	I can catch a music video instead of a commercial.
.71	3.8	2.08	I can catch videos of the top recording stars almost any time.
.71	4.0	2.17	I can see more music videos.
.70	4.0	2.11	it helps me get the most out of cable TV.
.62	4.6	2.00	it makes it easier to watch a greater variety of cable channels.
			Factor 5: Environmental Convenience
.72	5.3	1.66	I can adjust the sound to an appropriate level.
.71	5.1	1.75	I can turn down the sound when it gets too loud.
.54	4.8	2.10	it makes it easier to be a couch potato when I want to.
.53	5.1	1.80	it makes it easier to watch TV.
			Factor 6: News Scanning
.75	3.6	1.93	I can catch the news almost any time.
.67	3.6	2.05	I get to see more news.
.58	3.7	2.03	I can compare newscasts.

of the proportion of viewing time spent "watching television with the sound muted."

(5) Multiple program viewing was measured through a summed index (alpha = .76) of the z-scores for

(a) multiple program frequency (M = 2.6, SD = 1.2), which measured (on the five-point scale of "never" to "very often") how often the remote control was used to "follow more than one program at a time," and

(b) multiple program percentage (M = 19.8, SD = 25.7), which provided estimates of the proportion of viewing time "spent watching two or more programs at the same time."

(6) Grazing was measured through a summed index (alpha = .65) of the z-scores for

(a) channel change frequency (M = 3.2, SD = 1.0), which measured (on the five-point scale) how often the respondent changed channels in a typical hour of viewing,

(b) channel flipping frequency (M = 3.9, SD = 1.2), which measured (on the five-point scale) how often respondents "use the remote control to flip from channel to channel" when watching television, and

(c) channel flipping percentage (M = 32.6, SD = 32.5), which stemmed from estimates of the proportion of viewing time "spent flipping from channel to channel."

(7) Total RCD activity was measured through an eight-item index (alpha = .80) that summed RCD activities during "normal" (as opposed to "entry") viewing. The total RCD activity index sums the z-scores for commercial avoidance (Number 3 above), the two items (4a, 4b) that make up the muting index, the two items (5a, 5b) that make up the multiple program viewing index, and the three items (6a, 6b, 6c) that make up the grazing index.

RESULTS

Reporting of results is structured according to the three major research questions. First, factor analysis is used to assess the primary motivations underlying RCD gratifications. Second, the explanatory roles that desirability of control, novelty seeking, sensation seeking, television affinity, and technological affinity play in understanding RCD gratifications and RCD activity are examined through simple analyses of variance. Third, the question of how demographic, psychological, media affinity, media situation, television gratification, and RCD gratification variables compete in a transactional explanation of RCD activity is examined through hierarchical and stepwise regression analyses.

Underlying RCD Gratifications

The results of the factor analysis on RCD gratifications items are presented in Table 9.1. The six-factor solution that was chosen used principal components analysis with varimax rotation and resulted from a "best solution" strategy derivative of guidelines by McCroskey and Young (1979). A best solution was deemed to have a maximum number of factors, where all factors had a minimum of three items with primary loadings over .5 that did not have secondary loadings of more than half the primary loadings. The initial factor analysis was run with minimum eigenvalue set at 1.0 and yielded 11 factors, many of which had no items with primary factor loadings. Successive factor analyses were run specifying progressively fewer factors until the best solution criteria yielded a six-factor solution with minimum eigenvalue of 1.8 and accounting for 55.1 percent of the variance.

Factor 1—*selective avoidance*—included nine items and centered on avoiding unpleasant programming, particularly disliked news reporters or stories, politicians or political ads, and other "obnoxious things" or "objectionable parts." Factor 2—*aggressive play*—combined three items that focused on using RCDs to annoy or tease friends and family with two items that embraced "playing with the buttons" on the remote control as "something to do with my hands." Factor 3—*commercial avoidance*— linked two primary items outlining remote control use to exit commercials with items that characterized scanning "to see what's on all of the other stations" and avoiding "dull parts of a program." Factor 4—*music scanning*—centered on three items seeing RCDs as useful in catching music videos (as opposed to commercials) and two items that stressed RCDs' utility in accessing cable's variety of channels. Factor 5—*environmental convenience*—combined a base of two items that stressed RCD use to control (but not "turn off") the television sound environment with two items that highlighted RCDs' role in making the viewing situation "easier," including being "a couch potato" when that was desired. Factor 6—*news scanning*—included three items showing how RCDs facilitate catching and seeing more of news programs "almost any time" and comparing newscasts.

For further analysis, the items loading on each factor were multiplied by their loadings and then summed to produce six RCD gratification variables: selective avoidance (alpha = .93), aggressive play (alpha = .87), commercial avoidance (alpha = .82), music scanning (alpha = .86), environmental convenience (alpha = .72), and news scanning (alpha = .79).

Examining Psychological and Media Affinity Origins of RCD Use

High, medium, and low groups were constructed through an equal three-part division of the responses to each of the following variables: desirability of control (DOC), novelty seeking (NS), sensation seeking (SS), television affinity (TVA), and technological affinity (TCA). Simple one-way analyses of variance examined how group differences on these variables were predictive of RCD gratification and activity measures. Only significant results ($p < .05$) with significant ($p < .05$) post hoc Scheffe contrasts are reported. No significant results were found on RCD gratification or activity measures for the novelty seeking and technological affinity groups. Thus, results reported here focus only on desirability for control, sensation seeking, and television affinity.

Desirability of Control. Only one RCD gratification—environmental convenience—showed differences by DOC group ($F = 4.8$, $p < .01$). High DOC was mated with high environmental convenience ($M = 3.4$) and had a significant post hoc contrast with medium DOC ($M = 3.0$). Three of the RCD activity variables showed differences by level of DOC. A high muting score ($M = .45$) was seen in the low DOC group, contrasting significantly ($F = 3.9$, $p < .02$) with the low muting score in the medium DOC group ($M = -.27$). A high grazing score was also found in the low DOC group ($M = .54$), and the significant difference ($F = 3.8$, $p < .02$) came from the contrast with the medium DOC group ($M = -.48$). Finally, the same pattern was seen with regard to the total RCD activity score. Total RCD activity ($M = 1.3$) was highest in the low DOC group, and the significant difference ($F = 4.4$, $p < .02$) was attributable to lower RCD activity ($M = -1.2$) in the medium DOC group.

Sensation Seeking. Two RCD gratifications—aggressive play ($F = 7.4$, $p < .01$) and commercial avoidance ($F = 4.0$, $p < .02$)—showed differences by level of sensation seeking. The high level of aggressive play gratifications among high sensation seekers ($M = 2.2$) significantly contrasted with both medium ($M = 1.7$) and low ($M = 1.5$) sensation seekers. High commercial avoidance was found in high SS ($M = 3.7$), contrasting significantly with low SS ($M = 3.3$). Two RCD activity measures—RCD dominance ($F = 3.8$, $p < .03$) and entry scanning ($F = 3.3$, $p < .05$)—had evidence of differences by level of SS. The high RCD dominance seen in the high SS group ($M = 51.2$) contrasted with low RCD dominance in the low SS group ($M = 41.0$). Similarly, high entry scanning of the high SS group ($M = 4.3$) contrasts most with low entry scanning of the low SS group ($M = 3.9$).

Television Affinity. Three RCD gratifications—selective avoidance ($F = 13.6$, $p < .01$), aggressive play ($F = 5.3$, $p < .01$), and music scanning ($F = 9.6$, $p < .01$)—showed differences by level of television affinity. In each instance, high television affinity groups were higher in the RCD gratifications and contrasted significantly with both medium and low affinity groups. Four RCD activity measures—RCD dominance ($F = 19.6$, $p < .01$), multiple program viewing ($F = 3.4$, $p < .04$), grazing ($F = 5.4$, $p < .01$), and total RCD activity ($F = 5.4$, $p < .01$)—could be differentiated by TV affinity level. In each case, the high TV affinity groups were highest in the RCD activity and contrasted significantly with the matched low TV affinity groups. Only in the case of RCD dominance did the high TV affinity group also contrast significantly with the medium TV affinity group.

The Nature of the RCD Transaction

Regression analyses were used to understand how demographic, psychological, media affinity, media situation, television gratification, and RCD gratification variables compete in a transactional explanation of RCD activity. First, hierarchical multiple regression analyses (see Tables 9.2 and 9.3) with forced variable entry and with variable blocks entered according to the logic of Wenner's (1982; 1985; 1986) transactional model were performed on each of the seven dependent RCD activity measures. These hierarchical analyses examine all variables in the system, suggest which individual variables are most important within that system, and provide a clear look at the additive explanatory power of hierarchically arranged classes of variables. Second, for each dependent measure, a parallel stepwise regression analysis was used as a data reduction technique to isolate those variables that most deservedly belong in an explanatory system. The SPSS standard that combines both forward and backward "cycling" into the stepwise process (with $p < .05$ to enter the equation, and $p < .10$ to mandate being removed from the equation) is used for data reduction. The terminal F statistics for all of the fourteen regression analyses (7 dependent measures $\times$ 2 regression methods) reported are significant at the $p < .01$ level.

RCD Dominance. The hierarchical regression on RCD dominance accounted for 28.1 percent of the variance and shows that blocks of media affinity and media situation variables add significant amounts of variance when entering the equation (see Table 9.2). The beta coefficients show a strong affinity for television, the tendency to view alone, and a high motivation to use RCDs for commercial avoidance as best predictors of RCD dominance. The stepwise analysis (accounting for 23.2 percent of the variance) confirms these three variables as central.[4] Although they are not significant in the regression equations, each of the television gratifications, as well as a number of other RCD gratification and media situation variables, have strong Pearson correlations with RCD dominance.

Entry Scanning. Accounting for 28.4 percent of the variance in entry scanning, the hierarchical analysis found psychological variables, TV gratifications, and RCD gratifications each adding significant amounts of variance when entered into the equation. The hierarchical analysis suggests seven variables as most weighted in the aggregate equation. High motivation to avoid commercials, U.S. citizenship, low affinity for television, high novelty seeking, low number of channel options, low seeking of cognitive television gratifications, and white race rather than non-white race are linked to high entry scanning levels. When TV affinity and cognitive gratifications

Table 9.2
Hierarchical Regression Analyses on RCD Dominance, Entry Scanning,
Commercial Avoidance, and Muting

	RCD Dominance		Entry Scan.		Comm. Avoid.		Muting	
	r	Beta	r	Beta	r	Beta	r	Beta
Gender	-.10	-.06	-.01	-.06	.01	.08	-.04	-.02
Race	-.01	-.03	.01	.14[b]	-.00	.07	-.02	-.01
Income	.02	.03	.02	.06	.03	.10	-.05	-.05
Citizenship	-.03	-.02	-.12	-.22[a]	.08	.08	-.04	-.03
Household Size	.03	.05	.09	.11	-.00	-.03	-.07	-.06
Desirability of Control	.01	.04	.10	.07	-.02	.01	-.22[a]	-.24[a]
Sensation Seeking	.14[b]	.05	.16[b]	-.00	.14[b]	.04	.04	-.02
Novelty Seeking	-.00	.02	.24[a]	.17[a]	.10	-.07	.05	.20[b]
TV Affinity	.36[a]	.25[a]	-.07	-.20[b]	.10	.10	.07	.01
Technological Affinity	.04	-.03	-.04	-.06	.10	.14[b]	-.02	.01
Channel Options	.18[a]	.05	-.07	-.16[b]	.13[b]	.01	.13[b]	.09
TV Exposure	.21[a]	-.04	.00	.07	.04	-.07	.12	.15
Cable Viewing	.20[a]	.08	.00	-.00	.13[b]	.08	.12	.07
Viewing Alone	.29[a]	.21[a]	.02	.05	.07	.09	.07	.03
Program Guide Use	-.02	-.01	-.16	-.07	-.23[a]	-.17[a]	-.12	-.06
Cognitive Grat.	.17[a]	.14	.02	-.21[b]	-.03	-.09	-.09	-.24[a]
Diversion Grat.	.27[a]	.12	.06	.06	-.01	-.07	.06	.17
Personal Identity Grat.	.32[a]	.15	.11	.17	.05	-.06	-.03	-.13
Selective Avoidance	.22[a]	-.02	.16[b]	.12	.22[a]	-.03	.14[b]	.15
Aggressive Play	.20[a]	.02	.13[b]	-.06	.13[b]	.01	.09	.01
Commercial Avoidance	.27[a]	.19[b]	.35[a]	.30[a]	.60[a]	.66[a]	.14[b]	-.01
Music Scanning	.25[a]	-.02	.22[a]	.12	.31[a]	-.00	.09	-.05
Environ. Convenience	.17[a]	-.04	.12	-.07	.15[b]	-.11	.07	.04
News Scanning	.15[b]	.04	.15[b]	.00	.24[a]	.06	.14[b]	.18[b]

R^2 BY VARIABLE BLOCK:	RCD Dominance	Entry Scan.	Comm. Avoid.	Muting
Demographic Variables	.013	.026	.008	.011
Psychological Variables	.024	.073[a]	.027	.067[a]

Table 9.2 (cont.)

R^2 BY VARIABLE BLOCK:	RCD Dominance	Entry Scan.	Comm. Avoid.	Muting
Media Affinity	.125[a]	.006	.026[b]	.007
Media Situation	.067[a]	.027	.085[a]	.043
TV Gratifications	.025	.035[b]	.003	.026
RCD Gratifications	.027	.117[a]	.329[a]	.045
Total R^2 Accounted for	.281[a]	.284[a]	.479[a]	.200[a]

Note: a = significant at $p < .01$; b = significant at $p < .05$.

are removed from the equation, the stepwise analysis reduces the list of significant predictors to five while still accounting for 21.1 percent of the variance.[5] It is important to note that the effects of high novelty seeking are attenuated in the stepwise analysis.

Commercial Avoidance. The hierarchical regression on the frequency of using RCDs to avoid commercials accounted for 47.9 percent of the variance. The variable blocks of media affinity, media situation, and RCD gratification added significant amounts of variance when entered into the equation. It is not surprising that the hierarchical analysis finds the RCD commercial avoidance gratification as the most important explanatory variable. However, the hierarchical analysis points to only two other variables—low program guide use and high technological affinity—as important to explaining high levels of commercial avoidance. The stepwise analysis reduces accounted variance to 42 percent, but it reinforces the importance of these variables and adds a low cognitive gratification score as a key indicator of frequent use of the RCD to avoid commercials.[6]

Muting. In accounting for 20 percent of the variance in the muting index, the hierarchical regression points to only the psychological variable block as significantly adding variance when entered into the equation. Here a low desire for control and high novelty seeking combine with low cognitive television gratification scores and the tendency to use RCDs for news scanning to explain frequent muting. By centering on these variables and adding only the level of television viewing, the stepwise analysis drops accounted variance to 15.6 percent.[7]

Multiple Program Viewing. The hierarchical analysis accounts for 39.4 percent of variance in the multiple program viewing index (see Table 9.3). Two variable blocks—media situation and RCD gratifications—add significantly to the variance total when entered into the equation. The same five variables become central in both the hierarchical analysis and the stepwise analysis (accounting for 34.9 percent of variance).[8] A high RCD commercial avoidance gratification score, high television viewing, the tendency to view alone, low cognitive gratification seeking from television, and a high RCD

Table 9.3

Hierarchical Regression Analyses on Multiple Program Viewing, Grazing, and Total RCD Activity

	M.P. Viewing		Grazing		Total Activity	
	r	Beta	r	Beta	r	Beta
Gender	−.11	−.10	−.08	−.09	−.09	−.07
Race	.12	.09	.10	.11	.08	.09
Income	−.03	.05	−.03	.04	−.04	.04
Citizenship	.05	.06	−.01	−.01	.02	.02
Household Size	−.03	.01	−.04	−.02	−.05	−.03
Desirability of Control	−.01	−.03	−.10	−.11	−.12	−.13[b]
Sensation Seeking	.10	−.01	.07	−.09	.10	−.04
Novelty Seeking	.05	.07	.05	.13	.08	.14[b]
TV Affinity	.16[b]	−.08	.21[a]	−.01	.19[a]	−.01
Technological Affinity	.11	.05	.04	−.02	.07	.04
Channel Options	.16[b]	.00	.14[b]	−.07	.19[a]	−.00
TV Exposure	.36[a]	.32[a]	.33[a]	.27[a]	.32[a]	.27[a]
Cable Viewing	.24[a]	.14[b]	.28[a]	.19[a]	.27[a]	.17[a]
Viewing Alone	.32[a]	.24[a]	.22[a]	.15[b]	.25[a]	.17[a]
Program Guide Use	−.09	−.06	−.14[b]	−.08	−.18[a]	−.11
Cognitive Grat.	.07	−.14	.06	−.13	.02	−.20[b]
Diversion Grat.	.14[b]	.06	.15[b]	.02	.13	.07
Personal Identity Grat.	.12	−.06	.15[b]	−.05	.11	−.10
Selective Avoidance	.15[b]	−.03	.21[a]	−.03	.23[a]	.02
Aggressive Play	.07	.03	.14[b]	.04	.14[b]	.04
Commercial Avoidance	.37[a]	.34[a]	.49[a]	.44[a]	.51[a]	.43[a]
Music Scanning	.25[a]	−.01	.36[a]	.09	.33[a]	.01
Environ. Convenience	.13[b]	−.07	.22[a]	.01	.19[a]	−.03
News Scanning	.25[a]	.15[b]	.19[a]	.01	.27[a]	.13

R^2 BY VARIABLE BLOCK:	M.P. Viewing	Grazing	Total Activity
Demographic Variables	.028	.021	.018
Psychological Variables	.014	.025	.041[b]
Media Affinity	.023	.040[b]	.037[b]

Table 9.3 (cont.)

R^2 BY VARIABLE BLOCK:	M.P. Viewing	Grazing	Total Activity
Media Situation	.206[a]	.159[a]	.181[a]
TV Gratifications	.005	.008	.014
RCD Gratifications	.117[a]	.179[a]	.195[a]
Total R^2 Accounted for	.394[a]	.434[a]	.486[a]

Note: a = significant at $p < .01$; b = significant at $p < .05$.

news scanning gratification score combine as indicators of frequent multiple program viewing.

Grazing. Some 43.4 percent of the variance in the grazing index is explained by the hierarchical regression equation. Media affinity, media situation, and RCD gratification variable blocks all add significant amounts of variance when entered into the equation. RCD gratifications to avoid commercials, television and cable viewing, and viewing alone are all central, and positively related, to the level of grazing in the hierarchical analysis. The stepwise analysis (accounting for 37.2 percent of variance) agrees on three of these four independent variables as important.[9] The stepwise analysis replaces the likelihood of viewing alone with the tendency not to consult a television program guide prior to viewing as an important predictor of grazing.

Total RCD Activity. The 48.6 percent of the variance accounted for in the hierarchical regression on the total RCD activity index is the greatest amount of explained variance seen in this series of analyses. In the hierarchy, psychological, media affinity, media situation, and RCD gratification variable blocks all add significant increments to the variance total when entered into the equation. Here, seven variables surface as key indicators of high total RCD activity: strong RCD commercial avoidance gratifications, high television exposure, high cable viewing, frequent viewing alone, low cognitive TV gratifications, high novelty seeking, and low desire for control. The stepwise analysis (44.1 percent of accounted variance) adds RCD news scanning gratifications to this list, as well as weighing more heavily the contribution of high novelty seeking and low desire for control.[10]

DISCUSSION

The results from the varied analyses help to paint a broader picture of RCD gratifications and activities. With regard to the motivations underlying RCD gratifications, the picture that emerged is a clearer one that is consistent with earlier findings. Five of the six factors—selective avoidance, aggressive play, commercial avoidance, music scanning, and news scanning—mirror the results of Bellamy and Walker's (1990a) study. The remaining factor found here—environmental convenience—combines elements of the more ambiguous "finding out what's on" and "getting more from TV" factors found in Bellamy and Walker's (1990a) study.

By looking at the analyses of variance by levels of desirability of control, novelty seeking, sensation seeking, television affinity, and technological affinity, we learn a little bit more about the psychological origins of different kinds of RCD gratifications. However, what is most striking about the results from this series of analyses is how few of these RCD gratifications could be characterized by differences in the independent variables. No gratification was distinguishable by level of either novelty seeking or technological affinity. The findings concerning television affinity affirm those of Bellamy and Walker (1990a) and point to this variable as a key to understanding RCD use. Still, a high TV affinity link is found only with selective avoidance, aggressive play, and music scanning gratifications, but not commercial avoidance, environmental convenience, or news scanning gratifications. The only pattern that tentatively emerges here is that TV affinity is related more to the "newer" uses of the RCD as an aggressive weapon or to scan for music videos than to the more traditional "older" uses to avoid commercials and be a "couch potato." High sensation seeking seems to play a role in explaining only the tendency to receive aggressive play and commercial avoidance gratifications from RCD use. Although the aggressive play finding seems consistent with the goals of seeking intense sensations, the finding concerning commercial avoidance is more confounding, given that commercial avoidance is arguably an attempt to avoid the intense sensations of commercial bombardment. As well, the sole significant finding concerning the relation of desirability of control to environmental convenience gratifications presents a mixed picture. Indeed, the need for high control could explain the strong "sound adjustment" portion of this factor but has a less clear role in explaining the couch potato aspects of this gratification. This last finding calls for thoughtful re-evaluation of the perceived control of the stereotypically passive couch potato in the television environment.

The analyses of variance on RCD activity variables showed similarly limited sole impact of the psychological and media affinity variables. That the bulk of the findings point to a null result, and that levels of novelty seeking and technological affinity seem individually to be unrelated to any of the RCD activities, may be more important than the significant results. However, the finding that high sensation seeking was significantly related to RCD dominance and entry scanning tells us more about the "tool" versus "toy" character of these RCD activities. The results here point to the high intensity of affect associated with these activities. The null results of desirability of control on the variables paint a picture of the playful, rather than controlling, character of individuals who dominate use of the RCD or use it to scan the television environment as it is entered.

The significant analysis of variance (ANOVA) results for desirability of control on RCD activity point to three findings that are, at first glance, in conflict with one another. Low desire for control was linked to high levels of muting, grazing, and total RCD activity. Certainly, the fact that low desire for control predicts high grazing and total RCD activity can make good sense given that such RCD activities are little concerned with control. However, the low control associated with frequent muting can only be explained by looking at its implications in reverse. High desire for control may have more to do with watching what one intends to watch than in controlling one aspect of the viewing environment, such as muting the sound. Certainly, much remains to explain and confirm the low control but high muting finding. Finally, the ANOVA analyses again highlighted the importance of TV affinity in explaining a variety of RCD activities. RCD dominance, multiple program viewing, grazing, and total RCD activity all have positive and significant links to related levels of TV affinity. Equally important, however, are the findings that muting, entry scanning, and commercial avoidance are not explained by underlying levels of TV affinity.

The results from the series of regression analyses paint broad brushstrokes across the picture of RCD activity. Perhaps most important is the confirmation of Bellamy and Walker's (1990a) finding that demographic variables do not contribute in a meaningful way to explanations of RCD activities among students. Confirmed as well is the fact that RCD gratifications are very important in explaining such activity, even when entered last into a considerable list of independent predictors. Their findings concerning the importance of media affinity and media situation variables are also largely confirmed. As a class of variables, the media situation measures are significant in all but the explanations for entry scanning and muting. The media affinity group merits little importance in these fairly weak explanations and also fails to play a significant role in explaining multiple program viewing. One of the most striking findings concerning the impact of variable groups in explaining RCD activity was the meager impact of television gratification block. Only in one equation—for entry scanning—did the television gratification block add a noteworthy amount of variance when entered into the analysis.

A main feature of this study was the adding of psychological variables to Bellamy and Walker's (1990a) transactional explanation of RCD activities. Although ANOVA analyses for these variables point to a limited role in explaining RCD activities, the regression analyses suggest that their impact may be more significant. In three of the seven hierarchical equations— for entry scanning, muting, and total RCD activity—the psychological variable block makes a significant contribution to explaining the dependent measure. The stepwise analyses point to high novelty seeking as a key indicator of high scores on these dependent measures. In addition, low desirability of control is a significant predictor of high muting and total RCD activity scores. As has been suggested earlier, the low desire for control finding for high total RCD activity reinforces the novelty findings and points to a "toy" or play orientation associated with total RCD activity. The finding concerning muting appears to be more complex, and the high control pairing with low or medium muting seems particularly worthy of further investigation.

Some significant lessons may be learned about the variables that are most important in explaining RCD activity by examining other non-psychological variables that are left consistently in the equations for the seven stepwise analyses. A clearly dominant predictor of any RCD activity is the RCD gratification associated with commercial avoidance. This RCD gratification dwarfs all other RCD gratifications in the explanatory system. The only other RCD gratification left standing in any of the stepwise analyses concerns using the RCD for news scanning. High RCD gratifications for news scanning are significant in explaining high muting, multiple program viewing, and total RCD activity. Although television gratification blocks have little impact in explaining RCD activities, low levels of cognitive television gratifications are significant in explaining high levels of commercial avoidance, muting, multiple program viewing, and total RCD activity. However, these findings concerning the cognitive gratification should be approached with caution, because the Pearson correlations are consistently weak and often change sign when compared with the beta weights seen in the regression equations.

Also confirming Bellamy and Walker's (1990a) findings is the significant role played by media situation variables, especially habitual television and cable viewing levels, in explaining RCD activities. Viewing levels appear to play important roles in muting, multiple program viewing, grazing, and total RCD activity but are less significant in explaining RCD dominance, entry scanning, and commercial avoidance. The context of viewing also seems important to consider in future studies of RCD use. The tendency to view alone is significant in explaining both grazing and total RCD activity, and infrequent use of a program guide is indicative of high commercial avoidance and high grazing. Finally, the technological affinity measure, which had all but disappeared in the analyses (even though it appears to be a very reliable measure of the concept), seems to play an important role in explaining the likelihood of RCD use to avoid commercials.

The results of this study give a broader view of the RCD gratification and activity process. The results suggest that there are many different kinds of RCD gratifications and activities; and there are a variety of reasons for these differences. Findings concerning the underlying psychological states associated with RCD activities suggest that novelty seeking may play an important role in understanding frequent RCD use. More perplexing are the findings concerning desirability of control. Although this variable seems to make a difference in explaining some kinds of RCD activities, the findings suggest that much remote control use is not related to a strong need to control the television environment, beyond fleeing commercials. In sum, these preliminary results suggest that the RCD may often be more of a toy than a tool, and that the "control" in remote control can be a misnomer masked in the guise of novelty seeking. Although the results here need to be tested in a broader context to understand the workings of the remote operator's personal judgments, the heuristic value of the transactional approach and the theoretical importance of underlying psychological reasons for differential RCD use have been confirmed.

NOTES

1. Transactional models follow a straightforward logic. Wenner (1982; 1985) reasons that each model should first take account of the social and psychological origins of needs and values as general background since they are the most pervasive and, in good part, shape other influences. General foreground variables such as media affinities and beliefs that develop over years of media use enter next into the equation because they tend to set the tone for media reference background variables that characterize recent patterns of media exposure. Recent patterns of exposure in turn lead to and shape the current expectancies (or specific gratifications sought) and perceived satisfactions (or gratifications received) from engagement in media consumption. In this case, we conceptualized gratifications sought generally from television as modifying the specific gratifications obtained from RCD use. Although each test of the transactional model may specify different variables of interest, the basic logic of the model sees a dynamic and ever-changing system of variables wherein the influences of certain variables are antecedent to the influences of others. In this regard, the model is very conservative in its estimates of the role of gratifications in effects; self-reported gratifications become determinative only when they are non-redundant of the influences of other variables.

2. The following items were summed to form a technological affinity index.

1. When I go to buy a new appliance or piece of consumer electronics, I try to stay away from the models with all the advanced technical features.
2. I'm one of those people who quickly learns about how to use all the automated functions on new electronics equipment or appliances.
3. I've got some electronics gadgets around that I still haven't a clue how to fully operate.
4. I never seem to understand how to program the advanced electronic features of new appliances.
5. Using all the advanced features of a consumer electronics product is a pleasurable experience for me.
6. It's easy for me to figure out how to operate all the features of the newest consumer electronics products.
7. I really look forward to sitting down and figuring out how to get the most out of a new electronics product I've recently purchased.
8. I tend to be the kind of person who waits until everyone else has a new electronics product before I finally get one.

9. I become tense when I have to program some operation on one of my newer appliances or electronic products.
10. I get nervous when I have to set up the automated features on some appliance or consumer electronic product.
11. I'm one of those people who is always thinking of new ways to use all the features available on new appliances and products.
12. I'm frequently asked to show other people how to use the features they have on their consumer electronics appliances.
13. I tend to let someone else operate the advanced features on appliances and consumer electronics I own.
14. I tend to be one of the first people to get a new electronics product when it comes on the market.
15. I think it's important that the operational features on consumer electronics products are set up correctly.
16. I feel relieved when I've successfully set up some complex operation on an electronic appliance.
17. I always seem to need help from somebody else to get consumer electronics products operating the way they're supposed to.
18. I prefer to set up the automated functions on electronics products and appliances rather than having someone else do it.

The polarity for Items 1, 3, 4, 8, 9, 10, 13, 16, and 17 was reversed in scoring.
    3. The following RCD gratifications had split factor loadings:

I like to use the remote control because . . .
    It makes it easier to control what I see on TV.
    I can avoid things on television that really offend me.
    I don't miss as much of the good stuff on other stations.
    I can change channels without getting up.
    I can zap someone on TV that I don't like.
    I can turn off the sound fast.
    It makes television more interesting.
    I can check out what's on TV.
    I feel that I have more control over the TV networks.
    I can quickly avoid offensive things that pop up on the television screen.
    I can zap annoying commercials.
    I can kill the sound.
    I can catch sports coverage almost any time.
    I can avoid some of the obnoxious people on TV.
    TV doesn't have to be as boring.
    I can find out what's on without looking at the TV listings in the paper or the TV guide.
    It makes it easier to use my VCR.
    I get more out of watching TV.
    I can create my own unique program by choosing bits and pieces from many different shows.
    I like most electronic gadgets.
    I can catch just the good parts of a program.
    It makes it possible to control what others in the room are watching.
    I can avoid the boring parts of a program.
    You don't need a TV listing.
    I can catch the weather almost any time.
    It helps me control what programs my family watches.

4. In the stepwise regression analysis on RCD dominance, the following predictor variables produced significant Betas: TV affinity (*Beta* = .29), viewing alone (*Beta* = .24), and commercial avoidance (*Beta* = .22).

5. In the stepwise regression analysis on entry scanning, the following predictor variables produced significant Betas: race (*Beta* = .14), citizenship (*Beta* = −.21), novelty seeking (*Beta* = .19), channel options (*Beta* = −.13), and commercial avoidance (*Beta* = .36).

6. In the stepwise regression analysis on commercial avoidance, the following predictor variables produced significant Betas: technological affinity (*Beta* = .12) program guide use (*Beta* = −.15), cognitive gratifications (*Beta* = −.14), and commercial avoidance (*Beta* = .61).

7. In the stepwise regression analysis on muting, the following predictor variables produced significant Betas: desirability of control (*Beta* = −.26), novelty seeking (*Beta* = .19), TV exposure (*Beta* = .17), cognitive gratifications (*Beta* = −.30), diversion gratifications (*Beta* = .16), and news scanning (*Beta* = .23).

8. In the stepwise regression analysis on multiple program viewing, the following predictor variables produced significant Betas: gender (*Beta* = −.14), TV exposure (*Beta* = .30), viewing alone (*Beta* = .24), cognitive gratifications (*Beta* = −.19), commercial avoidance (*Beta* = .31), and news scanning (*Beta* = .18).

9. In the stepwise regression analysis on grazing, the following predictor variables produced significant Betas: TV exposure (*Beta* = .26), cable viewing (*Beta* = .21), program guide use (*Beta* = − .12), and commercial avoidance (*Beta* = .43).

10. In the stepwise regression analysis on total RCD activity, the following predictor variables produced significant Betas: desirability of control (*Beta* = −.17), novelty seeking (*Beta* = .18), TV exposure (*Beta* = .33), cable viewing (*Beta* = .17), viewing alone (*Beta* = .15), cognitive gratifications (*Beta* = −.20), commercial avoidance (*Beta* = .34), and news scanning (*Beta* = .16).

Part IV

Group Viewing in Remote Control Use: Family and Gender Issues

10

"OK, Where's the Remote?" Children, Families, and Remote Control Devices

Kathy A. Krendl, Cathryn Troiano, Robert Dawson, and Ginger Clark

A recent article in the popular press noted that the remote control device (RCD) has become "the most avidly used and fought over device in the electronic cottage" (Arrington 1992, 10). Audience use of the RCD has been referred to as "grazing" (Gilbert 1989), a constellation of behaviors that has stimulated considerable interest among academics. However, academic research has tended to focus primarily on the impact of the device in terms of industry concerns—that is, how programmers and advertisers can develop strategies to counter RCD use—rather than examining changes in the viewing experience for the audience. The strong industry orientation was established in early research on RCD use with studies of user profiles (Heeter and Greenberg 1985b) and reports of channel-changing patterns (Yorke and Kitchen 1985) and is evident even in more recent research, including the most detailed examination of RCD use to date, the *Channels* study that appeared in 1989. In this collection of articles, topics focused primarily on advertising and programming ramifications of the RCD (Ainslie 1989; Bollier 1989; Brown 1989; Snyder 1989b) and programming strategies for responding to RCD use (Selnow 1989).

Research examining the significance of the RCD for the viewer has been less evident in the literature. Examples include Morley's study (1986) of family television, which included an examination of RCD use by male and female family members in Great Britain; Snyder's report (1989a) of viewer anecdotes about the RCD-mediated viewing experience; Walker and Bellamy's work (1991a; 1991b; Bellamy and Walker 1990a) applying uses and gratifications to the study of RCD use; and Copeland's (1989) examination of RCD-induced changes in family viewing patterns. With the exception of Morley's work, all RCD data compilations to date have used survey instruments that rely on self-reporting techniques. Even Morley's study was based on what family members "said" about television and RCD use rather than what they "did" with the technology.

In addition to the heavy reliance on self-report data, research to date has adopted an exclusive interest in adult audience members. Some evidence regarding other audience members emerged from studies by Heeter and Greenberg (1985b; 1988b), who examined RCD use among preadolescents and adolescents as part of larger studies; however, even in these studies, children's perceptions and reports remained incidental rather than central. Researchers have neglected RCD interactions experienced by children within the family viewing environment. Virtually no work has examined the processes by which children have learned to use and understand the RCD.

The present study responds to these two limitations of previous research: the exclusive reliance on individuals' accounts of their RCD use and the focus on adult members of the audience. It does so by adopting a multiple methods approach (Webb, Campbell, Schwartz, Sechrest, and Grove 1981), combining survey interview, observational, and depth interview methods and by making children the primary focus. Because "TV viewing does not occur in a vacuum: it is always to some degree background to a complex behavior pattern in the home" (Bechtel, Achelpohl, and Akers 1972, 299), media use is always influenced by ongoing and dynamic relationships between and among individuals in particular contexts. The complex influence of the family viewing environment challenges researchers not to isolate and examine self-reports of RCD activities but to supplement these findings with direct observations of behaviors within their naturalistic context in order to understand them more fully.

Qualitative studies have been found to enhance our understanding of the complex interrelationships at work in the home when the integration of televisual technologies has been examined (see, for example, Lindlof, Shatzer, and Wilkinson 1988; Lull 1990; Rice and Sell 1990; Traudt, Chapter 5 of this volume.) Although these small-scale qualitative studies cannot provide a basis for generalization in the traditional sense, using a combination of research approaches can yield what Eisner calls "structural corroboration" (1991, 110). As he observed, "when multiple types of data are related to each other to support or contradict the interpretation or evaluation" of a phenomenon, the confluence of evidence "breeds credibility." In his extensive work in this area, Lull (1990) has proposed the combination of personal observation and depth interviews as complementary approaches that provide a fuller understanding of individuals' behavioral patterns. This combination of methods permits the researcher to observe behaviors within the naturalistic setting—the home—and to compare the observations with explanations and interpretations provided by the interviews. We contend that such combinations of approaches will yield a fuller and richer explanation of RCD use.

RESEARCH QUESTIONS

The present discussion, part of a larger study of new television technologies (VCRs and RCDs) effects on preschoolers' television use, focuses specifically on the RCD and adopts a multiple methods approach to address research questions in three areas:

1. How do preschool children integrate the RCD into their viewing behavior? (What access do they have to it? How do they use it? To what extent do parental rules control their use of it?)
2. How competent and knowledgeable are preschoolers with regard to the RCD? (How competent are they in using the RCD? How have they learned to use it? How well do they understand the capabilities of the RCD?)
3. What role does the RCD play in shaping family viewing styles?

In order to answer these questions, we designed a study combining research approaches. Our purpose was to acquire responses to the first set of general questions regarding preschoolers and RCDs in the home primarily from a general survey interview, and then to use in-home observations and depth interviews to explain and provide context for the survey results as well as to provide insight into the questions related to competence, knowledge, training/parental support, and family viewing styles. The two-stage investigation consisted of survey interviews with fifty preschool children followed by extensive in-home observations and depth interviews with parents and a target preschool child in each of three families.

METHOD

The two stages of the research will be discussed separately. We will first describe the procedures we followed in conducting the preschool survey. We will then discuss the procedures used in the in-home observation and depth interview components.

Preschool Survey

We contacted local preschools and asked for permission to come in and talk with children ages four to six. Three preschools representing a cross-section of Bloomington, Indiana, provided access to their facilities. At each preschool, each child participating in the study was invited into a room away from the distractions and activities of others to talk with one of the interviewers. We showed the children an RCD and asked them whether they had one at home, whether they used it, how much they knew about what it did, what they used it for, and what kinds of parental rules controlled their use of it at home.

Our questions were asked in an open-ended fashion; our pretests of the interviews with preschoolers indicated that children were able to answer the questions if we drew them into a conversation about topics of interest rather than trying to conduct a rigidly structured interview. Thus, the interviews were casual and discursive but covered all topics with each child. The entire interview lasted approximately 20 minutes per child.

In-Home Observations

The second part of the study involved observing children in a naturalistic setting, their home, to address the second and third research questions.[1] In order to qualify for the study, each family had to have at least one child between the ages of three and six, the target age group, and own a working television set connected to a VCR and RCD. The three families that agreed to participate ranged from lower-middle to upper-middle income, all were white, and all had two parents present in the home who both worked at least part-time outside the home. The three mothers all had careers related in some way to education—one taught preschool, one taught kindergarten, and one was a librarian. Two of the families had two children present; the third family had four children.

For the in-home observations, one researcher was assigned to each family for the duration of the study. The three families were visited five or six times over the course of one month for a minimum of three hours per visit. The total number of hours spent with each family ranged from 15 to 26, depending upon the family's availability. Because all the children were involved in at least part-time daycare, possible observation times were somewhat limited; we worked with the families to accommodate their routines and plans. We scheduled observations to include a variety of times and days, assuming that their viewing behaviors would, at least in part, be shaped by the programming options available at any one point in time. Thus, in each household we observed the target child's viewing at least once during each of the following time periods: late afternoon (3 to 6 P.M.), early evening (6 to 9 P.M.), and Saturday morning.

Researchers were instructed to focus their observations on the target child within each home, though other household members and their activities during the observation period were recorded as well. The first visit was designed to allow the observer to begin to develop a relationship with the family and the target child. During this visit, the observer watched television with the child and talked with the parents. On the second visit, the researcher and child viewed and discussed one of the child's favorite videotapes.

Early in the observations, the researcher conducted depth interviews with the child and with each of the parents individually. The interview with the child addressed questions similar to those in the preschool survey but used more probes and follow-up questions in an unstructured, open-ended style.

The interview with the parents covered areas such as how program selection was determined in the home; parental concerns about their children's television and video use; level of support and instruction they provided the target child for RCD, VCR, and television use; rules about television, RCD, and VCR use; and a description of viewing styles of the family members. On the last visit, at the end of the observation period the parents were interviewed together. The final interview encompassed discussion about and clarification of behaviors and details that emerged from the in-home observations.

RESULTS

Preschool Survey

The sample of preschoolers interviewed (N = 50) included slightly more girls than boys, ranging in age from four to six. In terms of direct access to the RCD, 88 percent of the children said they had RCDs in their homes. This percentage is quite close to Arrington's recent national estimate of 85 percent (1992). In addition, we asked the children who used the RCD in their home and whether they were permitted direct access to it. Fifty-two percent of the children said that they used the RCD themselves. In addition, they reported that 74 percent of their mothers and 76 percent of their fathers used the RCD.

None of the children mentioned specific rules related to RCD use. In addition, only three reported that they were "not allowed to touch" the VCR. The children indicated that their parents had rules regarding the amount of viewing (60%) and the content of programming (50%). Yet, when they were asked to articulate these rules, 30 percent could not identify specific rules related to the amount of viewing and 22 percent could not identify the content rules of their household. Of those who could articulate rules, the most notable response was that parents often prohibit "scary" and "sexy" content. Despite considerable changes in the viewing environment since the introduction of VCRs and RCDs to the home viewing environment, parental rules regarding television have not changed much since the 1970s (for review, see Dorr 1986).

We also asked the preschoolers about their understanding of the uses of the RCD. When they were asked to explain what the RCD does, 16 percent said they did not know. The two most frequent answers were that it "changes channels" (mentioned by 60 percent) and that it "turns the TV on and off" (54 percent). Comparisons of boys' and girls' responses resulted in no differences in terms of understanding the functions of the RCD, though 21 percent of the girls said they didn't know what the RCD did, compared to 10 percent of the boys. In addition, no clear differences emerged in relation to the child's age; that is, responses regarding the functions of the RCD from four-year-olds were similar to those given by five- and six-year-olds.

In-Home Observations and Depth Interviews

We now turn to the results of the in-home observations and depth interviews with the parents and target children. We were particularly interested in the processes related to RCD use—how do young children develop competence with the technology, what do they know about the technology and how have they learned it, and how has the RCD shaped family viewing styles?

The Smith Family. Michael and Janet live with their two children, Carie (age 4 1/2) and Ben (age 2 1/2), in a small city that is home to a large midwestern university. Both Janet and Michael hold master's degrees and work full-time outside of the home; Janet is a librarian and Michael is a media specialist.

The family room is the center of activity within the home. The TV is located in one corner on top of a modular unit that houses the VCR and the family videotape library, which consists of about thirty children's videos. In front of the television set is a small play table where the children eat their meals, watch television, and do art and other activities. Their media center is serviced by three RCDs: one for the TV, another for the VCR, and the third for the satellite antenna. The relatively complex configuration has resulted in a system that is characterized by a high level of parental control over both selecting and accessing content. Rigid and strict rules govern access to the technologies. The general rule is that the children are not permitted to touch the components of the system.

Both children are enrolled in full-time preschool programs. Parents and children return home in the late afternoon, and the children dominate television viewing from 5:30 to 8:30 P.M. Though the parents frequently share in and interact with their children while they view, the content selections during this time are designed to serve the children. Bedtime preparation takes approximately an hour more, which leaves little time for adult viewing in the evenings.

During the observations, typical viewing was characterized by the mother giving Carie and Ben a list of three or four choices from their video library; each child would select one of the choices offered. After selections were made, one of the parents, usually the mother, would insert the videotape and start it for them. Even matters such as controlling the volume or changing channels were typically handled by the parents—again, usually the mother. Consequently, Carie and Ben had little opportunity to interact independently with any of the televisual technologies in their home. During the course of the observations, the children never attempted to manipulate any of the components—RCDs, VCR, or television. As a result, their knowledge and competence with the RCD and the VCR are minimal. Carie understands that the RCD is used to manipulate the VCR but has little practical experience with the hardware.

During the interview with Carie, the observer noted, "I started off by asking her if she could tell me the name of the remote control device. She called it a 'clicker' but went on to say that it 'starts movies' and 'turns them up and down.' Her instant linkage of the remote to videotapes reflects the minimal use of television programming in this home." During the course of the observations, the children watched only one broadcast/cable program—"Inspector Gadget"— on a Saturday morning. All other viewing (and all other viewing choices presented by the mother) consisted of children's videos. Because Janet and Michael are always involved with the children's viewing activities and are available for assistance, neither child showed concern or frustration about their lack of expertise. As Carie observed at one point during the interview and after trying to insert a tape backwards, "I don't use it [the VCR] alone, so I don't need help."

Both parents, but mostly Janet, work actively to engage their children's interest in the selected content, for example, asking questions, directing their attention to the screen, watching and reacting along with the children. They teach their children to be active, engaged viewers. In addition, both parents are advocates of prosocial and educational messages within the media content consumed by their children. They have firm ideas of appropriate content, which must meet Janet's strict criteria. As Michael observed, "[W]e can't control what they view at their friends' homes, but we feel it is easier to maintain control here at home than it is to retrieve it once it has been relinquished."

Once Carie and Ben are in bed, Michael and Janet are free to watch their preferred content, and a different viewing style dominates. Michael enjoys cable programming, especially historical documentaries and miniseries. Janet disdains most TV content, saying, "I can't believe there are thirty-five channels and still nothing to watch most of the time. I wouldn't walk across the street to watch most network programming." Even when Janet does watch television, it is more of a background activity to accompany looking at catalogs or eating.

Janet and Michael may be infrequent users of television, but they enjoy the benefits of the RCD. Michael enjoys being able to scan through the channels or to fast-forward through commercials on previously recorded programming. Janet, though more of a purposeful user of the RCD who plans what she is going to watch, finds that she is now more likely to change to another channel at the end of a program rather than watching whatever comes on next. She explained that she would previously "lock in" to a certain station and stay there for the duration of her viewing time. Neither parent voiced concerns about the presence of the RCD in their home, compared to their considerable concerns about television content.

The rules in this home are unspoken. The observer recorded in her field notes:

Carie told me that her parents had no rules regarding how much television she could watch and, as for content, she noted that "they sometimes tell me things are too scary for me." My observations supported this view though I think it necessary to point out that the rules in this house appear to be the "unspoken" sort. Considering the amount of control the parents exert over the viewing situation, there really is no need for them to articulate rules to the children.

Both Michael and Janet have strong opinions about the potential effects of television. Michael feels that one important function of television is to introduce children to a wide variety of cultural information. He finds this opportunity is often missed by standard network fare. Janet worries about programming that may be inappropriate—too scary or too violent—for her children. For this reason, they carefully screen what their children watch. As a further check, the home's complex televisual configuration serves as an additional barrier to the children's exposure to possibly harmful content.

The children's viewing styles reflect both their parents' view of television and, to some extent, their parents' viewing styles. The vast majority of their viewing time is filled with videotapes, which their parents feel afford greater control over content than network or cable programming. Videos tend to emphasize the type of positive messages and lighthearted music and songs that Janet and Michael feel are appropriate for preschool children. Because control over content is retained by the parents during viewing (for example, starting the tape, stopping it, rewinding it, adjusting the volume, all performed with the RCD), the children never skip over parts of a tape; they tend to watch each tape sequentially. Carie explained how her mother would help them watch favorite parts: "we sometimes go back and replay favorite parts but we don't skip anything."

In addition, Carie's viewing style mimics that of her mother. Like her mother, who consults the program guide before turning the set on, Carie watches preselected content from a listing of choices recited by her mother. Like her mother, she watches it from beginning to end without changing channels, fast-forwarding through content, and so on. A final similarity in viewing style was Carie's tendency to use the television as background noise, as Janet did. The observer noted, "During my observations, Carie and Ben ate dinner, played with toys, read books, and talked with each other or their parents while viewing videos. Only during one visit did the children actually sit attentively and watch a videotape."

An interesting characteristic of viewing styles in this home was the strict segregation of child and adult program content. The viewing styles and content change dramatically in the home after the children go to bed. As long as the children are up, television content caters to their interests and is tightly controlled by the parents, in particular by the mother, not only to insure that no offensive materials appear but also to insure that positive content does appear. Once the children have been tucked in their beds, more mainstream content is likely to appear (though both parents deny watching much commercial television) and more grazing behaviors emerge as well. The actual style of viewing changes when the children are not present.

The Jones Family. An upper-middle-class suburban midwestern community has been home to Jenny and Tom for about a year. This most recent move followed a series of job relocations to Michigan, New York, and Connecticut. Both Jenny and Tom possess college degrees and work outside of the home—Jenny, part-time, as a nursery school administrator and teacher and Tom, full-time, as an engineer for a public utility.

Their four children, Sally (age 14), Jeff (age 12), Erin (age 7) and Jimmy (age 3) enjoy free access to a variety of viewing situations and options. The family has four color television sets located at different viewing sites: living room, family room, the oldest daughter's bedroom, and the parents' bedroom. The main viewing area is in the family room, adjacent to the kitchen. The family does not subscribe to any cable service. VCRs are connected to the TV in the family room and in Sally's bedroom. Both viewing sites are equipped with RCDs. Parental control over viewing content and quantity is minimal, and conflicts over program preferences are resolved by moving to another viewing site. Despite this practice, the family tends to view as a group in the family room, where all the furniture is arranged to permit an unobstructed view of the set.

This family, more than any other in the study, watched television and videos avidly and clearly enjoyed doing so. Jenny expressed some concerns about the quality of television content, and she is clearly the party who is responsible for monitoring and rule-making around television viewing, but any constraints on interaction with the medium or its add-on technologies are strictly temporary and limited in extent. For example, the observer noted, "When I asked about rules for television, Jimmy said that sometimes they have rules. He called it their 'summer rule,' when he can watch only his favorite shows. He was referring to a set of rules that his mother would later relate to me in which she had limited the children to one hour of programming during the day due to 'overusage of TV.' " In this family, rules around television were transient and context-dependent; the only rule that existed in relation to the RCD was related to positioning. Both parents expressed the rule that the RCD was supposed to be returned to the end table nearest to the television set, though both parents laughingly conceded that the usual position for the RCD was "lost."

Parental enjoyment of the medium has resulted in a rich media environment, providing the children with ready access to VCRs, RCDs and a Nintendo game system. During the family dinner hour, the entire family routinely watched and discussed a program as a group. The parents consider group viewing as serving a healthy, integrating function in their family; it keeps them talking to each other—parents, teenagers, preschoolers—around a common subject.

High parental engagement in television has contributed to the acceptance of RCD technology in this home. The device is perceived as a benign extension of the television. Its use facilitates what is already an avid interest in content. Tom and Jenny's acceptance and enjoyment of the RCD have affected the willingness with which their children engage the device.

In the Jones family, Jenny said that channel changing was the biggest change she and Tom had noticed in relation to the RCD. She described sampling TV on several different channels and described her husband, Tom, as being particularly active during sports programming. Tom contended that he was more likely than Jenny to be channel-loyal, having more of a tendency to "go with the flow" of TV, though he acknowledged being an active channel-changer.

Tom favors changing during a program's course, a practice made easier during sports broadcasts, which are structured with time-outs and penalty decisions that lend themselves to grazing behavior. Jenny favors using commercials as a grazing opportunity. Jenny related that following the action on more than one program at once is easy with content with which she is familiar—for example, old movies, "in order to watch the good parts"—a practice that Tom denies being capable of accomplishing.

Jenny related that she has been an active channel-changer since childhood, when she would sit right on top of the set and twist the tuner from station to station. She acknowledged that the RCD had only made easier what has been a lifelong viewing pattern. Another area made easier is volume control. In the past when the children got so loud as to drown out the TV, both parents said they would have to yell at the kids to pipe down. Now, they can maintain their seats and raise the TV's volume from a distance. The children, upon hearing the TV-generated reprimand, usually diminish their noise level without words ever having been spoken.

Finally, the parents noted that the introduction of the RCD into their home has been accompanied by the almost daily hunt for the "lost" remote. As Tom remarked, "It is usually in the couch cushions or just plain lost [rather than positioned on the end table closest to the TV]." In spite of the recurring problem of locating the device, both Tom and Jenny have no urge to go back to pre-RCD living. They like their RCD.

Though Jenny assists Jimmy, the target child, in many of the same ways observed in the Smith family, including tape set-up and encouraging active, engaged viewing (again, a job her spouse does not feel compelled to perform), there is no attempt to segregate his content from the rest of family content. At times, Tom and Jenny each encourage their children to join them for viewing their favorite content: "MacGyver" for dad and "Star Trek: The Next Generation" and afternoon soaps for mom. Jenny acknowledges that the older children, Sally and Jeff, are soaps addicts already, with Sally time-delay taping her favorite program on a daily basis. In spite of the sheer volume of viewing that does take place, it was common for members of the family to read while viewing—except for Jimmy, who lacks reading skills at this point.

Though Jenny and Tom did not set out to train their children in its manipulation, the sheer volume of opportunities to employ the RCD has led their children to master its functions. Older siblings demonstrated complete mastery of RCD functions and operated the device routinely in the home. The combination of the mother's support and assistance, as well as sibling support, in helping the target child with the RCD provides explicit encouragement of the younger child's facility.

Even at three years of age, Jimmy has mastered the basics of RCD use. Though he has some difficulty articulating its functions verbally, observations demonstrated that he has a clear understanding of the device. The observer noted,

He appeared to understand the uses of television technologies, such as the remote control device, the VCR, and the home video game system. He was neither intimidated by, nor unfamiliar with, either their form or function. He could identify both the components and knew how to make them work. His responses to my questions were simplistic in nature, but, later in the observations, it became clear that he possessed the mechanical skills necessary for manipulation.

He primarily uses the RCD to change channels on the TV in order to watch his favorite programs. He must ask for assistance with channel numbers because he does not yet recognize numbers. He must also ask for time-telling assistance, but when it is received, he knows if his program should be airing. Any advice sought was specific and limited, and the actual manipulation of the technology was done by Jimmy, not by siblings or parents. One example from the observations illustrates this pattern:

Jeff and Erin [the older siblings] came into the family room and sat and listened to our conversation. They turned on the television set and Jimmy brought the remote control to his mother for assistance. He wanted to know the station number to press in order to get his program. Jenny had to ask Jeff what channel "Teenage Mutant Ninja Turtles" was on and he replied "59." Jimmy then successfully manipulated the remote to the proper channel.

At times, the manner of Jimmy's interaction with the RCD appeared almost play-like, testing and experimenting to see what it could do. Though no grazing behavior was observed, there were times when he would "accidentally" locate children's content through a mistake in channel entry on the RCD pad. Play behavior and lucky content finds seem to lend themselves to exploring such behavior. The fact that Jenny and Tom graze, with Jenny being adept at following more than one program at a time, may contribute to Jimmy's future use of the RCD. For now, Jimmy shows interest in pre-selected content and in watching shows from beginning to end rather than grazing. Even when he was encouraged to fast-forward through a tape to his favorite part, he declined on numerous occasions. His fascination with the content was complete, and he watched it all.

The Roberts Family. Both Mike and Mary have advanced degrees: Mary has a master's degree in early education, and Mike is a graduate student. Mary works full-time as a kindergarten teacher. They have two children, Jan, the target child (age 4) and Tim (age 2). The remote control device plays a significant role in the family's televiewing activities.

The family has one television set, which is located in the living room. It is an older model color console and is the focal point of the room. The family subscribes to basic cable service, as well as The Disney Channel. Connected to the television is a VCR equipped with an RCD. Because this is the only RCD, the VCR is on constantly to enable the family to conveniently switch channels as well as control the VCR.

Mike and Mary pride themselves on having created a "close and connected" family, which they feel will remain unaffected by television. Though Mary has some reservations about television's potential for negative effects, she feels that rule-making is impossible since the TV set is on all the time when her husband is home. It is Mary who attempts to control the content her children view. Mary wishes that the television was not such a presence in her home but feels there is little she can do because Mike enjoys viewing so much.

The only rule that emerged around the RCD concerned the time-delay programming buttons. Jan was told she was not allowed to use these buttons. The family had an extensive repertoire of time-delay programming, for example, programs they want to watch but that air when they are putting the children to bed. They feared that Jan might inadvertently make changes in the programmed recordings and, therefore, prohibited touching those parts of the RCD. Regular taping included one of Jan's favorite shows, which aired while she was at school. In addition, Jan regularly inserted a tape and recorded one program, while watching another, after she got home from school. Thus, it became apparent that it was not taping functions that were restricted but rather potential situations that might disturb pre-set programming.

The children's RCD use can be understood through the way the parents use the technology. The parents' use of television, the RCD, and the VCR in the home greatly affects the rules about the children's access to and their level of competence with the RCD and the VCR. Mike watches television much more than Mary or the children. Because of his viewing style, television is turned on whenever he is in the room. It is Mike who controls the RCD most often in the home. He refers to it as his "third arm." When he is in the room, the RCD is never far from his side. All members of the family report that the device is always on the table next to his place on the couch when he is viewing.

Mike insisted this practice is not a "power thing" but a reflection of the different ways in which he and his wife grew up in regard to television. He described his superior viewing skills (e.g., knowing the channel numbers; adopting an attentive, critical viewing style; possessing more extensive experience in relation to television; and focusing on the television rather than on household chores, as Mary does while viewing) as justification for both his program choice authority and his television viewing style.

Mike admitted that he watches television in a variety of ways, grazing through the channels, viewing several programs at once, unless it is a program in which he is particularly interested. He also uses it to zip through commercials and uninteresting content on prerecorded material. Despite his propensity for grazing, this behavior does not occur often because he claims the kids usually have command of content during at least two hours of their evening viewing time. Mary was described by Mike and herself as seldom watching TV unless it is accompanied by other activities, such as doing household chores or reading the paper. Mike finds it annoying when Mary is inattentive to the screen. He insisted he watches three times more content than his wife but is affected by it less. He wants her to actively engage in a program, which he perceives to be a defense against any possible negative effects that TV viewing may yield.

Mary contended that the RCD had not affected her viewing habits to any great degree. She uses the remote to change channels in order to view programs she has preselected. More of a planned viewer, Mary usually knows what she wants to watch when she turns on the TV. She uses the channel listings guide more than her husband does. She will occasionally graze through the channels until she finds interesting content but acknowledges it is usually a stalling tactic to avoid housework. Once she finds interesting content, she tends to stay with it.

Mike's "constant switching of channels" irritates Mary. She feels that she is not able to watch television and prerecorded tapes without disturbance because of Mike's use of the RCD. For the most part, he will let her watch her favorite shows without interruption, but if he feels she is not watching intently, he will flip through the channels. For Mary, the RCD is a convenient way to switch channels when a program of interest comes on another station. Unlike Mike, she seldom uses it to search out something to watch.

This difference between the spouses, both in styles of viewing and in their perceptions of the impact of television, does generate conflict; Mary jokes that she "[doesn't] get to watch TV any more." She finds Mike's grazing to be annoying. If she picks the show, Mike always asks if he can check the sports scores. If they are actively engaged in one of their favorite programs, such as "LA Law" or "Cheers," he uses the RCD only during commercials.

Jan's use of the RCD is an interesting balance between the way her parents use the device. Her skill at using the RCD comes from her father's overt instruction. She is aware of what all the buttons on the RCD do. The observer noted,

When I asked her about the remote control device, she understood that it controlled the VCR, not the television. She understood that the VCR controlled the television. She explained that the RCD controlled the channels...and she knew what all of the buttons on it did. At the bottom of the RCD were buttons that controlled setting the machine for recording when you are away from the home. She said she was not allowed to use these buttons. Only her father used these buttons.

Mike is very proud of his daughter's skill at manipulating the device, and he encourages her to use it. She uses the RCD primarily when viewing prerecorded material. Jan records her favorite cartoons while she is at school and views them when she gets home. She uses the RCD to fast-forward through the "words" (credits), as these have little meaning for her since she docs not read. She also uses the device to fast-forward through "the boring parts" and to rewind the tape in order to watch her favorite segments over and over again. (Although this activity pleases Mike, Mary finds it somewhat annoying, since she is generally in the room monitoring content.)

In the early stages of the interviews and observations, Jan used the RCD much like her mother. That is, she used it to switch channels to watch a specific program. Like Mary, she seldom grazed and watched only when she knew something was on that interested her. However, her mother reported later that Jan had started to use the RCD in ways more similar to her father. Much to Mary's consternation, Jan started to watch television more often and to mimic Mike's habit of constantly flipping through the channels in an attempt to find something that interested her. Mary reported that, on occasion, Jan and Mike share control of the RCD when they are both in the room viewing at the same time. They both encourage each other to flip through the channels, regardless of who is watching what.

What causes Mary the most concern is when Jan flips through the channels when Mary is trying to watch a specific program. Jan's excuse for doing this is the same as Mike's: "You are not really watching it anyway." Mary may have more to worry about in the future. Although Tim, at two years of age, does not use the RCD, he understands its potential power with regard to televiewing. On one occasion he grabbed what he thought to be the RCD and ran in front of the television, pushing buttons in an attempt to change the channel. He understood the concept of the RCD but had picked up a calculator, mistaking its shape and buttons for the device.

DISCUSSION

Taking the results of the survey interview and the in-home observations and depth interviews together, this study suggests that preschoolers have ready access to RCDs in their homes and that they are active users of the device. Furthermore, if they have access to the RCD, even young children will learn the device's basic functions. Preschool children are able to use the technology even at very young ages (three being the earliest in this study). Reading, time-telling, and counting skills are not necessary for using the device effectively. Also, gender and age did not emerge as important factors in influencing understanding or use of the RCD. Access appears to be the key to establishing a basic level of competence. Access goes hand-in-hand with parental encouragement to achieve technological knowledge/competence either explicitly or implicitly. In addition, the findings indicate that the RCD is considered a nonthreatening tool, and parents do not feel the need to control its use in the same way as television. The device itself elicits little response from parents in terms of rules and limits.

Both the survey and the observations suggest that preschoolers use the RCD keypad in very basic ways to control the television rather than the VCR, changing channels, lowering the volume, and so on. On several occasions, children were observed going to the front of the VCR to stop/start or to rewind tapes rather than using the RCD to do so. It may be that the simplicity of the front plates of VCRs appear less intimidating than the RCD for these functions. Thus, despite the fact that they have ready access to the RCD, they tend to use the device in very basic ways.

Preschoolers' RCD use patterns are related to, but not a direct imitation of, their parents' RCD use. That is, grazing parents do not necessarily guarantee grazing children, at least in children in this age group. Child-specific content appears to have great appeal and is attended to from start to finish, in most cases. However, two factors appear to be directly related to the development of grazing behaviors. First, exposure to parents' and/or siblings' grazing habits and patterns appears to be related to the child's interest in grazing. Group viewing that includes different family members of different ages lends itself to the development of an interest in grazing in younger children. Second, when observation of parental or sibling grazing is coupled with overt instruction in how to use the RCD for grazing behaviors, direct modeling of the behaviors may begin to emerge, as we observed in the Roberts family. In this case the father served as a clear role model for the target child in determining how to integrate the RCD into her viewing style. The father's manipulation of the RCD was directly imitated by the target child, much to the mother's frustration. In addition, in the two homes where parents were more positive about commercial programming (the Jones and Roberts families), group viewing was more common, with its inherent exposure to others' viewing styles and habits. In these homes the children exhibited higher levels of competence with, knowledge about, and interest in RCD technology.

Our analysis of family viewing styles suggests that children play an important role in shaping family viewing styles and practices, just as parents play an important role in shaping children's viewing. In all the homes we observed, certain times of day were devoted exclusively to children's viewing. In one home this pattern was especially noteworthy because separate viewing styles and distinct uses of the RCD had been created around adult and child viewing, which were completely segregated activities. When the children were present, the medium was totally dedicated to children's content and no grazing behaviors were in evidence. However, after the children were put to bed, different content as well as different viewing styles and RCD uses appeared. In the other homes family viewing was the norm, but certain time periods were reserved for the children to assume control of the content and the technology. Parents were available for assistance and mothers constantly monitored content, but manipulations of the RCD, as well as content selections, were determined by the children.

The emergence of distinct viewing periods and styles as a function of the absence or presence of children appears to be directly linked to changes in the viewing environment, specifically to the introduction of RCD technology into the home viewing context. Previously, viewing styles tended to be more static (staying tuned to a particular channel) than dynamic, regardless of who was in the audience. However, the RCD offers the viewer enhanced control over content selections and facilitates dynamic viewing behaviors in the form of grazing. Clearly, many adults enjoy the control and power the RCD offers. However, for the most part they exercise this power after the children go to bed. While the children are present, the dominant viewing style caters to their needs and interests; that is, viewing tends to follow one program from beginning to end. Children's "basic" uses of the RCD suggest that they do not yet enjoy or appreciate the full capability of the device. Only in one home where parental instruction in technology use was emphasized and enthusiastically reinforced by the father did the child appear to take advantage of and pleasure in the empowerment offered by the RCD.

Once the children have disappeared from the viewing environment, a different viewing style appears to dominate, one characterized by much higher levels of grazing behaviors. Also, perhaps, this different style is more likely to fit Arrington's (1992) battleground description cited earlier. Our interviews with the parents suggested that it is when the parents viewed together that differences in RCD use and viewing styles became apparent. Fathers in these homes generally controlled the RCD more than mothers and, therefore, controlled the programming more often than the mothers when the two viewed together. The mothers consistently used the RCD in more purposive ways than the fathers, both for themselves and for their children. During the observations, only mothers consulted program guides.

Fathers, on the other hand, tended to use the RCD to scan for interesting shows. However, despite the differences in RCD use and viewing styles between mothers and fathers, we encountered only minimal levels of tension over RCD control in the homes we observed.

The observations and depth interviews make it clear that family viewing styles have been influenced, at least to some degree, by the introduction of the RCD. However, each family has integrated the device somewhat differently into their family viewing. The differences are especially compelling given the demographic similarities in these homes. Despite the homogeneity of the three homes we entered, we encountered three distinct viewing styles. For example, the "proper" location for the RCD was a clear signal about the role of the device in family viewing and about who was "in charge" of content selections. In one case, possession and control of the RCD was retained by the parents and content selections were controlled by the parents. In another home, the device "belonged" at the father's side and served as his "third arm." When he was at home, he controlled content selections as well as the RCD. In the other home, the RCD was supposed to remain on a table but always ended up "lost." Such differences in responses to the RCD do not appear to be a function of the demographic characteristics of the home or of the characteristics of the technology itself, but rather of the unique dynamics of family relationships.

We contend that direct observations of RCD behaviors within the home context can inform traditional research that relies on self-reports of behaviors by adult audience members. The richness of the observational data on routine behaviors and family interactions add depth and dimension to our understanding of how families respond to empowering televisual technologies. The combination of depth interviews and direct observation extended the findings that emerged from the preschool survey interview. The purpose of multiple methods research is to triangulate, to seek structural corroboration in the findings by combining methods. Though the present study represents only a modest effort in introducing such an approach to the study of RCD behaviors and influences, relying on a small sample of preschoolers and only three homes, we hope that the model of incorporating complementary approaches to enhance researchers' understanding of RCD behaviors within the home context will be deemed worthy of replication.

NOTE

The research presented here was supported by Children's Television Workshop through a grant to the senior author.

1. To ensure anonymity, the names of family members in the in-home observations have been changed.

11

Domination of the Remote Control during Family Viewing

Gary A. Copeland and Karla Schweitzer

Typically, media use is centered within the home and the family. The centrality of the family is often ignored because survey and experimental methods are better suited to measuring individual response than examining the ecology of the family unit. However, the family provides an additional and vital variable for researchers. The functioning of the family affects not just the members who are contemporaneously a part of the household but continues long after the members of the family break away either through natural maturing processes (going away to school, marriage, moving out) or catastrophic breakups caused by life events such as abandonment, divorce, and death.

Evidence of the family's potential for negative effect on a member's life can be seen in works by researchers such as Keitner and his associates (1990, 28), who found a "probable link between family functioning and recurrent suicide behavior"; McNamara and Loveman (1990), who concluded that family functioning helps predict who may become bulimic and who may not; and Saayman and Saayman (1989), who found that adversarial divorces have a negative effect on the psychological adjustment of the children of the divorcing parties.

Of all media choices, television is the most integrated into the family structure. Family life (e.g., meals, conversation, chores, bedtime) is influenced or punctuated by television (cf. Bryce 1987; Leichter et al. 1985). Family functioning also influences how the media are used and media's subsequent effects on individual members of the family. Lull (1980a) found that television provides both structural (environmental and regulative) and relational (communication facilitation, affiliation/avoidance, social learning, competence/dominance) uses for families. Singer and Singer's (1983) lon-

Figure 11.1
Televisions per Household

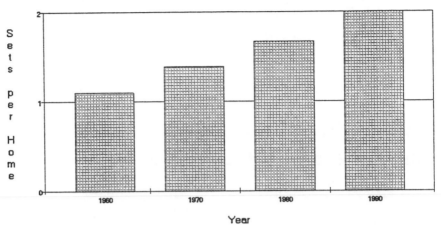

gitudinal study of 100 students over a five-year period led them to conclude that behavioral and cognitive patterns are affected by a combination of television and family variables. Simatos and Spencer (1992, 95) see television as "an active transaction between the viewer, the television, and the television environment. The uses and effects of television are, thus, closely intertwined with people's interpersonal relationships." Klapper's (1960, 8) conclusion from over thirty years ago still holds: The influence of television "functions among and through a nexus of mediating factors and influences," one of the most important of which is the family.

Initially, television (as radio before it) drew the family together in one place to share common experiences. However, the introduction of multiple television sets into homes has removed the centripetal nature of television viewing. The number of multiple set homes has been steadily climbing since the introduction of television. The rise over the last 30 years is illustrated in Figure 11.1, the data for which was drawn from the U.S. Census Bureau. Family viewing time still exists, but the predominate viewing context is not with the entire family. Lawrence and Wozniak (1989) reported that approximately 14 percent of children's television viewing is done with the entire family present, 30 percent with a sibling, 13 percent with the father, and 8 percent with the mother. McDonald (1986) reported similar findings.

PROGRAM SELECTION IN FAMILIES

Parental control of program selection—or the perception of that control—seems to have changed over time. Blood (1961) reported that among lower-class families competition over program selection in the family was usually won by the father but that in middle-class families fathers deferred to their wives and children. Smith (1961), on the other hand, described "housewives" as selecting the evening programming 45 percent of the time, husbands 14 percent, children 10 percent. Lull (1978) found that the most influential person in program selection was the father (41%), followed by the mother (34%) and then the children (25%). By 1982, Lull reported that fathers selected 36 percent, children 30 percent, and mothers 15 percent. Copeland (1989) found in a survey of families with children conducted in the same town as Smith's (1961) study that men were perceived as the person who selected the television program in 33 percent of the homes, children 25 percent, and women 19 percent. The differences between the early and later studies may be function of class differences, history, introduction of new media choices, or interaction among all three.

There is evidence that the selection process may be one of negotiation or democratic rules when authority is not invoked. Niven's (1960) early study suggests that the family as a group made the viewing decision more frequently than an individual. McLeod, Fitzpatrick, Glynn and Fallis (1982) viewed the experience as a reciprocal process within the family. Lull (1982) agreed that families often try to reach a consensus on program selection. However, the process by which program selection is accomplished is probably represented best by Gunter and McAleer's (1990) observation that family viewing patterns and selections are idiosyncratic to the family.

When democratic methods for program selection are not used, it appears that fathers tend to dominate. Lull's (1982) data show that fathers were the least likely to ask permission before changing channels. In terms of turning the set on, off, and changing channels, the father acted alone in making the decision about 90 percent of the time. Since 1982, the increasing presence of the remote control has made the ability to do all of these functions much easier.

REMOTE CONTROLS

Morley's (1986) study conducted in Britain indicates that men usually exercise dominance of the remote control. Morley notes that men do not have the competing exigencies of the home with which to deal and so maintain more authority over the use of the set. Morley also found that women were less willing to use VCRs and remote controls when their husbands were at home.

As indicated earlier, fathers were often viewed as the dominant force in program selection even before the remote control became prevalent in U.S. households. The introduction of the remote control into a home made explicit (through direct control) what may have been previously only implicit; the father controls what channel will be watched and when channels will be changed. Indeed, the ability to change channels with ease and frequency is causing discord in some families. Lindlof, Shatzer, and Wilkison (1988) note that friction from the unilateral use of the remote control can manifest itself nearly instantaneously in family interactions. The increased channel changing made possible with a remote (whether zapping or grazing) can make television viewing a chaotic experience for the individual who is not in possession of the remote. Copeland (1989) reported increasing friction within families over constant channel changing.

People recognize that such use of a remote control may be dysfunctional, as demonstrated in Walker and Bellamy's (1991a) gratifications study. The authors' "annoying others" gratification was the second factor to emerge, indicating that it accounted for a relatively large amount of the variance among the reported functions.

Another probable negative effect of the use of remote controls to change stations, especially during commercials, is a reduction in family communication. York and Kitchen (1985) report that the most common activity during commercials is conversation. Use of the remote to survey other programming probably reduces the opportunities for discussion among family members. The power of television to bring families together, to provide opportunities for discussions about mediated events and family events, seems to be reduced by the constant use of the remote control.

FAMILY COMMUNICATION PATTERN STUDIES

Previous studies have examined the family as a unit that uses television for togetherness, entertainment, information, and as a topic for family conversation (for an interesting historical review of television and its relationship to the family, see Spigel 1992). These studies often focus on the power relationships and rules that develop in the family's uses of television (e.g., Lull 1978; Wand 1968). Chaffee, McLeod, and Atkin (1971) examined ways in which parents attempted to influence the choices of their children in using television. Chaffee and associates found that the family communication environment influences how children interpret television's content and also influences children's program selection behaviors. Lindlof and Copeland (1982) determined how family viewing rules are linked with family communication patterns among expectant partners. They found that expectant couples could articulate rules for television use in both a prescriptive and proscriptive manner even before the birth of their child. They also found that partners who came from families with different communication orientations varied in their flexibility in enforcing prospective rules.

In order to study the pattern of family discussion about media and other related issues, Chaffee and McLeod in conjunction with their colleagues developed the Family Communication Pattern (FCP) scale (e.g., Chaffee, McLeod, and Atkin 1971; McLeod and Brown 1976; McLeod and Chaffee 1972). The FCP scale comprises two subscales that differentiate two distinct patterns of family communication. One subscale measures the socio-orientation of a family. Socio-oriented families stress peaceful intrafamily relationships and shun argumentative situations. Socio-oriented families strive to achieve family harmony at the cost of stifling diverse family opinion. The second subscale of the FCP measures how concept-oriented a family is. Concept-oriented families nurture and esteem the expression of opinions by family members, even when those opinions conflict. Concept-oriented families strive to foster independent thinking at the cost of momentary family harmony.

From these two dimensions a fourfold typology was constructed: laissez-faire families were those where neither socio- nor concept-orientation was emphasized. In laissez-faire families, children were most influenced by friends and peers rather than by the family. Protective families are those in which the family is high in socio-orientation but low in concept-orientation. These families stress the importance of family harmony over the individual. Consensual families show high scores for both socio- and conceptual orientations. Families support children's awarness of what is happening outside the home but still stress harmony within the family. Pluralistic families are high only in concept-orientation. In these families, the children are encouraged to challenge values and norms.

Abel (1976) found a strong positive relation between a mother's predictions of her child's preferences in programming and the child's expressed preferences in families who were high in socio-orientation. Lull (1980b) found that in high concept-oriented families parents did not use television as a means of stimulating family communication for cohesive purposes but used the media content to teach, explain, clarify, and help create positive controversy. Lindlof and Copeland summarized that "concept oriented families do not seem to accept television as readily into their lives as background or concomitant to their activities, but instead prefer to use it purposefully for commenting on larger issues" (1982, 469).

Copeland (1989) used the FCP in his study of remote control use in the family. He found that in families where the woman has possession of the remote control, there is a significantly higher socio-orientation score than in families where children or men have control. Socio-oriented families are those that attempt to reduce or control intrafamily conflict. Copeland speculates: "Mothers may take on the role of mediator between the conflicting program preferences of man [sic] and children. As the primary agent of socialization for children, the mother may literally take matters into her hands by controlling a possible source of discord in those families where harmony is important" (1989, 13).

A limitation of the FCP is that it provides evidence about four types of families along two dimensions. However, the family interactional environment is more complicated than the two dimensions represented by the FCP. A multidimensional measure of family differences is needed to provide a more precise estimation of the dynamics that may shape how television is used and how television is controlled within the family environment.

THE MCMASTER FAMILY ASSESSMENT DEVICE

The family is the primary source for the formation of our values and the definition of ourselves as individuals (Lindlof, Shatzer, and Wilkison 1988). The crucible from which the family and its constitutive individuals emerge is created from structures, functions, systems, and encounters (Anderson 1987). Anderson argues that in studying the family and its interaction with mediated communication, the intent "is to explain the presence, functions, and influence on the content and technology within the structures, functions, systems and interaction of the family" (163). The better one can understand the family system, the better one can understand the role of the media within that system.

The McMaster Family Assessment Device (FAD) (Epstein, Baldwin, and Bishop 1983; Miller, Epstein, Bishop, and Keitner 1985; Kabacoff, Miller, Bishop, Epstein, and Keitner 1990) was designed to collect "information on the various dimensions of the family system as a whole" (Epstein, Baldwin, and Bishop 1983, 171). The McMaster Model of Family Functioning (MMFF), from which the FAD is drawn (Epstein, Bishop, and Levin 1978), "describes structural and organizational properties of a family group and the patterns of transactions among family members" (Epstein, Baldwin, and Bishop 1983, 172).

The McMaster Model identifies six dimensions that the FAD operationalizes and measures: problem solving, communication, roles, affective responsiveness, affective involvement, and behavior control. In addition, the FAD contains a general functioning subscale that measures the family's functioning.

The problem-solving subscale measures a family's perceived ability to resolve problems. These solutions to family problems are seen as methods to both resolve the perceived difficulty and maintain effective functioning within the family. The task of making media selections is a problem that families must solve (Lindlof, Shatzer, and Wilkison 1988). The ability of the family to solve problems may be related to media selection procedures.

The communication subscale measures whether the family communication messages are clear and, more specifically, whether they are directed toward the appropriate individuals. It also determines whether feelings and emotions are discussed openly. Direct and emotional communication patterns are measured by the subscale. It taps a new dimension of family communication within the study of media use. The emotional element tapped by the FAD's communication subscale is related to affect tapped by the socio-oriented subscale of the FCP scale used in Copeland's (1989) earlier research.

The roles subscale measures whether tasks assigned within a family have been equitably distributed to various members of the family. The roles subscale is sensitive to the allocation of family resources, individual interests, and the distribution of tasks within the family. Finally, whether or not members are completing their assignments in good order influences the score on this subscale.

The three other FAD subscales (affective response, affective involvement, and behavior control) are dimensions that may prove useful in continued research on family functioning, domination of the remote control, and media selection. These areas do not have a sufficient set of links to the media use area to produce informed research questions or hypotheses. However, elements from each of these dimensions are included within the general functioning subscale.

The general functioning subscale comprises elements from each of the other subscales. It gives an overall measure of how well the family is functioning. It was created with items from each of the prior subscale domains. Since the general functioning subscale is a global measure of family functioning, it provides an opportunity to explore the effect of the mediating function of the family (Klapper 1960) on RCD use.

HYPOTHESES AND RESEARCH QUESTIONS

Lindlof and Copeland considered family television viewing as "an inseparable part of ongoing [family] communication patterns" (1982, 557). The work by Copeland (1989) suggests that differences in family communication patterns are related to RCD control. Specifically, Copeland's earlier results using the FCP scales suggest that family communication style is related to the issue of who has dominance of the remote control. Families in which the mother controlled the remote were significantly more likely to be socio-oriented.

Socio-oriented families are emotionally centered. This suggests that the FAD communication subscale, which measures how effectively the family can communicate about feelings, should behave in a similar manner.

> Hypothesis 1: The family communication pattern will be more direct in target and emotional in content in families where females dominate the remote control.

Copeland (1989) suggested that mothers dominate the remote control in order to restrain arguments and intercede between conflicting program preferences among the other family members, thus increasing problem-solving abilities in the home. Eakins and Eakins (1978) noted that women's communication strategies stress cooperation to achieve the welfare and goals of the group. How a family solves the problem of program selection when there are competing interests should differ by who dominates the remote.

Women who exert dominance of the remote control may do so in order to facilitate program selection decisions through their abilities to foster co-operation and harmony in the home.

> Hypothesis 2: The problem-solving functions of the family will be greater in families where the female dominates the remote control.

Lindlof, Shatzer, and Wilkison (1988) suggest that the use of video technologies may be dominated by one member of the family over the other based on tacit agreements about the appropriate roles for any given task within the home. Morley's (1986) and Lull's (1982) reports of men generally exercising dominance over most media may simply be a manifestation of the roles selected in the home, as Lindlof and his colleagues suggest. For those families where the women dominate the remote control, we would expect the family roles to be less well defined than for families where the men dominate.

> Hypothesis 3: The role functions of the family will be more defined in families where the male dominates the remote control.

Each of the preceding hypotheses focuses on the elements of communication, problem solving, and roles within the two-parent family. Epstein, Bishop, and Baldwin (1982) argue that the family should be viewed as a system. They postulate (from which the dimensions of the FAD are derived) that family functioning cannot be adequately understood by simply examining its parts. Rather, they posit that the structure and organization of the family must be examined as a whole as well. The general functioning scale of the FAD integrates the three dimensions previously examined from the McMaster Model of Family Functioning along with affective responsiveness, affective involvement, and behavior control. Epstein, Bishop, and Baldwin (1982) have argued that these elements constitute a well-functioning or "healthy" family. The relationship of family functioning to remote control domination is an interesting one that deserves at least a brief examination. A general research question is proposed as a starting point:

> Research Question 1: Is general family "health" related to the family member who dominates the remote control?

METHOD

Sample

Data were collected from 183 undergraduate students attending communication courses at the University of Alabama during the spring and summer of 1992. The sample contained twelve African-Americans and two students who were Asian foreign nationals; the remainder identified themselves as Caucasian. The two Asian foreign nationals were removed because of their small numbers and the assumption that they may come from a culturally distinct family setting. Of the 90 males and 91 females that remained, students who responded to the question, "Are your mother and father still living together?" with a "no" (n = 48) were also removed from the sample. Thus, the sample was limited to students with both parents in the home.[1] Those remaining in the sample were checked to verify that a remote control device was normally used to change channels in the home.

The final sample contained responses from 72 males (54.1%) and 61 females (45.9%). The disproportionate split in respondents' sex was not considered to be a crucial liability because information about the family rather than the individual was being gathered.

Procedures

Participants were requested to complete a booklet containing rudimentary questions about the respondent and the respondent's family's demographics. These questions were followed by specific questions about specific viewing situations; for example, when the family watches the television together, when the parents watch television together without the children, or when the children watch television together without the adults. Each scenario was followed by a series of questions as to who usually dominated the remote control and who usually made the programming decisions. Finally, the 60-item FAD was administered.

The analysis reported in this chapter focuses on the scenario of "when the family watches the television together." Results from other scenarios will be reported when they help clarify an issue within the family viewing scenario.

Criterion Variables

The original 53-item FAD had alphas ranging from .72 for behavior control to .92 for general functioning (Epstein, Baldwin, and Bishop 1983). In this study, the alphas for the four subscales were as follows: problem solving, .73; communication, .80; roles, .77; and general functioning, .87. All subscale alphas exceeded the minimum of .70 set by Nunnally (1978). A mean score for each subscale was calculated according to Epstein and colleagues' procedures. The *lower* the mean for the subscale, the *better* a family functions in that particular domain.

Usable responses to the question, "Who usually dominates (holds) the remote control when your family watches television together?" were coded into the categories of mother, father, son(s), daughter(s). The results showed

Table 11.1
Communication Subscale Means for Domination of the RCD

	Communication	Prob Solving	Roles	General
Daughters	1.49^{ab}	1.67^{ab}	2.25	1.49^{a}
Mothers	1.85^{c}	1.97	2.05	1.90
Fathers	2.16^{b}	2.11^{b}	1.98	1.79
Sons	2.37^{ac}	2.28^{a}	2.18	2.02^{a}

Note: Means with the same superscripts within the same column are significantly different from one another at $p > .05$.

that the father dominated the remote control in family viewing situations ($n = 83$, 60.1%), followed by son(s) ($n = 27$, 19.6%), mother ($n = 12$, 8.7%), daughter(s) ($n = 9$, 6.5%). The category "everyone/no one" had one response and was dropped from the analysis, as were the six families with responses missing on this item.

Statistical Analyses

To test the hypotheses, one-way analyses of variance were computed. The appropriate subscale score from the FAD served as the dependent variable, and the coded results from the open-ended question, "Who usually dominates (holds) the remote control when your family watches television together?" were used as the factors. A posteriori contrasts were made using Scheffé's tests. Data were analyzed using the subprograms of SPSSX. The significance level was set at $p < .05$.

RESULTS

Table 11.1 reports means for daughters, fathers, sons, and mothers for each FAD subscale. The first hypothesis predicted a more emotional/direct communication style in families where the females (mothers and daughters) dominate the remote control. The F ratio is significant [$F(3, 127) = 9.16$, $p < .0001$] on the communication subscale. An examination of the means for each factor showed that in families where the daughter usually dominated the remote control during family viewing situations, the family had the better scores in communication ($M = 1.49$). Families where the son dominated the remote control exhibited the lowest score ($M = 2.37$). The results of the Scheffé tests revealed that (1) the scores for families where the fathers and sons dominated the remote control were significantly worse than for families where the daughter dominated the remote control, and (2) for families where the sons dominated, scores were significantly weaker than for families where the mother dominated. Thus, Hypothesis 1 was supported.

The second hypothesis predicted that the problem-solving functions of the family will be better where the females dominate the remote control. The result of a one-way ANOVA for the problem-solving subscale of the FAD revealed a significant F ratio [$F(3, 125) = 4.72, p < .004$]. An examination of the data revealed a similar pattern to that of the communication subscale. Examination of the means for the four groups revealed, once again, that in families where the daughter dominated the remote control, the problem-solving functions were the best ($M = 1.67$); they were weakest for families with sons who dominated the remote control ($M = 2.28$). Once again, the Scheffé tests indicated that the problem-solving scores for families where the fathers and sons dominated the remote control were significantly weaker than scores from families where the daughter usually had control. Thus, Hypothesis 2 was supported.

The third hypothesis predicted that the role functions in homes where the men dominated the remote control will be more fixed than where the females dominated. There proved to be no significant relationship between who in the family dominates the remote and the roles subscale [$F(3, 123) = 2.16, p < .10$]. Thus, hypothesis 3 was rejected.

The research question asked if general family health is related to the family member who dominates the remote control. The one-way analysis of variance of the general functioning scale did reveal a significant difference for the families being studied [$F(3, 123) = 3.76, p < .013$]. The means showed that families where the daughter dominated the remote control ($M = 1.49$) were functioning significantly better than families where the son dominated the remote control ($M = 2.02$).

DISCUSSION

Morley's (1986) findings that males dominate use of the remote control are confirmed in the current research. Men have usually been viewed as the persons who control program selection, and domination of the remote control seems to make visually explicit what may have previously been implicit The possession adds additional weight to that dominance. The present findings show that it is most likely a male member of the family—either father or son—who will dominate the remote. In this study, females controlled the remote during family viewing situations in only 15.2 percent of families. Domination of the remote control also strongly suggests domination of the program selection process. As a post hoc validation of this assumption, contingency tables crossed the person who was perceived as usually dominating the remote control with the person who was perceived as usually selecting the program to be viewed by the family. (Men, women, sons and daughters were the choices for both variables.) The results of the chi square proved significant [$x^2(9, N = 107) = 74.21, p < .0001$, lamda = .30] when program selection is the dependent variable. These results support previous findings linking dominance of program selection with dominance of the remote control (Copeland 1989).

The remote control is clearly the ensign of command for program selection within the family. The data show that the person with the remote is perceived as the one who sets the viewing agenda for the family. However, whether the remote control merely goes to the authority figure (possession of the remote control as effect), or the remote control empowers an individual to set the viewing agenda (remote control as cause) is not discernible from the data presented here.

The first hypothesis, that the family communication pattern will be more direct in targeting communication and will contain more direct emotional content in families where females dominate the remote control, was supported. In families where the daughter or mother usually holds or dominates the remote control, communication is significantly more direct and emotions are discussed more freely. Women have traditionally been socialized to handle communication of emotions better than men (Deaux 1976). The ability to handle emotional messages may make the female the best person to dominate program selection in families where emotional talk is open. It seems unlikely that female domination of the remote control will cause an increase in the openness of the family to discuss emotions.[2]

The pattern seen in the communication subscale is repeated in the problem-solving subscale. The second hypothesis predicted elevated problem-solving abilities in families where the female dominates the remote control. The higher ability to solve problems and thus reduce conflict provides results similar to those found by Copeland (1989).

Copeland (1989) found that in families where the women dominate the use of the remote control, there is a significantly higher socio-orientation score on the Family Communication Pattern scale than where children or men dominate the remote control. Socio-oriented families attempt to reduce or control conflict. In families where problem solving is particularly valued, the women may take on the role of mediator of conflicting program preferences. Concomitant to the socio-orientation is the accentuation on emotion as emphasized by the need for harmony. Similar results for both communication and problem solving are not surprising within that view; thus, the domains of communication and problem solving are linked.

The rejection of the third hypothesis is surprising. Roles have played an important part in understanding the use of VCRs within the family (Jordon 1990), and it was assumed that the same would be true for remote controls. Possessing the remote control would seem to imply having a role within that particular viewing context. Perhaps the lack of significant findings is a function of the FAD's operationalization of roles. In particular, the role subscale that measures satisfaction with the distribution of tasks may be incapable of evaluating a specific role played by a single member of the family, such as the RCD controller.

The research question attempts to ascertain a measure of family health as measured by the FAD in relation to who dominates the remote control. The significant differences in scores between homes where the sons dominate and those where the daughters dominate continue to support the idea that homes where women dominate the remote control contain better-functioning families.

What seems to be a consistent finding is that in families where a female dominates the remote control (more specifically, the daughter), the family generally scores better than where males dominate. Our assumption is that elements of family functioning also influence who dominates the remote control. Unfortunately, the current study does not provide clues as to why in some families the daughter is the dominant user of the remote control.

A possible explanation is that in homes where the women dominate the remote control the family members are not as involved in stereotypical male/female roles as in other homes. Though they are not significant, the means on the role subscale hint that roles are not as well defined in families where the women dominate the remote control. Gender scholars have long argued that strongly masculine or feminine stereotyped individuals are not as psychologically healthy as those who have escaped the trap of these stereotypes (cf. Bey 1975; Bey, Martyna, and Watson 1976; Deaux 1976; Kaplan 1976). Future researchers may want to examine the gender roles of people who dominate the remote control and determine whether there is a relationship.

It was thought that daughters might have been socialized into dominance of the remote control by seeing their mothers dominate when both parents were viewing television alone. Analysis of the question, "Who dominates (holds) the remote control when your father and mother watch television alone?" shows that fathers dominate the remote control 56 percent of the time; mothers, 22 percent; and both, 22 percent. Thus, the explanation that the daughter simply has usurped or substituted for the mother is not valid.

This study solidly suggests that families where the daughter dominates the remote control are functioning better as a family than those where the males are dominant. Finally, both Copeland's (1989) study and the current study suggest that in homes where emotions are discussed and harmony is an important family goal, women will more likely dominate the remote control.

NOTES

The authors would like to express their appreciation to Rosemary McMahill, who provided valuable assistance in the preparation of this chapter.

1. Only two-parent families were included in the study so that the influence of

both mothers and fathers on remote control use could be analyzed. Of course, this decision restricts the generalizability of results to two-parent families.

2. We thought that daughter dominance of the remote control in a household might be the result of all siblings in the family being daughters. However, examination of the data revealed that this was not the case.

12

Gender Differences in Remote Control Use

*Elizabeth M. Perse
and Douglas A. Ferguson*

The popular media (e.g., cartoons, greeting cards, television shows) have satirized gender differences in RCD behavior by portraying men as channel hoppers (The battle 1991; Kissinger 1991). The image of the man in the recliner with a beer in one hand and the remote in the other has become a cultural icon. The popular media image is that men control the television set and dominate use of the remote control device. On May 30, 1991, the ABC program "Primetime Live" speculated on why men are channel hoppers with the remote. Comedian Jerry Seinfeld offered his explanation: "Men hunt and women nest. And that's why we watch TV differently. Because we're still hunting. Men are still hunting. But there's nothing to kill anymore. This [the RCD] is the only weapon left that men have, on a nightly basis, with which they can still hunt" (Sawyer 1991).

Can something with so much face validity be wrong? This chapter focuses on gender differences in the use of remote control devices. We undertook this study to identify which attitudes and behaviors showed significant gender differences and what motivations were behind the differences. Taking into consideration different approaches to explaining gender differences, we anticipated that differences in socialization would minimize some differences in remote control use for younger adults. But we expected that inherent male-female differences in information processing would be revealed in differences in the reasons for changing channels.

RESEARCH ON GENDER DIFFERENCES IN RCD USE

Men and women approach and use the remote control device differently. Several studies have noted gender differences in perceptions of RCDs, frequency of use, and motivations for changing channels.

Perceptions of RCDs

The view of the remote control device (RCD) as a part of the male domain has been reinforced by research. Gray, for example, asked women to describe household technology as either pink (feminine) or blue (masculine). This strategy "produces almost uniformly pink irons and blue electric drills" (1987, 42). Video technology is usually described in mixed colors: VCR "record" buttons are usually lilac but the timers are usually blue. However, "the blueness of the timer is exceeded only by the deep indigo of the remote control" because it is almost always controlled by men.

Males view the remote control device as a source of power. In a series of focus groups, Ferguson observed that several male participants admitted to fighting over the remote control: "My roommates and I fight over the remote. When we leave the room we hand it off to another guy to make sure someone else doesn't get it. Sometimes we'll hide it. Reminds me of people who call the remote God [because it] controlled their life" (1990a, 2). Ferguson and Perse (1991) also found that men are more likely than women to feel powerful when they are in control of the RCD. Walker and Bellamy (1991a) noted that males were also more likely to use the RCD to annoy others.

Women, on the other hand, view the remote control as a source of frustration. One of the six themes to emerge from focus group research (Ferguson 1990a) was frustration over control as a part of RCD use. Females reported a sense of frustration directed at the person (always male, in this sample of women and men) who controlled the remote control:

My dad is a cruiser. He'll flip it back and forth and it gets real irritating. My dad does that, just something fierce. It makes me so mad. 'Cause I'll sit down and he'll be watching something and I'll watch it and just at the point—I don't know how he does this—just at the point when I'm getting in to it, he'll flick it to something else. Then I'll watch that, and I'll just be getting into it, and he'll flick to something else. Everyone gives him a hard time, but he thinks they're kidding him. (Ferguson 1990a, 2)

The frustration that women feel because of a loss of control over their television viewing may lead women to have more negative feelings about the remote control device. Ainslie observed that "more than half of women viewers (who are often forced to graze by their spouses or children) . . . say they enjoy TV less while grazing" (1988, 57).

Frequency of Use

Some limited research suggests that males use RCDs more than women. Heeter (1985), for example, reported that adult males change channels more and engage in several other behaviors that reflect higher levels of channel changing. Males use viewing guides less, watch more different channels, engage in less concentrated channel use, and are more familiar with different channels.

Heeter (1988b) also noted that males are more likely to change channels before settling on a program to watch, during commercials, and in the middle of programs. Moreover, Heeter found other gender differences that may be due to greater use of remote control devices. Men exhibit less television viewing loyalty. Ten separate studies using a variety of methods revealed that females are more likely to watch the same daily and weekly programs and that men are less likely to plan their viewing before turning on the television set.

Ferguson and Perse (1991) observed several gender differences in remote control use. Men changed channels more. Women, on the other hand, were less likely to graze (flip channels) during their favorite programs. Ainslie summarized that "men graze more than women and enjoy it significantly more" (1988, 54–55).

Motivations for Changing Channels

Several studies have also identified gender differences in the reasons for changing channels. Consistent with the findings that males change channels more, males are more likely to endorse reasons for changing channels.

In general, men are more likely to change channels to avoid commercials (Ainslie 1988; Ferguson and Perse 1991), to watch two or more shows at the same time (Ainslie 1988; Ferguson and Perse 1991; Wenner and Dennehy 1990), and to check what is airing on other channels (Ainslie 1988; Ferguson and Perse 1991). Walker and Bellamy (1991a) found that college men were more likely to change channels to avoid certain types of content, especially political ads, and to watch news or weather.

Summary

Heeter (1988b) noted that men seem to prefer greater variety, rather than familiarity, in television viewing. And remote control devices make it easier for men to achieve that variety. Thus, studies reveal that males have more positive perceptions of remote control devices, use them more, and are more likely to endorse reasons for changing channels that focus on power or variety seeking. However, few scholars have speculated about the underlying causes of these gender differences.

THEORETICAL PERSPECTIVES ON GENDER DIFFERENCES

Feminist writers have identified three perspectives on gender differences: liberal, radical, and socialist (Steeves 1987; van Zoonen 1991). In general, different explanations are based on the socialization of children, biological and psychological characteristics, and social and economic power. Each perspective has implications for RCD use.

The liberal perspective holds that there is no inherent biological or psychological basis for most gender differences. The strongest factor in creating differences between males and females is socialization. Stereotypical roles are pervasive in society; children learn these roles from parents, schools, peers, and the media. An important implication of liberal perspectives is that gender differences can be eliminated through social learning. Societies can eliminate gender-based stereotyping through education and social action.

Conversely, the radical perspective holds that there are profound biological and psychological differences between men and women. Men and women differ greatly in physiology, and some scholars argue that there are physiologically based gender differences in information processing (Meyers-Levy 1989) and ethical reasoning (Gilligan 1982). This perspective is considered "radical" because its proponents believe the following: Because female characteristics are belittled in patriarchal societies, women can realize their goals only when they separate from men.

The socialist perspective posits that women's social roles promote gender differences. The patriarchy creates and maintains these roles to maintain economic and political power. The domestic roles occupied by women, focusing on nurturing and concerns for family, are accorded less societal power. According to this view, gender differences are socially based and can be eliminated only by societal upheaval. Like the liberal perspective, the socialist perspective is concerned with gender differences leading to gender inequality. The two perspectives differ, though, in level of concern and assumptions about society.

The liberal perspective focuses on reducing gender differences through changes at the individual level—equal socialization of children and elimination of gender stereotypes. The liberal perspective is rooted in social tradition and affirms the value of existing societal structures. The socialist perspective, on the other hand, holds that individual change can occur only through changes at the societal level. Gender differences are based in social, economic, and class divisions reflected in family and work structure. Thus, the socialist perspective argues for change in the existing social structures.

Explaining Gender Differences in RCD Use

Liberal Explanations. The evidence suggests that differences between men and women's use of remote control devices reflect differences in socialization. In recent studies, adult respondents, socialized in an earlier era of strong gender differentiation, exhibited clearer differences in RCD use than younger respondents. Heeter (1988b) found many gender differences in adult samples across ten separate studies, but only few differences in three samples of fifth and tenth graders. Ferguson and Perse (1991) noted several gender differences in RCD behaviors and attitudes in men and women, but these differences were not apparent in young women and young men (Ferguson 1992a; Walker and Bellamy 1991a; Wenner and Dennehy 1990). This reduction in gender differences found in samples of younger viewers is consistent with findings associated with mental abilities (e.g., verbal, spatial, and mathematical) and social behaviors (e.g., influenceability, helping, aggression). Hyde, for example, found that research on social behaviors over the past fifteen to twenty years has shown "a decline in the magnitude of gender differences" (1990, 72). She used d scores, where $d = M_m - M_f/s$, yielding an effect size (positive when male greater, negative when female greater). Between 1966 and 1973 her meta-analysis showed gender difference effect sizes $d = .53$, but only $d = .41$ between 1978 and 1981. Female advantage in verbal ability among pre–1973 studies was $d = -.23$ but only $d = -.10$ after 1973.

The liberal view suggests that older adults acquired their media use attitudes and learned television behaviors when U.S. society was more sex-delineated. Thus, females in general would be expected to use the RCD less. But the behavior of younger women raised in more feminist times should reflect fewer gender differences.

Radical Explanations. Another possible explanation for RCD-related gender differences highlights differences between males and females in attentional styles, information processing, and judgment. The superior verbal development of females, which is exhibited at an early age, allows them to listen to television without looking more often than boys do. However, males have superior visual skills. Alvarez, Huston, Wright, and Kerkman (1988) reported several experiments and secondary analyses that demonstrated consistent differences between boys and girls in visual attention. They concluded that boys focus more on the visual content of television and girls focus more on the verbal auditory content.

Other researchers have studied gender differences in attention and recall. Anderson, Lorch, Field, Collins, and Nathan (1986) reported that men looked at the television set more than women. Although Stauffer, Frost, and Rybolt (1983) found no gender differences in the recall of network television news programs, Gould (1987) noted that younger females recalled more television commercials than other male and female groups. Gould attributed such findings to greater self-consciousness about inner thoughts and feelings and greater social anxiety in the presence of others among younger females.

Meyers-Levy (1989) presented an extensive review of the literature on information processing. Meyers-Levy was able to reconcile sometimes contradictory findings by postulating a selectivity hypothesis: Males do not comprehensively process all valuable information, relying instead on highly available and salient heuristic cues, while "females generally attempt to engage in a rather effortful, comprehensive, piecemeal analysis of all available information" (1989, 221). Although neither of the two is a superior information-processing strategy, Meyers-Levy found support in the research literature for gender differences on several levels of information processing: interpretation, play behavior, other-directed interactions, spatial versus linguistic skills, and influenceability. In general, women are distracted more by irrelevant details and competing information (Halley 1975). Men, on the other hand, are better able to ignore information that does not help them meet their goals.

Meyers-Levy's argument assumes that there are inherent psychological gender differences. It suggests that men use the remote control more often because of their more rapid (though not necessarily better) decision making and ability to discard irrelevant information. Women, on the other hand, should find the frequent content shifts because of changing channels annoying and distracting, unless they are changing channels to seek or avoid specific content.

Socialist Explanations. There are several explanations for gender differences in RCD behavior that are grounded in disparities in social power and social roles. First, because males control the production of media content, most television characters are male (Comstock, Chaffee, Katzman, McCombs, and Roberts 1978; Greenberg, Simmons, Hogan and Atkin 1980), creating a male bias that extends to masculine sex-types content and masculine connotations. Because of this overriding male bias, male viewers may be interested in a wider variety of television content and actively seek additional stimuli via the remote control device.

Second, the home is the location of domestic work for women and the site of relaxation for men. Cleaning, cooking, and child care are often part of the rhythm of women's television viewing (Modleski 1983). Gender differences in channel changing might be explained by women's greater distraction by household concerns while viewing.

Third, men traditionally wield greater power in the family. Men generally control media use (Morley 1986). Males have greater say in both program selection (Lull 1982) and technology purchase (Harvey and Rothe 1986). Presumably, males' superior understanding of technology leads them to control these devices, including VCRs (Cohen and Cohen 1989) and remote control devices.

Research Expectations

This study focused on gender differences in channel changing and tested explanations drawn from three different perspectives. First, a liberal perspective suggests that gender differences are based on sexist socialization.

Because research notes that more equal socialization of men and boys is leading to fewer sex differences (Hyde 1990), we expected that gender differences in RCD behaviors would be present only for older viewers.

Hypothesis 1: Older males will change channels more than older females. Younger females will change channels as much as younger males.

Second, the radical perspective on gender differences holds that there are intrinsic biological and psychological differences between men and women. Because Meyers-Levy's (1989) research suggests that males may make channel selection decisions more quickly because they rely on highly salient visual cues, we might expect more rapid and, thus, more channel changing in males. But differences in channel-changing behaviors may be more evident in the reasons for changing channels. Men, who attend more to visual information and can process information more quickly, are more likely to change channels to increase visual stimulation and variety and avoid boredom. Thus, males should be more likely to change channels for stimulation-related reasons such as the following: to follow more than one program at a time, to see if something better is on, and to avoid boring programs and commercials. There should be fewer differences in changing channels to seek (or avoid) specific sorts of television content, such as news, music videos, and other specific programs.

Hypothesis 2: Men will change channels more for stimulation-related reasons.

Third, a socialist perspective on gender differences suggests that gender differences arise from societal roles. Because women are more likely to watch television while being involved with competing household chores, we expect that channel changing will be lower for women who are engaged in distracting activities while watching television.

Hypothesis 3a: Engaging in greater levels of distracting activities while watching television will be associated with lower levels of channel changing.

Gender differences also arise from different social power, according to a socialist perspective. Men more often control media selection and use. Thus, we expected that gender differences in RCD use would be greater in women who are viewing with others and do not control the remote control device.

Hypothesis 3b: Gender differences in channel changing will be greater in viewers who are watching with others.
Hypothesis 3c: Gender differences in channel changing will be greater in viewers who do not usually control the remote control device.

These hypotheses were tested with data collected in two studies: a quota sample from the East Coast and a random-digit telephone survey from a town in the Midwest (Ferguson and Perse 1993; Perse 1990). The use of two samples and two methods of data collection might strengthen the generalizability of our findings.

METHOD

Study 1: East Coast

Procedure and Sample. In Spring 1988, research assistants enrolled in a research methods course at the University of Delaware were given course credit for collecting the data for this study. The 180 assistants, trained in questionnaire administration and ethics, were instructed to recruit adults in six age and gender quotas (male and female, by ages 18–34, 35–49, and 50 and above) to complete questionnaires. Within a two-week period, 566 self-administered questionnaires were completed.

The sample was 50.6% male (coded 1) and represented ages 18 to 85 ($M = 40.44$, $SD = 15.07$). Respondents were drawn from a wide geographic area; 158 different zip codes were represented. The sample membership was somewhat well educated. Overall, 20.8 percent were high school graduates, 32.8 percent had attended college, 27.7 percent were college graduates, and 14.2 percent had attended graduate school. Respondents' occupations were coded into seven categories: 1 = professional, 7 = unskilled labor (Warner, Meeker, and Eells 1949). An independent coder recoded 10.0 percent of the occupational responses. Intercoder reliability was 89.5 percent. Average occupational level was 3.03 ($SD = 1.48$). Respondents watched an average of 2.89 hours of television a day ($SD = 1.72$).

Because this study considered gender differences in channel-changing behaviors, only respondents who owned a remote control device were included in the sample. Of the sample 75.4 percent ($n = 427$) owned a remote control device. The sample differed only slightly from those surveyed but not included in the analyses. Those with remote controls had higher-status occupations ($M = 3.04$) than those without ($M = 3.48$, $t(532) = 2.87$, $p < .01$). Remote control owners were also more likely to subscribe to cable than nonowners.

Channel Changing. Channel-changing frequency was not measured directly in this study. Instead, we assessed likelihood of changing channels by asking respondents to indicate whether or not they changed television channels while they watched: "between television programs"; "when commercials come on"; and "in the middle of shows—even when commercials aren't on." Because these items reflect types and locations of channel changing, the responses were treated as Guttman scalograms. Of the total sample, 1.8

percent never changed channels (coded = 0), 23.5 percent changed between programs (1), 44.3 percent changed when commercials came on (2), 30.4 percent changed in the middle of shows (3).

Changing Motivations. Respondents indicated how closely thirteen reasons for changing channels drawn from previous research (Ainslie 1988; Heeter and Greenberg 1985b) matched their own reasons for changing channels (5 = exactly, 1 = not at all). Nine reasons focused on changing channels to seek stimulation and avoid boredom: to avoid commercials (M = 3.12, SD = 1.17); to watch more than one show at a time (M = 2.25, SD = 1.06); to check what else is on (M = 3.43, SD = 1.02); because of boredom from watching the same program (M = 2.64, SD = 1.04); to see if something better is on (M = 3.47, SD = 1.08); to see something different (M = 3.12, SD = 0.98); to seek variety (M = 2.86, SD = 1.05); to see what's on the other channels (M = 3.22, SD = 1.08); and to see what they're missing on the other channels (M = 2.81, SD = 1.14).

Four of the changing motivations concerned channel changing for content-related reasons: because they don't like what they're watching (M = 3.38, SD = 1.03); to watch a particular program (M = 3.66, SD = 1.08); because someone else asks them to change the channel (M = 2.93, SD = 1.04); and because they don't like the program they're watching (M = 3.39, SD = 1.10).

Distractions. To assess distractions while viewing, respondents indicated how often (5 = very often, 1 = never) they engaged in seven distracting activities: reading a book, newspaper, or magazine (M = 3.31, SD = 1.13); preparing food (M = 2.93, SD = 1.21); eating (M = 3.65, SD = 1.00); doing housework or chores (M = 2.70, SD = 1.17); doing needlework or hobbies (M = 2.23, SD = 1.25); taking care of children (M = 1.88, SD = 1.14); and doing homework or paperwork (M = 2.75, SD = 1.23). Distractions ranged from 1.00 to 5.00 (M = 2.77, SD = 0.70, median = 2.71, Cronbach alpha = .71). The scores were split into two groups around the median.

Study 2: Midwest

Procedure and Sample. A random-digit-dialing telephone survey was conducted in Spring 1991 among adults living off campus in Bowling Green, Ohio. Out of 813 valid attempts (excluding business numbers, no answers, and ineligible persons), there were 615 completions and 198 refusals, giving a 75.6 percent completion rate. The sample was 45.1 percent male and ranged in age from 17 to 93 (M = 36.27, SD = 17.01). The average respondent had completed 14.45 years of education (ranging from 8 to 20 years, SD = 2.45). Hollingshead's two-factor social position index measured occupational level (Miller 1983) and ranged from 11 to 73 (M =

46.50, SD = 18.52), with lower scores representing higher status. The typical respondent watched 2.98 hours of television a day (SD = 2.24).

Once again, because the study focused on gender differences in channel-changing behaviors, all analyses included only those respondents who owned remote control devices (73.5%, n = 452). The RCD-owner subsample was not substantially different from nonowners, but owners (M = 45.80) had higher occupational status than nonowners (M = 49.59) and were more likely to subscribe to cable TV (76.5%) and own VCRs (82.4%) than nonowners (45.0% and 54.5%, respectively).

Channel Changing. Ferguson (1992b) reported on the unreliability of asking respondents to indicate how many times per hour they change channels. For example, people are more likely to remember "how often" they glanced at their wristwatch yesterday than "how many times" they performed such a mundane behavior. Because of the difficulty in precisely recalling a similarly mundane behavior, respondents with RCDs described their frequency (1 = never, 2 = seldom, 3 = often, 4 = very often) to the question, "How often do you flip channels?" The mean score was 2.37 (SD = 0.81).

Channel-Changing Motivations. Respondents indicated how often they changed channels (4 = very often, 1 = never) for nine reasons adapted from RCD motivations identified by Ainslie (1988) and Walker and Bellamy (1991a). Five motivations focused on stimulation-boredom reasons: to watch two or more channels at the same time (M = 2.11, SD = 0.93); to avoid commercials (M = 2.63, SD = 1.09); out of boredom (M = 2.56, SD = 0.85); to annoy others (M = 1.47, SD = 0.72); and to peek at other programs out of curiosity (M = 2.59, SD = 0.82). Four motivations focused on seeking specific content: to watch music videos (M = 1.75; SD = 0.92); to watch news (M = 2.35, SD = 0.87); to avoid seeing certain persons on television (M = 2.58, SD = 0.90); and as a substitute for printed TV listings (M = 2.42, SD = 0.99).

Viewing Content. Respondents indicated how often (4 = very often, 3 = often, 2 = seldom, 1 = never) they watch television alone. Most (30.2%) respondents seldom watched television alone. The mean score was 2.73 (SD = 0.81), reflecting that most respondents were sometimes alone. The four response categories were collapsed into a "seldom" group (44.1%) that included "never" and "seldom" and an "often" group (55.9%) that included "often" and "very often."

Respondents also indicated the person in their household who most often operated the remote control device. Most respondents (50.9%) reported that they operated the RCD most often, followed by respondent's husband or other male (23.5%), wife or other female (9.0%), decision by consensus (6.9%), two or more children (2.4%), or nobody in particular (2.2%). The remaining respondents (5.1%) did not know or would not answer. This item was recoded to reflect self-controlled RCD (50.9%) or other-controlled (49.1%).

Statistical Analysis

Following scale construction, there were several stages to analysis. We tested the hypothesized interaction between sex and age on channel-changing levels with a 2 (sex) by 2 (age) analysis of covariance using educational level and occupational status as covariates. Because of our concern with socialization differences between younger and older respondents, age was dichotomized into two groups, those age 29 and younger and those age 30 and older.[1] A 2 (sex) by 2 (age) analysis of covariance using educational level and occupational status was also used to explore gender differences in reasons for changing channels.

There were several steps to testing the third set of hypotheses. First, a t-test was used to examine male-female differences in engaging in distracting activities during television viewing. Second, a 2 (sex) by 2 (distraction) analysis of covariance (once again using education and occupation as co-variates) explored the influence of distraction on channel changing. Third, a 2 (sex) by 2 (viewing context) analysis of covariance tested the impact of group viewing on channel changing. Last, a 2 (sex) by 2 (device control) analysis of covariance examined the impact of device dominance on channel changing.

RESULTS

Study 1: East Coast

Testing the Liberal Perspective. The first hypothesis predicted that gender differences in channel-changing behaviors would be found only in older viewers. The cell means for Study 1 are summarized in Table 12.1.

Analysis of covariance supported the hypothesis. Sex had a significant effect on channel-changing location and type: $F (1, 385) = 11.71, p < .001$, eta squared $= .14$). Males changed channels more than females. Age also had a significant effect: $F (1, 385) = 11.86, p < .001$, eta squared $= .18$). Younger respondents changed channels more.

Consistent with the first hypothesis, however, there was a significant interaction between age and sex in the East Coast study: $F (1, 385) = 6.71, p < .01$. As expected, gender differences were reduced for younger respondents.

Testing the Radical Perspective. A radical perspective to gender differences is based on inherent differences between men and women. We expected

Table 12.1

East Coast, Analysis of Covariance: Channel-Changing Motivations as a Function of Sex and Age

	Males		Females		F	F	F
	<30	30+	<30	30+	Sex	Age	Inter-action
Channel Changing	2.22	2.12	2.27	1.74	11.71***	11.86***	6.71**
Stimulation							
Avoid commercials	3.64	3.26	3.68	2.84	8.43**	23.59***	6.05*
To watch more than one show at a time	2.60	2.56	2.53	1.75	36.32***	11.94***	12.12***
Check what else is on	3.85	3.42	3.83	3.15	5.27*	23.10***	1.30
Bored watching the same program	2.96	2.56	2.67	2.50	3.18	3.70	1.41
To see if something better is on	3.83	3.51	3.72	3.28	4.89*	8.50**	0.24
I want to see something different	3.30	3.10	3.16	3.11	0.55	0.64	0.43
I like variety	3.22	2.89	2.91	2.69	6.80**	4.01*	0.31
To see what's on other channels	3.63	3.25	3.51	2.96	6.61*	14.13***	0.64
To see what I'm missing	3.22	2.88	3.12	2.46	11.16***	13.36***	1.66
Content							
I don't like what I'm watching	3.33	3.24	3.39	3.46	1.61	0.01	0.33
To watch a particular program	3.46	3.55	3.55	3.87	5.15*	2.53	0.92
Because I don't like the program I'm watching	3.35	3.29	3.49	3.50	2.64	0.02	0.09
Someone asks me to	2.89	2.78	3.09	2.91	1.65	1.52	0.17

*$p < .05$
**$p < .01$
***$p < .001$

those differences to be reflected in the reasons that people changed channels. We hypothesized that men would change channels more for stimulation-related reasons. There was partial support for the second hypothesis. The cell means are reported in Table 12.1.

Men in the East Coast study were significantly more likely to report changing channels to avoid commercials, to watch more than one show at a time, to check what else is on, to see if something better is on, because they like variety, to see what's on other channels, and to see what they're missing.[2] Contrary to the hypothesis, there was no difference between males and females in reporting changing channels out of boredom or to see something different.

There were few gender differences in content-oriented changing motivations. Women were significantly more likely to report changing channels to watch a specific program. Several non-hypothesized relationships emerged between age and changing motivations. Younger respondents were more likely to change channels to avoid commercials, to watch more than one show at a time, to check what else is on, to see if something better is on, to seek variety, and to see what's on other channels. In two cases, there were significant interactions between age and sex. Gender differences were apparent only in older respondents in changing channels to avoid commercials and to watch more than one channel at a time.

Testing the Socialist Perspective. The third set of hypotheses concerned the influence of social roles on channel changing. Hypothesis 3a was tested in Study 1. Hypothesis 3a predicted that women's typical responsibilities in the home would lead them to engage in more distracting activities than men while watching television. This expectation was supported in the East Coast study by t-test. Women ($M = 2.97$) reported more distracting activities than men ($M = 2.62$); $t(418) = 6.93$, $p < .001$.

Our next expectation was that distracting activities would be associated with lower levels of channel changing. Because the East Coast study did not directly assess channel-changing frequency, we tested whether distracting activities would affect the location and type of channel changing. This hypothesis was not supported. Although sex was a significant influence on location and type of channel changing ($F(1, 369) = 12.62$, $p < .001$, eta squared $= .16$), distractions were not a significant factor ($F(1, 369) = 1.60$, $p = .21$).

Study 2: Midwest Study

Testing the Liberal Perspective. The liberal perspective was tested in Hypothesis 1, which predicted that gender differences in channel-changing behaviors would be found only in older viewers. The cell means for the Midwest study are summarized in Table 12.2.

Analysis of covariance supported the hypothesis.[3] Sex had a significant

Table 12.2
Midwest, Analysis of Covariance: Channel-Changing Motivations as a Function
of Sex and Age

	Males		Females		F Sex	F Age	F Inter- action
	<30	30+	<30	30+			
Channel Changing	2.75	2.36	2.64	1.99	14.83***	33.00***	4.38*
Stimulation							
Watch two or more channels	2.47	2.12	2.22	1.81	11.18***	12.32***	0.19
Avoid commercials	3.14	2.45	2.89	2.28	5.49*	26.68***	0.05
Boredom	2.92	2.82	2.39	2.31	1.19	33.45***	0.02
Annoy others	1.80	1.60	1.39	1.24	10.38***	19.89***	0.07
Peek at other programs out of curiosity	2.98	2.53	2.76	2.32	9.07**	23.77***	0.03
Content							
Music videos	2.15	1.49	2.20	1.43	0.87	43.40***	1.48
News	2.64	2.37	2.11	2.26	10.69***	0.53	6.94**
Avoid certain persons	2.70	2.69	2.44	2.47	0.07	3.41	0.02
Substitute for listings	2.64	2.64	2.56	2.07	6.16*	13.29***	5.72*

* $p < .05$
** $p < .01$
*** $p < .001$

effect on channel changing in the Midwest study ($F(1, 423) = (14.83, p <$ .001, eta squared = .19). Once again, males changed channels more than females. Age also had a significant effect: ($F(1, 423) = 33.00, p < .001,$ eta squared = .34). Younger respondents changed channels more.

Consistent with the first hypothesis, there was a significant interaction between age and sex: ($F(1, 423) = 4.38, p < .05$). As expected, gender differences were reduced for younger respondents.

Testing the Radical Perspective. In terms of the influence of inherent differences between men and women on channel changing, the second hypothesis predicted that men would change channels more for stimulation-related reasons. The cell means are reported in Table 12.2.

Once again, there was partial support for the second hypothesis. Men in the Midwest study were significantly more likely to report changing channels to avoid commercials, to watch two or more channels at a time, to annoy others, and to peek at other programs out of curiosity. There was no gender difference in changing channels out of boredom. There were some gender differences in content-oriented changing motivations. Men were more likely to change channels to watch news reports and as a substitute for printed listings.

As before, several non-hypothesized relationships between age and changing motivations were uncovered. Younger respondents were more likely to change channels to watch two or more channels, to avoid commercials, out of boredom, to annoy others, out of curiosity, and to watch music videos. There were two significant interactions between sex and age. Gender differences in changing channels to watch news were shown only in younger respondents (younger men were more likely than younger women to change to see the news). Older females were least likely to substitute channel changing for printed TV listings.

Testing the Socialist Perspective. Hypothesis 3b expressed our expectation that women would change channels less because they watch television with others who tend to control the set. We predicted that gender differences would be greater in viewers who typically watch with others. The hypothesis was not supported. Once again, sex was a significant factor ($F(1, 422) = 23.03, p < .001$). Males ($M = 2.55$) changed channels more than females ($M = 2.25$). Watching television alone or with others was a near-significant factor in channel changing ($F(1, 422) = 3.47, p = .06$). Those who watched alone changed channels less ($M = 2.30$) than those who watched with others ($M = 2.45$). Contrary to the hypothesis, there was no significant interaction between sex and viewing context: $F(1, 422) = 0.36, p = .55$.

Hypothesis 3c predicted that gender differences in channel changing would reflect male domination of the use of the remote control device. Thus, we expected that gender differences would be greater in viewers who do not usually control the remote control device. This hypothesis also was not supported. Differences in channel changing were not a function of control of the remote by the respondent ($M = 2.47$) or another ($M = 2.30$): $F(1, 423) = 1.28, p = .26$. Also, there was no significant interaction between sex and control: $F(1, 423) = 0.50, p = .48$.

DISCUSSION

Part of the promise of the new media environment is that unbounded choice replaces the homogeneity of the "old media" (Webster 1986). In addition to cable television and the videocassette recorder, the remote control device (RCD) is a choice-facilitating element in the new media environment. This study examined RCD use as a function of gender differences.

Overall, the results of our study are consistent with previous research that identified gender differences in channel-changing frequency and motivation (Ferguson and Perse 1991; Heeter 1988b; Walker and Bellamy 1991a). Men changed channels more readily and more frequently than women. Men were also more likely to endorse more reasons for changing channels than women. Similar to earlier findings, men were more motivated to change channels to seek variety and stimulation and to avoid annoying or boring content.

Our study considered three explanations for gender differences arising from liberal, radical, and socialist frameworks. We found a good deal of consistency across our two studies in our findings in changing levels and motivations. In general, we found support for liberal and radical perspectives.

The liberal perspective argues that there are no inherent differences between men and women. Differences that have been identified are due to the stereotypes that exist in and are reinforced by society. As these stereotypes are reduced, children will be socialized more similarly and gender differences will disappear. Our study found that differences in channel-changing frequency appear to be decreasing for younger viewers. Although older men change channels more than older women, younger males and females did not differ significantly in how often they changed channels. Moreover, younger respondents from the East Coast did not differ in their desires to change channels to avoid commercials and to watch more than one show at a time.

But the results of our study also offer support for a more radical view of gender differences. This perspective argues for inherent biological and psychological differences between men and women. We expected these differences to be reflected in motivation to change channels. Consistent with our hypothesis that men would change channels to increase stimulation, we found that men were more likely to change channels to avoid commercials, to watch more than one channel at a time, and, in general, to seek variety in their television viewing. Women, on the other hand, were more likely to change channels only to watch a particular program.

These findings differ somewhat from prior research. Ferguson and Perse (1991) found that males were more likely to avoid commercials, but Walker and Bellamy (1991a) found that sex was not related to that motive for changing channels. Both Ainslie (1988) and Ferguson and Perse (1991) noted that women were more likely to change channels to peek at other programs, for curiosity. In our studies, that motivation was more strongly endorsed by males. Clearly, research should continue to explore the nature of gender differences in reasons for changing channels.

According to the radical feminist perspective, the real differences between men and women make it impossible for women to achieve self-actualization in a gender-mixed society. Gender differences in television program preferences and attitudes about and use of various television technologies appear to be real. Future research should explore the impact of mixed-gender television viewing on satisfaction with television. Just as romance novel readers enjoy private time reading (Radway 1984), female television viewers may find more satisfaction with television when they can choose programs and change channels themselves (see also Gantz 1985).

We found little support for a socialist perspective to explain gender differences. This view holds that differences between men and women arise from roles created by societal structure. Although women engaged in more distractions while watching television, distractions had little impact on type or location of channel changing. Sex did not interact with viewing context to influence channel changing. There are two possible explanations for these null findings. First, our methods might not have been sensitive enough to locate the subtle influence of societal power. Most research based on the socialist perspective has used in-depth interviews and observations (Gray 1987; Morley 1986). Second, the social roles created for women may be so powerful that they may continue to influence their viewing across a variety of viewing contexts.

The results of our study support the views of writers who have conceptualized the remote control device as both a tool and a toy (Bellamy and Walker 1990b; Wenner and Dennehy 1990). For the men in our samples, the RCD appears to be a tool that eases location of stimulating television content. But because men use concrete props to facilitate play (Meyers-Levy 1989), the RCD may also be a toy. Future research should explore the content and process gratifications of remote control use (Cutler and Danowski 1980).

These studies' results point out that the concept of stimulation may be useful to future media research (Christ 1985). Males seem to use the RCD to seek variety and stimulation and to avoid unpleasant content. Research has observed that sensation seeking, a personality trait that leads people to seek risks and excitement (Zuckerman 1979), is linked to watching horror movies (Edwards 1991) and some reasons for watching television (Conway and Rubin 1991). Research should explore the influence of sensation seeking on reasons for changing channels (see Wenner and Dennehy, Chapter 9 of this volume).

The implications of how men and women use RCDs differently to view television have practical impact on television programmers and theoretical importance for television choice models (Heeter 1985; Webster and Lichty 1991). Research might explore gender differences in attention levels during commercials. Older women might be more attentive, because they are less likely to change channels to avoid commercials. On the other hand, distracting activities may detract from awareness of commercials (Perse 1990). Printed and on-air promotions should be aimed at women, because they are more likely to seek specific programs when changing channels. Finally, advertisers who want to attract male attention should increase the stimulation appeal of their commercials.

NOTES

We'd like to thank Charles Pavitt for arranging data collection.

1. The median age was 36 in both studies. Age 30 was chosen to mark the split between the two groups because it traditionally marks the end of adult youth. Also, persons in their thirties in 1988 and 1991 were socialized before the rise of feminism in the 1970s. Thus, they reflect a theoretically significant young-old split, rather than just a chronological one.

2. The subtleties in wording are worth noting. The phrase "what else is on" suggests mild dissatisfaction; "see if something better is on" implies stronger dissatisfaction. The phrase "see what's on other channels" may only denote curiosity.

3. Occupational status was a significant covariate in only the Midwest study. Educational level was not significantly related to channel changing.

Part V

The Impact of Remote Control Devices on Media Industries

13

The RCD's Impact on Television Programming and Promotion

*Susan Tyler Eastman
and Jeffrey Neal-Lunsford*

Programmers have traditionally assumed that their key concern should be *audience flow*, the movement of audiences from one program into the next. Strategies such as scheduling powerful lead-off programs and strong lead-ins and lead-outs, blocking similar programs throughout a daypart, and spending top dollar for hit off-network series all depend, at least in part, on the assumption of audience flow from program to program (Head, Eastman, and Klein 1993). But the remote control device's widespread diffusion makes flow assumptions far less tenable in the 1990s (Beschloss 1990). Even without cable television, viewers now jump between pairs of programs, graze along dozens of channels, and generally show little station or network loyalty, paying scant attention to choosing a single source for a daypart's viewing (if, indeed, they ever consciously "choose" a channel or network to view). The theory of least objectionable program—the idea that viewers watch the program that creates the least outcry among co-viewers (Klein 1976)—becomes even more untenable in light of grazing and multi-channel viewing. What are programmers doing to defeat the effects of the remote control device? What experiments in programming, production, and promotion have been successful in countering the remote control's impact? How are programmers adapting to new audience viewing patterns? Are most station programmers even aware that grazing and jumping pose problems for them? What are promotion directors and producers doing differently today in direct response to grazing? This chapter seeks answers to these questions in the scholarly and trade press and original interviews with ninety-six programmers, managers, and producers.

Most studies involving remote control devices (RCDs) reflect either the interest of scholars in how viewers interact with the device or the interest of television professionals in how grazing affects the viewership of commercials. However, complaints about the RCD's likely negative influence on program ratings appear regularly at industry meetings and in trade articles (Selnow 1989; Sylvester 1990). One widely recognized strategy for stations to minimize grazing's impact is to seek a low channel number. Research has repeatedly shown that the lower dial positions are searched more frequently than the higher numbers (Bollier 1989; Ferguson 1992a). But one area that has not received much attention from scholars is the RCD's influence on daily programming practices. Acknowledging the overall grazing problem, in 1989 *Channels* magazine put together the most comprehensive assessment of the remote control's impact to date (*How Americans Watch TV: A Nation of Grazers*), but even this mammoth report had little to say about strategies for combating the RCD in programming, especially at the local level. With the A. C. Nielsen Company reporting that nearly 80 percent of American homes now have television sets equipped with RCDs (Carter 1991), it becomes evident that the relationship between RCD usage and industry programming practices merits closer scrutiny. That the RCD alarms producers of dramatic shows is evident from the ironic words of Barney Rosenszweig, producer of "Cagney & Lacey" and "The Trials of Rosie O'Neill": "I can see it now. Gotta have 14 car chases per reel; gotta have jeopardy in every scene. We'll start getting notes like that from the network. . . . We'll go back to McLuhan—the medium is the message" (Ainslie 1988, 62).

Although some research indicates that using RCDs does not necessarily result in increased grazing (Ferguson 1992a) or impair the networks' ability to maintain audience shares (Davis and Walker 1990), it is clear that RCDs affect the way in which many people experience television, which in turn must affect programming strategies aimed at capturing high ratings. To date, the television industry has not shown great concern about possible effects of the RCD, yet the programming landscape is nonetheless changing in response to the device (Carter 1991). Although the terms "compelling programs" and "quality programs" repeatedly appear in the trade press as appropriate response strategies, their definition remains problematic. Preliminary assessment of scattered comments (and complaints) suggests that strategies for combating the effects of grazing can be grouped in two areas: (1) changing the style or content of programs, and (2) altering the ways in which program schedules are structured and presented.

PROGRAMMING STYLE

Of key concern to programmers and producers is grabbing the viewers' attention at the beginning of a program, which has intensified in response to the RCD and changed how programs are structured. The goal is to instill a sense of loyalty or commitment to the program in the viewer, and to do this as quickly as possible. To create this loyalty, programmers and producers have begun emphasizing *top-loading*, a strategy wherein high production values are emphasized at a program's beginning to gain the audience's attention. Producer Steven Bochco describes the need for and goal of top-loading:

The competition is fierce. Viewers are fickle. They sit there with their zapper, and they can access 50 channels without getting up off their behinds. And if they don't like what you're [the producer] doing, then in 90 seconds you're history. And they don't come back because there are just too many other things to access. And in that climate, I can't imagine a fresh idea not generating interest. Zapping does not bother me. It's a complete waste of time for any of us to bemoan what once was. Besides, I'm one of those guys that sits there with the zapper clicking through those channels. And you'd better grab my ass fast or I'm looking for the next ball game, you know? As a writer, as a producer, I have to find ways to adjust what I do to that reality. So I'm a big believer in designing shows and writing shows in a way that will freeze your thumb within a minute or two (Steven Bochco: Taking risks 1991, 28).

One form of top-loading involves the use of expensive, eye-catching opening credits to attract attention, as is the case with the programs "Davis Rules" and "Home Improvement." Another form of top-loading utilizes a cold opening, starting right in with the program, as in "Wings" and "Walter and Emily." Opening credits are run later than usual, and the first commercial break is postponed for several minutes, to allow the audience to develop enough interest to stay with the program. To be effective, top-loading requires compelling opening segments as content beginnings. Thus, programs are structured to begin with longer, more fully developed scenes to ensure viewer involvement, as opposed to the traditional method in which a program begins with a short segment that may or may not have relevance to the rest of the program (Davis and Walker 1990).

One effect of wide RCD usage is a movement toward faster-paced programs with an increased emphasis on quick edits. As one scholar describes it, "TV is now only bits and pieces. Very often the picture and sound are only slightly related" (Sanoff and Kyle 1987, 56). Some of this change in program pacing and editing is a result of copying the MTV style of unconventional graphics and rapid editing techniques. This influence stems not only from the music videos shown on the cable network but from MTV's other programs, including "Liquid Television," "Totally Pauly," and "The Week in Rock." According to Marshall Cohen of MTV, "Programming is responding to grazing, but it's more a matter of style than content. There is more cutting, shorter scenes, faster-paced shows, and more shorthand visual techniques" (Bollier 1989, 47). Some network programs, such as NBC's former hit, "Miami Vice," and Fox's "In Living Color," overtly adopted the MTV style in order to appeal to viewers reared on music videos.

In fact, to appeal to a younger audience, much of the Fox schedule shows MTV's influence.

More recently, Comedy Central's "Short Attention Span Theater" was structured so that continuing viewer attention would not be required to enjoy the program. As opposed to programs with a linear storyline, such as sitcoms and dramas, "Short Attention Span Theater" is constructed of brief, mostly discrete program segments such as stand-up comedy sketches and clips from programs like "Saturday Night Live." Since the various segments have little relationship to each other, viewers are tacitly encouraged to flip to other channels, knowing they can rejoin "Short Attention Span Theater" at any time without losing the thread of the show. Cable networks such as CNN Headline News, MTV and its lookalikes, shopping channels, and The Weather Channel are structured in much the same way. Programming throughout the day is broken down into short, regularly scheduled segments repeated each hour or half hour that allow viewers to "drop in" at their convenience without having to follow a program from its beginning. According to Merrill Brown, vice president of The Law Channel and former *Channels* editor—who coined the word "grazing" to refer to channel hopping—grazing actually encouraged the formation of VH–1, Comedy Central, and The Weather Channel because they are designed to take account of the habits of people armed with RCDs (personal communication, November 10, 1991).

Many in the television industry feel that viewers, bored with many of the programs they see, need almost constant visual and/or aural stimulation, and that boredom induces some viewers to begin grazing (Ainslie 1989). William Rhodes, president of Insight Cable in Salt Lake City, complained, "The typical viewer wants something new, but it is only new for a few moments. After the newness wears off, they are back to flipping again" (personal communication, November 11, 1991). By increasing the pace of programs, it is hoped that viewers will not have time to become bored with a particular program (or cable channel), thus reducing the urge to graze. Some research indicates that the typical viewer stops at each channel for as little as two seconds while grazing (O'Connell 1989), which leads some programmers to believe that fast-faced programs will become a necessity, regardless of the effect of such pacing on the content of programs.

Others in the television industry argue that grazing is not primarily a function of boredom; it is instead a method of sampling, of rapidly checking out what is available from many sources (Bollier 1989). Thus, grazing has positive advantages for the less frequently viewed cable-only networks and independent stations. It may indeed be a boon for public television, which need not then rely on its "educational" image but can capture viewers with its programs (Fuller 1993; LeRoy and LeRoy 1988). Shopping channels also benefit from grazing and try to attract samplers with high-profile guest hosts (for example, Joan Rivers, Susan Lucci, Pete Rose). Another new practice, viewing two programs at a time either by jumping between them or inserting one in the corner of another, called *schitzing* by Marshall Cohen (Bollier 1989), also favors less well-known channels.

The programming style of various networks and stations seems to affect the amount of grazing that occurs. One (network-sponsored) study found that the three broadcast network programs were less prone to grazing than cable networks, independent stations, and Fox affiliates (Carter 1991). Whether this was because the traditional networks tend to be more stylistically conservative in their programming than flashy, contemporary cable networks such as Fox and Lifetime is not clear. Walker (1988) also found network viewers conservative, and Davis and Walker (1990) speculate that the more adventurous viewers (in other words, those who graze) have abandoned the traditional networks, leaving an audience less likely to graze.

Certainly the style of some specific program genres lends itself to grazing. As ABC programming executive Robert Iger put it, "The remote control device has hurt dramas more than anything else. Comedies require less of a commitment on behalf of the viewer to watch" (Tyrer 1991, 8). In a similar vein, others believe that what makes programs graze-resistant are their ability to inspire empathy in the audience. CBS vice president for research David Poltrack cites empathy-based programs such as "thirty-something" and "The Wonder Years" as examples of series that are relatively resistant to grazing because their content induces strong viewer involvement (Bollier 1989). However, Jane Zenaty of Leo Burnett contradicts this view, holding that overall quality has always mattered more than attributes such as empathy (Bollier 1989).

Many studies and critical comments point to sports programs as likely candidates for grazing (Carter 1991; Coe 1992; Eastman 1993). As a viewer explains it, "Baseball is a half-watching kind of experience. Remote control is something I've been waiting for all my life. I can watch three games at once and never miss a pitch" (Snyder 1988, 58). A factor that contributes to increased grazing of sports programs is that males, who are more prone to graze, make up the majority of the audience for all televised sports events (Ainslie 1989; Schlosberg 1987).

PROGRAMMING STRUCTURE

Although opening credits may become more elaborate to attract the viewer's eye, closing credits may well become an endangered species. It is widely believed that between-program clutter such as credits, commercials, promos, and public service announcements are an invitation to change channels. Interstitial, or non-program, matter facilitates grazing as viewers look for more interesting fare or avoid selling messages. To keep viewers from reaching for their RCDs, programmers and producers increasingly focus their efforts on rapid and arresting transitions between programs. The reduction of clutter or improvement of interstitials is part of a larger strategy to improve audience flow between adjacent shows. Moving the audience rapidly from one program to the next is considered essential in combating grazing.

One method, called *living end credits* in the industry, seeks to minimize and possibly glamorize closing credits by running them over the last scene of an episode or movie; "Roseanne" and "Newhart," for example, have used a mix of motion and freeze-frame to entwine program and end credits. Another method, called *squeezed credits*, uses a digital video effects device to squeeze the picture in one corner of the screen, employing the remaining space for promotional announcements that would ordinarily follow the closing credits. This saves time by speeding the transition to the next program and can add visual interest.

To keep viewers from straying during the transition, many local stations and some cable networks have adopted an even more extreme practice variously called *hot switching* (moving directly from one program to the next) or *seamless programming* (eliminating virtually all credits and interstitial material at the hour and half hour).[1] Especially in prime time, some networks move from one program to the next in thirty seconds or less, as opposed to the traditional one- to two-minute commercial pod between programs (Davis and Walker 1990). The seamless ploy, combined with top-loading, seeks to keep the audience continuously captivated by the programming to decrease the likelihood of grazing behavior.[2]

In 1992, ABC became the first broadcast network to announce a formal plan to cut back on closing credits as part of its clutter reduction policy (Coe 1992; Garron 1992), and NBC has experimented with seamless movement from some prime time programs into others. According to program director Margaret Shadburne of WAVE-TV in Louisville, NBC has promised its affiliates to eliminate closing credits by 1994 (personal communication, February 21, 1992). Many local stations have found ways to deal with closing credits without eliminating them altogether. As the practice of shortening or manipulating closing credits becomes more widespread, however, problems will arise with unions such as Directors Guild of America (DGA) and the American Federation of Television and Radio Artists (AFTRA), whose contracts guarantee their members a certain amount of exposure through credits. NBC may not find negotiations easy, and even if the unions become convinced of the need for change in the future, it is unlikely that they will agree to cut credits on reruns and already-produced movies.

Another structural alteration in programming used first by Superstation TBS is *lagged scheduling*, in which programs are begun not at the top of the hour or half hour but at five minutes past. This practice was initiated to make WTBS's schedule stand out in television guides by having its programs listed under separate times, rather than being grouped with all other shows starting at a particular hour. Lagged scheduling has the added benefit of carrying the WTBS audience through other channels' commercial breaks and program transitions (the *bridging* strategy), at the top of the hour and half hour, times when grazing is rampant (Eastman 1993).

RATINGS IMPACT

The RCD, by precipitating new ways to watch television, has forced a change in traditional strategies for ratings interpretation. New viewing habits have compelled leading programmers to reassess their schedules, with the result that program *turnover* (rapid replacement of weak shows), already at a high rate, has become even more pronounced (Adams, Eastman, and Lewine 1993). One reason for so much cancellation is that RCDs, and the viewing behaviors they engender, are a factor in causing the ratings for marginal and low-rated programs to drop even further while increasing the ratings for programs in the Nielsen top ten (Sanoff and Kyle 1987). What results is an even shorter time for new programs to establish an audience before cancellation. This problem especially affects the broadcast networks. Already suffering audience erosion as an outcome of stronger competition from cable television, Fox, and VCRs, the broadcast networks are watching their hard-won viewer loyalty slip away as viewers employ the RCD as a convenient way to sample competing programs. This undercuts traditional scheduling ploys such as hammocking and tent-poling intended to boost ratings for weak programs (Adams, Eastman, and Lewine 1993). According to Stipp (1989), however, the amount and type of grazing is far less than generally believed, and it is unlikely that strategies such as strong lead-ins and hammocking will completely lose their effectiveness. At any rate, the RCD has turned the networks' attention to new strategies such as cold openings and seamlessness to counteract grazing between programs (Garron 1992).

PROMOTIONAL IMPACT

Since commercials and promotional spots are a necessity for most stations and networks, new strategies have arisen to help carry the audience through a commercial break and back to the programming. One such strategy is contesting. Contests are nothing new to television, but new forms of contests are being tried in an effort to get viewers to pay close attention to commercial breaks and promote programming in a way that viewers will find entertaining to watch (Slakoff, Helper, and Neal-Lunsford 1991). Increased production values in promotion, the use of brief storyline vignettes in promos (Zahradnik 1987), and contesting are elements copied from advertising that apply to on-air promotion. Some contests unite a network and advertiser in a mutual promotional scheme. CBS/K-mart and NBC/McDonalds are prominent examples (Bellamy 1992). Syndicated programs such as "Live with Regis and Kathie Lee" have used a similar device: Viewers must watch the program over a period of time to learn a series of code words, which must then be sent in to be eligible for the contest. This type of contesting helps neutralize grazing, at least somewhat, by encouraging long-term sampling in the hope that viewing will become a habit.

Cable networks are also using contesting as a way to hold viewers through program breaks. A 1992 Nick at Nite contest used a double-barreled approach in which promotional announcements informed viewers of the contest and its prizes but required viewers to watch for another promo that contained the information needed to enter the contest. Such approaches are likely to be successful with those who enjoy contests, but viewer interest quickly diminishes if they require too much time and effort. Contests have proven popular thus far and will continue to be an important tool for cable audience retention and program promotion (Eastman and Trufelman 1991).

In addition to self-contained *promos* (promotional spots), the traditional form of program promotion, more aggressive on-air plans for stations and networks involve increased use of announcements to entice viewers to stay put (Bollier 1989). *Teases* (tantalizing visual plugs for upcoming news stories), *tags* (short audio-only stay-tuned messages), *bumpers* (short visual stay-tuned messages), and *billboards* (alphanumeric lists of upcoming program titles) are nothing new, but they are being utilized more effectively than in the past (Eastman 1991; Minnucci 1991). CNN Headline News, for example, plays teases of upcoming stories before every commercial break, and it also runs a daily news quiz that sandwiches the breaks. The pay-cable movie channels continuously billboard their upcoming films, as do the broadcast networks their prime time schedules and affiliates their early fringe sequence of programs.

NEW QUESTIONS

It appears there are programming strategies for adapting to or counteracting the effects of the RCD, but how widespread is their use? Is there agreement on which programs are most vulnerable to grazing? Do local programmers and program producers recognize the relationship of strategies and practices such as cold openings, top-loading, and seamlessness to the new grazing habits of the public? If not, managers can expect erratic support for these strategies at the local level and only infrequent incorporation of them in newly produced programs (unless or until network pressure overrides the artistic concerns of producers). If not, managers can expect seemingly incomprehensible ratings and minimal improvement in station promotional practices. Scholars of programming theory need clear understanding of the role of these changes in program content and scheduling practices to guide their assumptions about programming.

Program Decision-Makers

Broadcast and cable programmers have three main responsibilities: the selection, scheduling, and evaluation of programs. With input from ratings research and in consultation with others in management, programmers choose which newly produced shows, movies, or syndicated reruns to put into a program lineup and in what order to schedule the shows; later, they evaluate each show's ratings performance and demographic appeal. Promotion directors (also called "creative services directors" and "marketing directors") produce, schedule, and evaluate on-air and print promotion for programs. Their perceptions about the number of viewers utilizing remote controls and the ways viewers use them affect, to some degree, how on-air promos are produced and scheduled and the mix of external media purchased to promote specific programs. Even more crucial to understanding television programming trends are the views of program producers. They actually make (or hire the writers and directors who make) most of the original television programs for the Hollywood studios and independent producers that are, in turn, licensed to the country's 1,500 television stations and 100 or so domestic broadcast and cable networks. Station managers, general managers, and corporate executives influence the thinking of those below them in business hierarchies, and their views on the importance and impact of remote controls set the agendas for change within the industry.

Interviews with Industry Practitioners

To find out how well informed industry practitioners were about ways to combat or adapt to grazing, Eastman and Neal-Lunsford (1992) utilized the strategies and practices suggested in the scholarly and trade literatures to counteract or adapt to the RCD in an analysis of nincty-six interviews with industry programmers, managers, and producers to get a sense of the scale of the television industry's concern about the RCD. This study shows the degree to which the new viewing realities described by scholars and industry leaders have been incorporated in television's day-to-day practices.

The ninety-six industry practitioners were asked open-ended questions about the RCD's impact on (1) program selection, (2) program scheduling, (3) types of programs affected by grazing, (4) ratings, and (5) promotional practices. Data were collected on market size, whether the service was national (Hollywood studio) or local (television station), and network affiliation (ABC, CBS, Fox, NBC, PBS, or independent). Most interviews (94%) were conducted by telephone (6% in person) by trained college students who tape-recorded the conversation (if permitted) in order to report the subject's words verbatim.[3] Comments relating to programming, promotion, ratings, and specific programs were transcribed and analyzed by faculty researchers to ascertain how deeply the programmers had considered RCD-

Table 13.1
Distribution of Interviews

Job Title	Station	Indep.Prod./Studio	Network	Total
Programmers*	56	2	2	60
Managers	11		1	12
Producers	2	22		24
				96

*Seven of these were promotion managers and four were operations directors; the rest had programming titles such as program director or assistant program director.

related issues; which program selection, scheduling, and promotional strategies were recommended; which program types were assumed to be negatively or positively affected by the RCD; and how production tactics were changing.[4] Table 13.1 shows the distribution of interviews by job title and industry affiliation.

Both local and national and small, midsized, and large markets are represented. About one-quarter of the interviews (26%) took place with programmers and managers at small-market stations (markets 101+), just over one-quarter (28%) with mid-market personnel (markets 26 to 100), and under one-fifth (18%) with large market staff (markets 1 to 25).[5] Another quarter-plus (28%) of those interviewed (mostly producers) worked for national program production companies (major independent producers or large Hollywood television production studios[6]).

Initial Reactions to RCDs

A stunning 60 percent of the ninety-six respondents thought RCDs were not a problem for themselves or the television industry. This finding illustrates the gap between the few trailblazers at the national and large-station level and the rest of the television industry. Only 16 percent of small-market programmers/managers admitted RCDs were a problem for them (and only 15 percent thought them a problem for somebody else—such as the networks or producers); in contrast, 44 percent of large-market programmers/managers acknowledged a problem.[7] (Even a surprising 41 percent of producers insisted that the RCD was irrelevant to their work, although they were producing for network prime time or first-run syndication.) Only 20 percent of the ninety-six industry practitioners interviewed acknowledged concern about grazing and associated viewer behaviors, some quite forcefully, and thus thought the industry (or their station or production house) needed to work on strategies for combating or adapting to the RCD.[8] Despite publicity from ABC (Garron 1992) and attempts at seamless programming by NBC,

Table 13.2
Programming Style Recommendations

	Top Loading	Quality	Pacing	Targeting	Localism	Blocking
Programmers	27%	18%	10%	8%	8%	1%
Managers	58%	58%	17%	8%	33%	-
Producers	42%	38%	25%	8%	-	8%

only six of twenty-six ABC and NBC affiliates connected the two networks' interstitial efforts to audience grazing; most seemed to have their heads in the sand, talking disjointedly (or sometimes quite smoothly) about traditional audience flow strategies as if the programming world was unchanging. On the local level (N = 69), only about one-quarter of stations (28%) thought the RCD was of any concern to them.[9]

Some respondents (10% overall) brought out the point that RCDs encourage sampling of less well-known channels. Public television programmers consistently mentioned its positive benefit, and Fox network executives and cable programmers (and those producing for Fox and cable) referred to this desirable attribute of grazing.

Programming Style Recommendations

Although most programmers, managers, and producers claimed that the RCD had no impact on programming strategies and practices (for example, "I haven't even considered the RCD, let alone given any thought to it being a problem," and "My colleagues [at a cable network] act as though the remote control doesn't affect them"), Table 13.2 illustrates the range of suggestions for counteracting grazing given by respondents (multiple answers were coded). Some respondents who claimed RCDs were not their worry nevertheless had ideas for countering their impact (thus, some percentages exceed 40).

Clearly, most who had any recommendations at all were focused on the style of program openings and the overall quality of programs. Rather vague terms for attention-grabbing openings such as "dynamic," "visually stimulating," "more effects," and "high energy" showed up repeatedly. But the key concept here was top-loading, especially cold openings—long story-related segments that give the viewer a chance to become committed to the program and that postpone opening titles and credits until well into the program. One vice president urged that "we have to become conscious of getting in and out of programs."

Program quality was described as needing to be compelling, of high visibility, and requiring more participation. Indeed, several producers thought the RCD was having a negative impact on program quality. Although thirteen stations in the study were CBS affiliates, only one large-market programmer mentioned Poltrack's concept of "empathy" (Bollier 1989). Other than the ideas listed in Table 13.2, respondents suggested programming strategies such as controlling audience expectations, taking risks with oddball program concepts, moving rapidly to split screens, multiplexing more than one network channel so that stations could select among network offerings (like syndicators), having more newsbreaks, and increasing stunting, especially crossover appearances by major stars.[10] Several local programmers were taken with the idea of "appointment TV," by which viewers plan ahead to watch programs that are important for them. However, grazing probably takes over when expectations are not met.

It is not surprising that producers were especially concerned about the pace of shows. Program pacing has picked up in recent years; shows generally have shorter segments and more compact treatment. One producer noted that viewers want "fast visual stimulation"; another called the same characteristic the need for "instant gratification"; still another talked of "time-crunching techniques" to shorten screen time but still tell a story. Here again, the most notable point is that three-quarters of the producers did not bring up pacing as a changing element in storytelling related to the remote control.

Five producers and station programmers brought up the classic strategy of blocking as a solution to grazing, but two others mentioned that it no longer was so effective. The ABC network itself has experimented with abandoning flow strategies such as lead-in and blocking in some situations, hoping to capture grazers. For example, placing the zany "Into the Night Starring Rick Dees" after a serious Ted Koppel on "Nightline" surely exemplifies such a disjuncture (Beschloss 1990). Public television and commercial independent stations also counterprogram more than they depend on flow from program to program in prime time, hoping for the "traveling" audience.

It was in analyzing the program genres most/least affected by RCDs that the study found the most unanimity and the most contradiction in responses. Sporting events were overwhelmingly seen as the most vulnerable to grazing, especially if a game was especially slow (baseball) or a blowout (football). Male-oriented programs were widely assumed to be the most affected by RCDs. But, curiously, respondents were evenly divided on whether 60-minute shows or 30-minute shows were most prone to grazing; several producers noted that it was becoming increasingly "hard to keep viewers' attention for an hour." Moreover, as many programmers (four) pointed to slow programs as producers (four) pointed to fast programs when asked what types were most prone to grazing.

Seven programmers and producers argued that a storyline protected a program; eight others claimed that nothing protected any kind of program and that comedies (or movies or dramas) were most vulnerable. In general, most respondents worried about situation comedies, seeing them as too predictable, not funny enough, and repeated too often to hold viewers. One programmer said that sitcoms give "more opportunity to flip around at the end," probably referring to wrap-up scenes and end credits. It is interesting that situation comedies are generally more female- than male-oriented, although the opinion was nearly unanimous (among those that responded) that male-oriented programs are grazed more. One manager asserted, "Males hold the RCD, so male-oriented shows will take precedence in prime time and weekend ratings." Respondents were also evenly divided (two/two) on whether children's cartoons were most or least vulnerable to grazing. Perhaps these comments reflect some confusion between who holds the RCD and what is viewed.

Unexpected conflict showed in responses regarding local news: Eight programmers and managers thought news (and local public affairs) were "grazeproof." Others were less sure: Ten others claimed news was most susceptible. There was widespread agreement that soaps were safe and talk/magazines were not. One programmer accounted for channel hopping during newscasts in this way: "People like to compare stories [on competing newscasts]." Eight station programmers pointed to the need for increased targeting of programs, and one-third of managers stressed localism as a solution for widespread grazing.

Four programmers noted that specials, particularly ones that did not live up to their hype, would foster grazing and that reruns of anything quickly make some viewers restless. Programmers mentioned that head-to-head competition among the three or four networks with the same type of program, as in all movies, brought RCDs into play. Two producers pointed to programs not requiring much concentration (such as game shows) as especially vulnerable to grazing; however, two managers claimed that "participation programs" (such as games) were least susceptible. Another tidbit came from one programmer who claimed that series with the same introduction (opening background under credits) season after season, such as "M*A*S*H," attracted grazing.

Program Structure Recommendations

Many suggestions for change related directly to program structure, focusing on transitions between programs. As Table 13.3 shows, programmers especially want seamless transitions with a delayed first commercial break. They particularly want hot switching from the last program directly into the following show, leaving no time for commercial spots, IDs, promos, or any other interstitial non-program material. Implementing this, of course, means either more or longer commercial pods within programs, but the lone cry from one programmer (in these interviews) for shorter commercial

Table 13.3
Program Structure Recommendations

	Seamless Transitions	Cut End Credits	CounterSch. Breaks	Lagged Timing
Programmers	30%	8%	12%	1%
Managers	17%	42%	-	17%
Producers	-	8%	-	-

pods seemed doomed. Nearly all the one-fifth of respondents that had heard of the seamless approach appeared to be enthusiastic proponents; lamentably, however, four-fifths of respondents had no idea what it had to do with them or with grazing. In weighing the percentages shown in Table 13.3, it is important to remember that 60 percent of programmers, managers, and producers, especially in small and mid-sized markets, thought the whole subject pretty much irrelevant. It was odd, for example, that writer/producers for "The Commish" and "The New WKRP in Cincinnati" had little or no concern, whereas producers for "True Colors" and "MacGyver" saw the problem.

However, one programmer claimed that his small-market station was already using a seamless approach into its local news and that it wasn't making much difference. It remains an open question whether this approach matters more for prime time or fringe entertainment programs or must become widespread across the dial to have an effect.

Managers of stations (general managers, station managers, vice presidents) were strongly in favor of eliminating or modifying closing credits. Along with cold openings and quality programs, doing something about end credits was deemed essential by most who recommended any response to the grazing problem. Specific suggestions for what to do about closing credits ranged from squeezing them to shortening them or using living credits to cutting them entirely. Indeed, relief was clearly expressed by three NBC affiliate managers that NBC had definite plans for getting rid of closing credits in a couple of years, and several ABC and CBS managers also brought up the NBC solution as a likely successful strategy. One programmer noted that her station's parent company already had decreed "no local credits" on locally produced shows.

Nearly one-quarter of programmers (23%) pointed to shifting the time of commercial breaks (counterscheduling them) as a measure to prevent grazing. Placing news segments and breaks at different times from competing stations' gives a station some advantage. If only one or two stations offset their breaks, they would benefit from grazing during the other stations' breaks. On the other hand, they might well lose fickle viewers at their own commercial time, but low-viewership independent station managers and programmers presumed they would gain more than lose. The same might be true of the less-viewed cable networks.

Only one programmer brought up multiplexing time-shifted versions of the same programming on different channels as a solution to grazing, but this idea clearly has appeal for the cable networks. (HBO, Cinemax, and Showtime began multiplexing in 1992; and The Discovery Channel, MTV, ESPN, USA, and The Family Channel have announced future plans. See MTV announces 1991.) It might work for broadcast stations if sufficient channel space was available. The idea of multiplexing is to dominate more of the dial, to have a presence at several locations on the dial (either bunched or spread), so that grazers have several chances to see portions of one's programming.

Five managers brought up the topic of lagged scheduling, pointing out the advantages for Superstation TBS and for public television (which sometimes makes use of it). It was suggested that one broadcast network experiment with it in prime time. Two programmers pointed out that it is "necessary to change viewers' habits and expectations" to make lagged or seamless approaches work well, and they appeared to view this as a difficult task. In addition, two managers spoke of "early starts" to newscasts as a reverse-variant on lagging. Beginning a local newscast at two minutes to the hour and continuing smoothly through the traditional break time is a type of seamlessness or bridging that worked well for them.

Producers said little about scheduling solutions, thinking of them as local station and network problems, not their own. But even some of them had heard of proposals to cut or otherwise modify closing credits and spoke of such changes as partial solutions to the grazing problem. All this suggests that there is a great deal of confusion in the industry. Decision-makers are groping blindly to produce for and program the country's stations and networks. These data suggest that even the best, most ratings-based recommendations of the networks (and other programming advisors) are not finding fertile ground.

Ratings

One producer for a major studio claimed that "the networks just use the RCD as an excuse to dump an expensive show with bad ratings. They can't ever admit they've aired a bad show." But most respondents (73% of the two-thirds who commented) seemed to agree that the RCD had had a definitely negative effect on the interpretability of ratings. Most (44%) claimed that ratings were now much less accurate and that diary-based ratings had become virtually worthless, because, they said, viewers simply could not keep track of rapid channel changes and think in terms of the seven-minute time periods the ratings companies define as "viewing a channel" (for diary analysis).[11] Four programmers and managers pointed out that the viewing of two programs (either by jumping or on-screen insertion) would usually be counted as viewing only one program. Seven large-market programmers, who have overnights and peoplemeter-based ratings, noted that grazing had forced them into minute-by-minute examination of daily ratings. Such programmers uniformly claimed that the RCD was having a definite impact on strategy. One executive yearned for "passive meters that can track grazing."

Respondents were equally divided on whether more sampling was a negative or positive phenomenon. Naturally, this tied closely to whether the person worked for (1) a traditional network affiliate or (2) an independent, Fox or public station, or cable network. One Fox affiliate programmer claimed that as a result of the remote control, his station was being programmed more like an affiliate with its top programs in prime time. Programmers and managers for public stations mentioned that "people tune in by accident" and catch, for example, a state college basketball game they would never have expected to find on a non-commercial station. However, three programmers noted the special difficulties of non-theme cable networks; one said, "Non-theme channels are hurt by zappers because they go among the channels they can identify with." Making the same point, one producer noted that "grazing helps capture viewers who didn't intend to watch Home Shopping Network." One general manager made the telling point that infomercials induce grazing when viewers discover they are not "real programs" but sales messages; he asserts that infomercials should appear only in unimportant (to ratings) time periods.

The RCD's impact on ratings is generating bizarre new programming concepts. One small-market general manager predicted the imminent arrival of "Zap News," 30-second news programs that are not teases but assemblages of extremely brief but complete news stories, each newscast being different from the last. Such an approach to news is a big step beyond "24-Hour News Stations" that mostly give one-minute headlines (for example, WISH in Indianapolis). Another ratings strategy influenced by the need to counteract the RCD is all-night theme programming, in which prime time entertainment and the following newscast focus on a single theme, treating it in fiction and then in real-life stories, even documentary. The best example to date was NBC's "Hurricane Night" (November 9, 1991). NBC aired three sitcoms back to back that all had storylines about hurricanes: "Golden Girls," "Empty Nest," and "Nurses." A variant on this was "Hostage Night" on one CBS affiliate: After CBS aired an episode of "Knots Landing" in which a couple was taken hostage, one manager said his station included a segment on a real-life hostage taking in the late evening newscast and followed this with an expert's analysis of whether the fictional couple or real couple had responded properly to the situation. More thematic ties seem likely between adjacent programs (as in "all-day horror movies" or whole days of westerns or science fiction monster movies) and even late news programs.

Cable systems, one general manager explained, can't "defeat zappers, but we may be able to use them" by scheduling channels in related clusters. In other words, some types of tiering may actually confine a certain class of viewer to a band of channels because all his or her favorites are there. In that case, grazing makes little difference to the cable operator (though it still matters to the individual cable networks and broadcast stations). Eastman (1993) lists four kinds of clustering: by similar content (all news, all shopping); by similar audience appeal (all male-oriented but mixing news and sports, for example); by cost (all pays together, all broadcast together); and by a mixed arrangement in which there is something for every member of the family/household in a single tier.[12] At any rate, the proliferation of RCDs (accompanied by fiber penetration, digital compression, and the prospect of 150- and 300-channel cable systems) is fostering strong interest in experimenting with tiering concepts.

Promotion

According to one large-market programmer, "Promotion has become 100 times more important than five years ago because of remote controls," and 60 percent of programmers and virtually all managers agreed that "RCDs make promotion more essential"; two even said that promotion was "the only practical solution to channel hopping." (Most producers, 83%, didn't answer the question.) Programmers want "clusterbusters," promotion that is eye-grabbing, provocative, upbeat, and faster-paced. Four programmers noted that promos will have to pack in even more information in a shorter time while still grabbing viewers' attention at the start. On the negative side, three pointed out that on-air promos have become even less visible in the RCD environment "because so many people graze during commercial breaks," necessitating even more repetition to have an impact.

There was widespread agreement that on-air promos will become shorter (10 seconds rather than 30 seconds), that IDs will become even shorter (from 3 to 5 seconds down to 2 seconds), and that promotion will become more frequent. As expected, greater use of teases, bumpers, and billboards was advocated by most respondents (who mentioned better promotion), and more use of computer graphics and special effects was championed. Promotion managers claimed that viewers will see more use of "Next" headlines and more IDs within multiple promos.[13] More vertical promotion (touting upcoming shows) and more promotional tie-ins between network and local programs are expected. For example, ABC took advantage of digital video technology in 1992–93 to create new promotional opportunities; it began squeezing program credits into a corner of the screen and using the remaining space to promote its upcoming programs. Thus, ABC adds to its promotional inventory without having to bump paid commercial spots from its schedule.

Three respondents agreed that the best strategy was "to get promos in first" in commercial pods (though one manager advocated the last position in breaks just before the hour so that the promo would hit "on the hour" grazers). Also, one programmer noted, "Placing promos at the top of the hour gives us a better chance of capturing those viewers who have just tuned in." This is, of course, a traditional strategy that goes counter to seamlessness.

One recent innovation in promotion that was mentioned by only two programmers was the tiny, semi-transparent on-screen logo. USA Network, CNN, The Family Channel, and other cable networks have used it for some time, and some broadcast stations are now copying the practice. On-screen logos are thought to aid in proper identification in diaries and in building a recognizable image for a channel.[14] Another innovation that was mentioned was Fox's use of an on-screen clock during "In Living Color" in 1992 to let Super Bowl viewers know when halftime was over; called the "Zap-Time Party," the idea behind the on-screen clock was to keep viewers from constantly jumping back to check for the start of the Super Bowl's second half. It must be remembered that even though some programmers/managers had these specific suggestions, 40 percent of programmers asserted that the RCD had negligible impact on promotional practices.

DISCUSSION

Grazing has both a positive and negative side for programmers, managers, and producers. Grazing helps capture viewers for little-watched channels such as shopping services and public television; it increases sampling for independent stations and Fox affiliates (especially when they have low channel numbers on cable systems). At the same time, it offers viewers many options other than the traditional network affiliates and makes the job of promoting program viewing even more difficult. Dial position (channel number) will take on even greater importance because, according to some station managers, most RCD users—at least when they are bored and looking for something to watch—usually do not punch in a channel number; they flip up or down through several adjacent channels. Rationales for clustering cable and broadcast channels in tiers of some sort should receive much attention in the 1990s, including widely varying experiments conducted by cable operators and howls of complaint from repositioned broadcasters.

On the production side, it is clear that grazing hurts shows that take a long time to develop. The remote control will continue to have considerable impact on pacing and program style. Shows will become more compact, more tightly knit, with shorter segments and less filler, and enormous attention will be given to grabbing the viewer in the opening minutes. Crossovers by well-known stars will become common to strengthen audience flow and promote pairs of programs effectively. Glitz and special effects near the start will be used to attract attention, and many programs will begin with big emotional tugs (such as are achieved in the most award-winning commercial spots). Long opening segments will be lavishly produced in order to capture viewers and forestall sampling of other channels.

Closing credits in their present form are clearly on their way out, despite outrage from the production community, and commercial breaks will be postponed until programs have a fair start. This does mean, of course, more or longer breaks within programs to permit the same amount of advertising—a battle yet to be fought. Audience fickleness will force programmers to develop more effective means of increasing flow between adjacent programs. Seamlessness on the hour and half hour, hot switching from one program into another, and cold starts are definitely the patterns of the future.

Promotion will require bigger bites of station and network budgets and receive greater attention. Innovative promotional techniques will have to be devised to capture viewers' attention. It is probable that placing on-air promos at the beginning of commercial pods (within programs) has better value than other placements for combating the impact of RCDs. Ratings data will need to be broken into minute-by-minute segments in all competitive markets, encouraging the movement of peoplemeters into far smaller markets than has been anticipated. As the number of viewing options increases, peoplemeters will become essential because of the diminished value of diary data resulting from RCD penetration. Indeed, "winning a time slot" may become impossible, and the focus of attention may shift to winning *most* or even *part of* a time slot. Scheduling practices will have to change to give programs more time to prove themselves.

Without a doubt, programming strategies that have sustained the television industry for decades are losing their effectiveness, and traditional practices are rapidly being altered. What is becoming clearer is that the industry needs to undertake more effective self-education so that huge numbers of programmers and managers do not get left behind; they must understand what they are doing and why in order to realize new programming and scheduling concepts effectively. Otherwise the industry will see immense turnover and compaction. The networks and syndicators have a stake in successful station programming. At the same time, more and more programming is likely to be taken over by station representative firms (reps) and group-level programmers to take advantage of innovative thinking and conclusions based on large-scale ratings analysis; local station programmers will be relegated to non-decision-making roles or will disappear entirely. Even in the country's largest market, New York, a Fox station recently combined the jobs of programmer and promotion. This move not only illustrated promotion's increasing importance but also revealed that programming decisions are actually made at the highest level, not by program-mers. At the networks, programming decisions move up from programmers to the highest executive levels. We are seeing the erosion of programmers' autonomy throughout the industry. The remote control is one of several factors making programming more costly and more risky in the 1990s.

NOTES

1. Although the two terms are similar, *hot switching* refers to the practice of cutting from the end of one program to the start of another and postponing com-mercials; it is a practice that networks and stations can adopt with current programs. *Seamlessness*, on the other hand, entails elimination of interstitial clutter but sets a broader, long-term goal of restructuring program closings and openings to foster flow.

2. Seamlessness had a precursor in radio called "no goodbye, no hello," which was employed by many FM stations during the 1960s and 1970s at the switchover from one disc jockey to another. Its goal was to continue uninterrupted music across the hour (from, say, 2:55 to 3:05) to prevent listeners from changing channels for the start of other programs.

3. Specific stations and studios were not assigned because of the difficulty of locating an appropriate person willing to be interviewed. Efforts were made to achieve wide geographic and market size representation, and interviews ranged from Los Angeles to New York to Florida to several states in the Midwest and South.

4. Two faculty researchers coded all interview data and computed intercoder reliability by calculating the percentage of agreement after separately coding five interview reports (5 percent of data). Intercoder reliability exceeded 95 percent.

5. Market size was categorized according to A. C. Nielsen divisions in ratings books.

6. For example, MGM TV, Paramount TV, Witt-Thomas-Harris Productions, Ruby-Spears Enterprises, The Disney Channel, Fox Television, New World Tele-vision, Aaron Spelling Productions, Landsburg Company, and several independent producers.

7. Only 26 percent of mid-market programmers/managers acknowledged that RCDs were a problem for their stations.

8. Another 7 percent gave no codable response.

9. Stations were represented roughly equally by affiliation, with fewer PBS af-filiates and just slightly more ABC affiliates than average: independents = 10; ABC affiliates = 16; CBS affiliates = 13; Fox affiliates = 11; NBC affiliates = 13; and PBS affiliates/members = 5. Only one cable system manager was included.

10. *Crossovers* are appearances by one program's star(s) in another program, as when "Cheers" characters appear on "Wings."

11. Diaries are broken into 15-minute segments (quarter-hours), and at least one channel must receive more than half the segment (in other words, 7 minutes) of viewing for the quarter-hour to be attributed to any channel.

12. In discussing tiering, it is important to disassociate the idea of tiering and the idea of having signals on adjacent channels; a tier could be scattered on the dial, just available for one price.

13. Multiple promos advertise several programs and generally last 30 seconds or more. Without internal on-screen IDs, it is easily possible for viewers to see part of a promo and never know what time and what channel it will be on. It is acknowledged that zappers graze even during promos, especially long multiple spots; the typical pattern is for the viewer to watch promos for programs he or she likes and then change channels when the promo is for an unwatched program or genre.

14. On-screen logo/identification is especially important for stations that appear on different channel numbers on cable rather than on the broadcast band.

14

Remote Control Devices and the Political Economy of a Changing Television Industry

Robert V. Bellamy, Jr.

More than 80 percent of U.S. households have a remote control device (RCD) for either a television set or a videocassette recorder (VCR) (TV remote 1992). As all VCRs and over 95 percent of the color television sets sold in the United States now come equipped with RCDs (Benjamin, Chapter 2 of this volume), the total number of households with remote controls is certain to increase as replacement equipment is acquired (Color TVs 1992).

The audience is using RCDs to expand and enhance its television viewing experience, often at the expense of traditional television outlets. Perhaps the best evidence of this can be discerned from the dwindling audience shares of network television. Whereas the Big 3 networks as recently as the late 1970s commanded approximately 90 percent of the viewing audience on most evenings, they now battle over shares that averaged 63 percent in prime time in the 1991–92 season (Network rating 1992). Most of the "lost" audience has moved to non-broadcast outlets such as cable and home video (Mahoney 1990).

The shift of audience and parallel drop in network revenues have had serious economic implications for the U.S. broadcast television industry, which traditionally has been dominated by the close-knit oligopoly of the networks (Lindheim 1992). The change of ownership, ongoing financial restructuring, and changing acquisition strategies of each of these companies in the 1980s is evidence of the reaction of the oligopoly to the new television business environment. Of course, such business activity cannot be attributed solely to the diffusion of new television technology. The regulatory policies (or lack thereof) in the U.S. government and in other nations have encouraged corporate reorganization and consolidation through a weakening of traditional domestic and international economic barriers to entry (McQuail 1990).

The purpose of this chapter is to demonstrate the linkage of changes in the U.S. television industry with the widespread diffusion of RCDs, along with the accompanying growth of cable, VCRs, and myriad new programming outlets. This linkage is central to an understanding of both the restructuring of the domestic and international media economy and changes in the power relationship of television outlet to television viewer.

THE RCD AS TOOL TECHNOLOGY

Diffusion of innovations has long been of interest to mass communication scholars. As explained by Everett Rogers, the most prolific of the communication diffusion scholars, a key concept of diffusion is the idea of social change wherein the "structure and function of a social system" is altered (1983, 6). As television is an important part of that system, the increasing penetration and use of alternate television technologies have contributed to changes in that system. Although the RCD is fundamentally different from cable and VCRs, it has been a major factor in this alteration.

The RCD differs from other "new" television technology in two major ways. First, the remote control device is not a programming conduit. The RCD allows the user to more conveniently choose from the programming options available but does not in itself provide programming. Second, the RCD, like the VCR but unlike cable, provides the means of non-linear viewing. With an RCD the user can conveniently choose to watch more than one channel at a time and alter the order of program presentation. In essence, the RCD is a tool that gives users more control over their viewing environment by allowing them to design individualized television menus.

Thus, the RCD is the most vital component of the phenomenon of grazing, whereby viewers "flip, zip, and zap with frequency, passion, and determination, altering viewing patterns, programming strategies and even the look, sound, and feel of programming services" (Gilbert 1989, 5). Given this pattern of use, the RCD fits Rogers's description of a "tool technology," a technology that invites reinvention: "the degree to which an innovation is changed or modified by a user in the process of its adoption and implementation" (1986, 121). The viewers' re-invention of television viewing through the use of RCDs has strongly influenced many of the recent changes in the television industry.

There has been no identifiable change agent in the diffusion of RCDs; rather, the increased use of remote controls has developed from "the practical experience of certain individuals in the client group" for VCRs and cable television (Rogers 1983, 7). As such, considerations of the impact of RCDs cannot be divorced from the diffusion of these other technologies, as remote controls would have limited utility as a modifier of media industry and user behavior without the increased programming offerings made available by cable and videotapes. However, without the RCD, both cable and VCRs would no doubt be less popular and economically viable.

Theorizing the New Television Environment

Despite their first commercial appearance on television sets in 1955 (Burghi 1988), RCDs are considered to be a new technology (Bellamy and Walker 1990b; Heeter and Greenberg 1985b). As such, any consideration of them must be tied to various conceptions of media technology. One view holds that technology is a positive good that is a key element in "the doctrine of organized universal betterment" (Dizard 1982, 16) and "a new social revolution based upon information rather than power" (Dordick 1987, 20). The opposition view is that media technology provides a major element of the means by which "private economic control over the entire information sector is exerted and concentrated" (Schiller 1987, 23–31). Between these two poles are arguments that new media are extensions of existing institutions and are unlikely to lead to radical changes for either good or bad (Williams 1989; Winston 1986). Despite the divergence of viewpoints, all point to the critical role of societal and governmental organizations in the development and diffusion of new technology. These conceptions and accompanying arguments are central to recent attempts of mass communication researchers to understand the impact of such technology.

Although there have been varying shades of opinion and analysis of the government/industry relationship in the United States, basically these can be divided into the pluralist and neo-Marxist (or radical) approaches. In the former, perhaps best exemplified in the earliest edition of Krasnow and Longley's *The Politics of Broadcast Regulation* (1976), the governmental regulatory apparatus is seen as a relatively neutral forum in which various vested interests air their disputes until consensus is reached (the best-case scenario) or one side wins. No interest or institution theoretically is more powerful (in terms of winning the argument) than any other. Media organizations, in this view, are generally autonomous from the governmental arena. In stark contrast, scholars from the radical tradition argue that capitalist society is characterized by class domination that, while allowing media to serve as an outlet for arguments on class, ultimately sets the terms of these debates in such a way that the media usually (if not always) present the views of the dominant class (Curran 1990, 136).

More recently, there have been attempts to re-think and synthesize these broad theoretical approaches. Essentially, this is occurring through a combination of pluralists adopting and adapting many of the ideas of the neo-Marxists on the inequality of resources and the role of the state (Streeter 1987), and the neo-Marxists' recognition that the audience is worthy of more consideration than has heretofore been the case (Curran 1990; Schement and Lievrouw 1987). The blending of views and institutional roles and functions is the theoretical touchstone of this essay.

The basic contention here is that economic considerations are the primary factor in understanding the actions of and events in an industry (Curran, Gurevitch, and Woollacott 1982; Mitnick 1980; Murdock and Golding 1979). As such, the government and major media interests in the United States have worked in concert to force changes in the regulation of television delivery services in order to allow these interests to gain an increased degree of market power. Media institutions have their own power base in capitalist societies and economies. As Akhavan-Majid and Wolf have argued in their "elite power group model," the power of the media continues to increase due to the "mutually reinforcing structural characteristics" of ownership concentration, relationships with other power elites and control of the regulatory process (1991, 149).

However, such regulatory actions took place at a time of high diffusion of new technology, which (1) caused tensions in the relationship of the state and industry, (2) opened up opportunities for new entities to gain the resources necessary to enter the television program delivery business, and (3) afforded the viewer a level of autonomy in her/his relationship with the television industry not previously available.

Unintended Consequences

Winston has argued for "the 'law' of the suppression of radical potential," which states that every new invention or innovation that is introduced into the capitalistic marketplace is controlled by existing social and economic patterns and organizations to the degree that its use is limited to a pre-established link with existing technology (1986, 23–24). Although this argument can be accepted as an element of a political economic perspective, there is a problem with the timeline implied by Winston. The RCD and related technologies have been introduced and used in ways not at all palatable to existing economic interests. The technologies discussed here have "broken the law" in becoming integral parts of the media mix of millions of consumers without the consent of powerful interests. In addition, the unintended consequences of regulation (and deregulation) resulted in a lessening of economic barriers to entry in the traditionally oligopolistic television industry, which in turn changed the organizational structures and power relationships within that industry. Such consequences have been cited by Horwitz as a major "irony" of recent U.S. telecommunications regulation (1989, 6–7). However, there is little doubt that powerful economic entities will attempt to close the "window of opportunity" that is the result of regulation (or lack thereof) and a high rate of technological diffusion.

INDUSTRY REACTION TO AUDIENCE EMPOWERMENT: MYTH AND REALITY

An underlying but important theme of almost all RCD audience studies has been the idea that the RCD allows the user to exert a new level of autonomy in her/his relationship with the traditional television industry (Ainslie 1988; Bellamy and Walker 1990a; Greenberg and Heeter 1988b; Walker and Bellamy 1991a). In fact, the user is seen as empowered to change the nature of that relationship by constructing individualized media menus. Semiologist Umberto Eco, for instance, has been quoted as saying that the RCD makes the "viewer a Picasso," able to create a new and unique television environment (Stokes 1990). Obviously, such a perception is not what the advertising and television industries with to hear. The television audience, after all, has traditionally relied on discrete programming units (series) presented in a linear and predictable fashion (through the establishment of rigid scheduling) designed to expedite flow from program to advertising to program. Indeed, one researcher has argued that the networks are "ill-suited and ill-advised to compete in this narrow audience market" resulting from "deep and permanent changes" in the industry (Selnow 1989, 39).

The idea of audience empowerment also has appeared in the popular and trade press, with accompanying discussions of how program suppliers and advertisers fear the newly powerful viewer, who before the RCD was regarded as a relatively docile receptor for the wares of the two industries (Arrington 1992; Knopf 1992; Larson 1992). What often is ignored in these scenarios is the ability of "power elites" such as television and advertising entities to exert their strength through the manipulation of the regulatory process and ability to enter into new economic arrangements.

The audience increasingly is an active participant in designing individualized television menus containing programming from an ever-expanding variety of sources (Becker and Schoenbach 1989; Boyd, Straubhaar, and Lent 1989; Heeter and Greenberg 1988b; Levy and Gunter 1988). Future development of "smart" RCDs and VCRs that will automatically zap commercials (Heeter, Yoon, and Sampson, Chapter 7 of this volume; Mandese 1992, 30), and "Interactive Television Operating Systems" that will allow the user to "conveniently capture, index and watch specific programming independently of the transmission schedule" will offer more ways for viewers to design individualized viewing experiences and further erode the power of television program and advertising suppliers to reach an audience (Franklin 1992, 14). However, a closer look at the arrangements being consummated within the increasingly international television industry demonstrate the ways in which the television industry seeks to re-exert its control over the audience.

The Re-exertion of Control

Becker and Schoenbach have argued that the question of who controls the choices that are available to the audience is critical to considerations of the impact that new television outlets have on audiences (1989, 19). To date, the reaction of the major U.S. television entities to competition for that control has consisted of the interlocking strategies of domestic economic integration, international partnerships, and the shift of costs to the audience. The cable industry's rise to economic prominence in the 1980s created much interest on the part of the Big 3 networks to gain entry into the industry. After some early failed attempts to develop their own cable programming services (ABC and Group W's Satellite News Channel, CBS Cable), the networks moved to partnerships (NBC/Cablevision Systems, ABC and Hearst's A&E Network) and majority buy-outs such as ABC's 90 percent ownership of ESPN (Clayton 1990; Mermigas 1990). This horizontal economic integration recently has been joined by the vertical integration represented by General Electric's acquisition of RCA/NBC, the Time/Warner merger, and Sony's acquisition of Columbia Records, an excellent example of hardware/software integration (Mermigas 1989). Although deregulation (complemented by technological diffusion) has allowed new entrants, it also has allowed such large mergers to be consummated with minimal government interference. Important here is the blurring of the boundaries between the broadcast and cable industries. Established by different technology and regulation, these boundaries increasingly are regarded as irrelevant by both the industry and the government, which see the product and not the delivery mechanism as the most important element in the television business. The result is a series of programming and ownership/operational co-ventures between broadcasters and cablecasters (Halonen 1992b; Tyrer 1992a). Recent regulatory action that will allow telephone companies to provide video services will present more opportunities for various joint ventures (Halonen 1992a). In essence, broadcast stations and networks continue to seek regulatory relief from the cable industry while at the same time seeking and gaining entry into the industry.

The Sony/Columbia deal is reflective of a burgeoning multi-billion dollar international electronic media marketplace (Loftus 1988, 53; Stilson 1989c). McQuail attributes the increasing international activity (particularly that in Europe) to the "global logic of deregulation," driven by right-wing economic policies combined with the failure or inability of governments to deal with changing technology (1990, 321). The result is that the Big 3 and major cable entities such as MTV and Turner are actively making deals with existing firms and creating new international television services (Forkan 1989; Greenstein 1990; Halonen 1990; Stilson 1989a; Stilson 1989b; Tyrer 1992b). International television industry activity is not solely the "invasion" of indigenous industries by U.S. firms, as many foreign firms are now actively engaged in acquiring U.S. companies (Mahoney 1989a; 1989b; 1989c). This activity is an indicator of how the drive for an enhanced financial position is now a global activity, aided and abetted by governmental policies.

The increasing growth and promotion of pay-per-view (PPV) television is the most obvious way in which the costs of television are being shifted to the user. Although the most popular PPV offerings to date have been events that most likely would not have appeared on advertiser-supported television (e.g., championship boxing matches, rock concerts) and are thus promoted as supplements to "regular" television, there are increasing attempts to shift other forms of television to PPV. Recent discussions on the likelihood of "à la carte" offerings of now basic cable services, video-on-demand (VOD) services, and interactive television offer further evidence of the cost shift occurring in the television industry (Knopf 1992; Maddox 1992a; Walley 1992b). In addition, the argument that television stations need a dual revenue stream like cable (i.e., advertising and subscriber fees) is central to recent regulatory activity that would force cable companies to negotiate payments to television stations for the use of their signals (Maddox 1992b). Without strict cost regulation, such fees are likely to lead to increased subscriber costs.

Of course, the shift of costs to viewers does not in itself change the relationship of the advertising industry to television, or, more specifically, allow advertisers to more easily reach an increasingly non-captive television audience. In order to do this, new forms of advertiser-supported television are being developed. One of the newer innovations in advertising is place-based media, which developed in print with direct mail and controlled-circulation magazines targeted to specific demographic targets. In television, companies such as Whittle and Turner Broadcasting System (TBS) have developed highly specific demographically targeted video services that are available in public and semi-public spaces such as classrooms, airports, supermarkets, and truck stops (Walley 1992a). This attempt to reach viewers in a relatively captive environment is a result of television providers' need to offer the advertiser the predictable, measurable, and relatively homogeneous audience that can no longer be ensured by television in the home.

The erosion of the traditional lines between programming and advertising is another way in which the television industry is attempting to both maintain and enhance its attributes as an advertising medium. Besides the obvious and ubiquitous program-length commercials and home shopping programs/cable services, the television industry is now active in supplying "value-added" marketing packages to advertisers for programs such as sportscasts. In such a package, the advertiser gets stadium signage, scoreboard spots, luxury boxes, and a variety of in-program plugs in addition to advertising spots (Reynolds 1992). This linkage of advertiser to program is meant to permeate the telecast to such a degree that even a zapping viewer is exposed to the advertiser's message. This is an example of how the television industry

is spending increasing amounts of time and money on devising more atten-
tion-getting and "zap-proof" programming, promotion, and advertising
(Eastman and Neal-Lunsford, Chapter 13 of this volume; Freedman 1988).

POTENTIAL OUTCOMES

Without question, both the domestic and international television industries are in an unprecedented state of flux. Previous patterns of industrial
and governmental action and the logic of the capitalistic marketplace allow
for some reasonable speculation on the ultimate outcome of this industrial
uncertainty. First, there is a strong likelihood that fewer and economically
more powerful entities will develop primarily as combinations of existing
firms in new guises or configurations. Second, now that the transnational-
ization of economic entities is encouraged by most governments, these new
entities likely will tailor more of their offerings for global audiences. At the
same time, there will be a continuing shift of costs from the television and
advertising industries to the television viewer, and an increasing blurring of
the lines between program and advertising content.

Although economics are of primary importance in understanding the
actions and events of recent years in the television industry, they can not
be regarded as the sole determinant. Rather, the control of economic resources (e.g., technology, audiences) accrues to the most powerful interests
in a society (Murdock and Golding 1979, 20), with the exceptions of (1)
the times when the diffusion curve outpaces the attempts of institutions to
control new technologies (as in the case of cable, VCRs, and RCDs); and
(2) when regulation either cannot keep pace with technological change or
is being used for purposes that have unintended consequences such as opening up the media structure for new entrants and affording the audience an
altered relationship with the providers of programming and advertising.

Although the media elites almost certainly will re-exert power in the
relationship with viewers through a shift of costs and control over programming choices, the parallel diffusion of cable, satellites, VCRs, and the
RCD has fundamentally altered the nature of that relationship. With the
power to select a large number of offerings and, more important, actively
avoid the traditional form of advertising messages, the television user
increasingly expects the industry to provide programs that meet her or
his needs. The economic survival of the industry depends on its ability to
do so.

At the same time, audience power over the television industry is a matter
of degree. Although audience power is more influential in determining programming, the programming function is not (nor is it likely to become) a
democratic exercise in terms of deciding on the types of programs that will
be made available to the audience. Such decisions are the purview of a small
group of corporations whose primary function is to maximize profit. Al-

though the audience has more options of what to watch at any given time, the choice of specific program content is still in the hands of an increasingly international class of capitalists. Any discussion of audience empowerment must be seen in this context.

Owen and Wildman have argued that the transformation of the structure of the television programming industry into a "highly competitive, pluralistic" model similar to that of the magazine industry is a positive good because it reduces the power of a traditionally oligopolistic industry (1992, 1). What is left unstated by such analyses is that the shift of costs to the television user, combined with more sophisticated appeals to the "right" demographics, will disenfranchise rather than empower those without the money or spending patterns to attract the attention of advertisers. In fact, market segmentation, a hallmark of the "new" television, can be seen in many respects as socially divisive. Gillespie and Robins, for example, have warned of the "spatial bias" of new technologies whereby the application of these technologies can actually increase inequality among both individual users and nations (1989, 7). Klein has argued that because market segmentation "targets those qualities that distinguish people from each other" rather than similarities, it is more difficult to "build a sense of common values" (1992, 22).

Although any technological device or change in industrial structure that encourages a multiplicity of content has positive attributes, the ability of RCD users to systematically avoid unpleasant stimuli encompasses far more than advertising messages. For example, the active avoidance of political information has been found to be a significant use of RCDs (Walker and Bellamy 1991). When this is combined with the lack of access to an increasing amount of programming on the part of those of less economic stature, it is easy to see how the continued use of RCDs and the subsequent change in television programming services are likely to contribute to increased levels of public apathy and disillusionment. The ultimate result, then, seems likely to be more choice for those viewers who have economic value for the program providers coupled with a general increase in social divisiveness hidden by the guise of programming pluralism.

Part VI

Critical Perspectives on the Remote Control

15

Remote Control:
Mythic Reflections

David Lavery

Television is the most relentless purveyor of the messages that constitute
and perpetuate our severely fragmented public consciousness. It slices
our attention span into increments too infinitesimal to get up and measure.

Kruger 1987, 402

TV gives us infinite information about choice—it celebrates choice as
a great blessing, which it is, and over the course of a single day it lays
out a nearly infinite smorgasbord of options. As much as it loves choice,
though, it doesn't actually believe in choosing. It urges us to choose
everything—this and this and this as well.

McKibben 1992, 185

My children wanted The Disney Channel. Its free promotion had convinced
us that the entire family might enjoy it enough to justify the cost of installation and the "premium channel" charge that the local cable monopoly
would put on our already large monthly tab. As I watched the installer set
up our new Sanyo cable-ready, remote control television set for proper
reception, sorting through the mass of cables (from the TV, two VCRs, the
cable connection), placing a strange, new piece of equipment—a switch
box—on the top of the set, the implications of what he was doing slowly
became clear. Without this box, it seemed, we could not bring in Disney;
although my TV could bring in HBO or Cinemax without additional equipment, Memphis Cablevision did not have the capacity to deliver directly to
my home the unscrambled Disney signal. But the obligatory black box had
a major side effect. It made my remote control device unusable. When I

broke my incredulous silence to complain to the installer, I was informed that if I wanted to continue to use my remote, I would need to rent a special remote from the cable company for an extra charge! Stunned at the audacity of this scheme, the suspension of one of my inalienable human rights and its reinstatement in exchange for a monthly fee, I immediately cancelled the installation and showed the installer to the door. Complaints to customer service, both at Memphis Cablevision and at Disney Channel headquarters, went unheeded. My children were disappointed, but as a family we agreed that doing without remote control was way too high a price to pay for acquiring The Disney Channel. We didn't want to return to the old days.

Only 17 percent of U.S. households had a remote control device in 1979; at the end of the 1980s, 72 percent did. Over 60 million households now no longer have to leave the sofa to change the TV. As this "living room gadget of the decade" (Shales 1989, G–12) has multiplied in Malthusian fashion in our living rooms, its image abounds in our popular culture as well:

- Chauncey Gardner of "Being There," expelled, as childlike as Kaspar Hauser, from his lifetime hermitage, his only knowledge of the outside world via TV, tries to zap away some muggers with his remote control.

- Garfield, that ultimate couch potato, sits on the sofa, trying without success to use John's RCD to turn the pages of a book.

- On MTV's resolutely mindless quiz show "Remote Control," three party-animal college student solipsists sprawl in lounge chairs, remotes in hand (they double as answer buzzers signaling their responses when pointed at the "Mother TV" on the game board) and respond to questions about—what else?—television. At break time, munchies fall from the sky like manna into the contestants' proffered cereal bowls. In the end, the lead point-getter stretches out in a Craftmatic Adjustable Bed and plays for more prizes (which often include, of course, a remote control) by identifying all of ten music videos regularly played on MTV, the channel of choice, after all, to which many zappers in the contestants' age group turn for instant release from the dull and uninteresting.

- A newspaper columnist (Diebold 1989) insists, tongue firmly planted in cheek, that remote controls cause violence, judging by the evidence of his own household. He has, he reports, actually seen his own children come to blows while struggling for possession of the family remote.

- In Wes Craven's horror film *Shocker* (1989), a serial killer escapes his electrocution when a power surge miraculously transforms him into pure energy. Able to transport himself over the airwaves from one television set to another, he goes on another crime wave. In the end, however, his nemesis "blows him away" with an RCD, turning off the TV in which the killer is momentarily trapped before he has the chance to escape. Like the western gunfighter, he expresses his satisfaction with a classic gesture, blowing the smoke away from the barrel of his "weapon" and placing it back in his holster/pocket.

- On an episode of Steven Spielberg's short-lived "Amazing Stories" entitled "Remote Control Man," a poor slob addicted to television to escape a nagging wife and awful family buys a new state-of-the-art set whose remote allows him to transform his family into characters from TV (June Cleaver, the Hulk, Ed McMahon, Gary Coleman, Richard Simmons).

- Jay Leno tells about his recent purchase of a brand new TV, complete with remote, as a present for his mother and father. The parents of a star, Leno explains, should be brought into the modern age—whether they want to come or not. Visiting months later, Leno discovered, however, that though the TV was in use, the remote was buried in a drawer. It seems his mother was afraid to use it, terrified that its misdirected beam, like a "Star Trek" phaser, might shatter a nearby vase or, horror of horrors, his father.

Now the stuff of which cartoons and monologues are made, remote controls are nevertheless approaching mythic status. Under the tutelage of Roland Barthes's reversal of the poles (1957), we now can see myth as a way of understanding that is no longer problematic, as a kind of thinking or doing that has become so inextricably part of our cultural consciousness that it seems almost invisible: a form of being that has come to seem entirely natural.

Television itself is already mythic in Barthes's sense. As Neil Postman has noted, "We are no longer fascinated or perplexed by its machinery. We do not tell stories of its wonders. We do not confine our television sets to special rooms" (1985, 79). Already it takes the strange mind of an artist like Nam June Paik or filmmaker Nicholas Roeg to bring us even a glimpse of television's uncanniness.[1]

Now, after only a few short years of widespread use, after only three decades of actual existence, the remote control appears more than ready to go the way of its companion instrument. The fascination that numinous new media/new technology induce in the so-called primitive mind—recorded, while it still could exist, by Edmund Carpenter in his media ethnography, *Oh, What a Blow That Phantom Gave Me!* (1973)—cannot exist for long in today's culture of technosophisticates. Leno's mother is clearly an oddity of the time, distinguished by her age. Already, many of us can no longer conceive of non-remote television viewing. The Paik-like cover of John Fiske's *Television Culture* (1987), an image of an extreme close-up of a remote control device filling the frame of a television, set against the ground of (1) a newspaper guide to TV viewing, and (2) the self-same RCD, seems an accurate rendering: Inside and out of our televisions the ever-present remote is "what's on."

The following reflections are offered with the intent of demythologizing the remote before its complete transformation into a mere household appliance, its dissembling into the guise of the ordinary, is complete, while still a hint of mystery clings to this tiny box of buttons in our hand.

As a result of a "fundamental weirdness," contemporary mass, exoteric culture now often mimics the formerly esoteric styles of experimental art (Polan 1986). It is not surprising, then, that remotes enable users to feel creative. Umberto Eco has suggested that use of remotes may be a way of increasing aesthetic satisfaction by subverting the closed texts of individual programs and single channels into the open interpretation grazing requires. By allowing us to "transform something that was meant to be very dog-matic—to make you laugh, to make you cry—into a free collage," remotes, Eco claims, "can make the television into a Picasso" (Stokes 1990, 39–40).[2]

In an essay exploring the proliferation of the hyper-genre of simulation on television, Michael Sorkin notes that the "flow" of television has much in common with a surrealist exercise known as "the Exquisite Corpse" (1987, 162). Exquisite corpses are collaborative works, both drawings and poetry, in which individual contributors work together to create a work without having any knowledge of their predecessor's input. At the top of a piece of paper, for example, one artist may draw a figure or design, in whole or in part, and then fold the paper so that the next in line cannot see the beginning. The next adds his drawing, again folding the paper to obscure the first two contributions, and turns it over to a third . . . and so forth. (Poets can easily play a similar game.)

Like the "Exquisite Corpse," Sorkin writes, "TV is about juxtaposition. Television's formal environment thrives on the multiplier effect of accidental collaborations among a community of propagators and users" (1987, 162–63). An evening's prime time viewing

is structured by a dialectic of elision and rift among the various windows (commercial scheduling, programming, "news") through which images enter the broadcast and are combined as television. "Flow" is more of a circumstance than a product. The real output is the quantum, the smallest maneuverable broadcast bit. And, with the spread of cable, VCRs, computer games, and the power to zap, "broadcasters" are accelerating toward the relinquishment—or rather the transcendence—of interest and investment in sequence. Any arrangement of bits will ultimately produce the same effects. (Sorkin 1987, 163)

As we regard "the minisculization of TV's combinable bits," we begin to grasp television's true sense of order. According to an old thought experi-ment, enough monkeys randomly typing on enough machines would even-tually turn out the works of Shakespeare. But "television's logic," Sorkin suggests, "accelerates toward a boldly economic resolution of this difficulty. The system, by definition, cannot make an illegible artifact: every chimp is a Shakespeare. No combination is lost to meaning" (1987, 163).

Sorkin's essay does not specifically address the question of the effect of remotes on this logic, but clearly the process he describes can only be exponentially accelerated by their growing prominence.[3] Several commen-tators have noted that channel switching enables viewers to make up their own mosaic of images, but "mosaic" hardly captures the strange, surreal nature of the activity. We should think, rather, of the hybrid, random creations of the grazer as exquisite corpses. Thanks to the remote, the revivification of the exquisite corpse becomes, for the inveterate remote user, a nightly pursuit of a new order "as beautiful as the chance encounter of a sewing machine and an umbrella on a dissecting table."[4] Each grazer is in fact a re-animator; each night before the TV, a night of the living dead.

Permit me, if you will, to display before you only one such corpse, brought to life via Memphis Cablevision at 7:35 P.M., Central Standard Time, on Thursday, June 25, 1992. (I will attempt no autopsy.)[5]

A small boy at Saint Jude's Hospital is fed intravenously during chemotherapy; on "A Different World," college women talk of "reappropriating the symbols of our oppressors." On a cable access channel, local experts talk about home insurance; on "Drexell's Class," two teachers meet at a drinking fountain; whale watchers track killer whales; students remodel a house; a spokesman for Sears makes a full disclosure about recent charges of fraud in automotive repair; Lloyd Bridges narrates an unidentifiable documentary in which a man plays Santa Claus; a posse tracks some outlaws; the name of a QVC winner is selected from a clear plastic barrel; Burger King claims they "are the one"; Michael Kuzak (Harry Hamlin) addresses the jury on "L.A. Law"; the fast delivery of Domino's Pizzas is touted; Robert Conrad pretends to have a French Canadian accent; toy dancers powered by "today's Duracells" outlast the competition; a radar image of the Memphis area reveals impending thunderstorms; Sgt. Joe Friday interrogates a suspect on "Dragnet"; on "This Is Your Life," Jeannette MacDonald is reunited with the minister who married her; prices are dramatically slashed in a Going Out of Business Sale at Shoe Biz; CNN Headline News reports on the popularity of "hash" running in New York City; CNN reports on a man who has been stalking Janet Jackson; the Color Match Car Care System is promoted in an infomercial; professional painters are said to always start with Sherwin-Williams; Hurricane Celia's progress is charted; Rep. Jim Slattery (D-Kansas) speaks on the floor of the United States House of Representatives; Ho Frat Ho performs (in a rap video) the Ho Frat Ho Swing; Senator Warren Rudman (R-New Hampshire) speaks on the floor of the United States Senate; Dick Van Dyke speaks of preserving television's "heritage" through re-runs of "I Love Lucy" on Nickelodeon; in an interview, Kurt Russell talks about *Bull Durham*, which was based on his life; we learn the 800 number for Super 8 Motels; a woman demands the keys of her obviously drunk male companion, as we learn not only that "Friends Don't Let Friends Drive Drunk" but that "Cable Television Cares."

Such excursions into Wacky Land may be undertaken at any time of the day or night, each time producing different results. The German electronic composer Karlheinz Stockhausen has created an ever-evolving work he calls *Kurzwellen* ("Shortwave"), in which a group of musicians responds intuitively and resonantly with bursts of shortwave reception selected by a mastermind (Stockhausen, of course) of the radio dial; each performance, as aleatoric as the broadcast spectrum, is thus completely different from the last. Every grazer can pretend to be the mastermind of a similar, though televisual, creation. Yet so accustomed are we becoming to the myth of the remote that the tacit acceptance of a "dialectic of elision and rift" required by such a spacy adventure comes more and more naturally.

Surveys continue to show that some people—more often women than men, more often old than young—do not graze and see no merit in it. They indicate as well that even dedicated grazers often become irritated when someone else masterminds the grazing as if their masturbatory art has no audience but the artist, as if flippancy is best performed alone. Yet the more we watch TV, the more our obsessive selection, our manic search via remotes and smart windows, discloses odd couplings and strange transmutation, the more our viewing is governed by a meta-irony. In all its range, the one thing we seldom see on TV, as Barbara Ehrenreich has noted, is people watching television. In fact, it may well be that "We watch television because television brings us a world in which television does not exist" (1987, 9).[6] Remote, flippant, the couch potato is a creature of paradox.

In Philip K. Dick's *Do Androids Dream of Electric Sheep?* (1968), denizens of a future, post–nuclear-holocaust, totally artificial Earth (people lavish great affection on simulated, robotic pets, and renegade, killer androids roam the streets) are equipped with special Mood Organs by means of which they can program their own feelings as the stresses of the day demand. One popular setting, we learn, is "the desire to watch television no matter what's on." Our primitive remotes have no such settings as yet and cannot program our desires, but they certainly do come in "handy" when the mood hits us to watch television no matter what's on.

Snyder quotes a retired executive's approach to grazing, an approach that must be fairly common: "I have my idea of what I want to look at. If it doesn't meet my specifications, I flip through the stations. If I still can't find anything to watch after five or ten minutes, I turn it off" (1988, 58). Many grazers are not so fast with the off button; they continue grazing, ever in search of something to watch, just "watching television." "Entertainment gives us what we want," a media critic has noted, while "Art gives us what we didn't know we wanted" (Youngblood 1978, 60). However, grazing necessitates a modification of this simple but eloquent definition: Grazing is entertainment as the search for what the viewer wants—entertainment as the search for entertainment.

Like Jeff Jeffries in Hitchcock's *Rear Window*, we have the potential to become immobilized spectators, voyeurs, before a multiple window exhibition. Hitchcock's voyeur, bedridden with a broken leg, became a Peeping Tom as a result of forced boredom. We, however, choose the couch. Jeffries lived too early—the film was released in 1954—to make use of even a primitive remote (though a turn of the head enables him to change channels), but he clearly stands as an ancestral figure of the couch potato. Today, if we have the right equipment, we can even open, with the touch of a remote, a "smart window" in the picture at hand and examine two offerings at once.

In a "culture of instinctive semioticians" (Eco 1986, 210), it has become more and more the case that one channel cannot satisfy. Grazers speak of enjoying the challenge of following more than one plot at a time, of moving back and forth not just across channels but between different genres and distinct forms, trying to keep them all "straight" (Snyder 1988). But we must be careful, if we are to avoid falling prey to myth, not to take these developments as natural or value free. Our gadgets disclose our motives; our use of them can exhibit a psychological style. Snyder (1988, 58) quotes a woman's annoyance with her husband's inveterate grazing: "He lies on the couch and plays the piano on the cable box. Every second it's switchy-switchy. It drives me crazy. It has something to do with a short attention span or hyperactivity. He claims it's how he relaxes, but it's very aggressive. I guess he feels in control. Anything he doesn't like, whammo, it's gone."

It is an illusion to believe that technological devices send merely technical messages. "Flippancy," this woman knows, may in fact be a form of domination, a dream of manipulation. Convinced that pleasure is best attained through mastery (Slater 1974), American culture appears firmly committed to a strange hedonics; and the remote control device, appealing as it does (like all forms of fingertip control) to fantasy of infantile narcissistic omnipotence, complements it perfectly.[7]

In his attempt to think through the nature of human movement and develop the principles of "kinetography," dance theorist Rudolf Laban has written (1988, 79) of a form of "elemental action" he labels, simply, "remote." When we are remote, Laban suggests, we are the opposite of "near." No longer present to things in need of our "warm impact or careful consideration," no longer required to express "strong attachment" or even "superficial touch," we experience instead a "detachment which may include focus on self or universal attention, together with restraint or abandon" (79). Are we not "remote" when we use the remote? Does not remote control immerse us in this mode? In a culture of narcissism, waffling between self-obsession and "universal attention"—the modern psyche, Hannah Arendt shows in *The Human Condition*, is engaged in a "twofold flight": "from the Earth into the universe and from the world into the self" (1958, 6)[8]— the remote confirms us in our flippancy, allows us to act it out while still inert in our living rooms.

The painter "takes his body with him," Paul Valery once noted (Merleau-Ponty 1964, 162). Does the grazer? "Tubers," according to 1980s' slang, are "couch potatoes," that is, they are vegetables: individuals without use of their body. To use a remote is to have an out-of-body experience.[9]

In "Where Am I?" philosopher Daniel Dennett (1981), a prominent authority on the nature of the human mind and the development of artificial intelligence, offers a "thought experiment" in which NASA removes a man's brain from his body—placing it, "disembodied in Houston," in a life-support system at the Manned Spacecraft Center—so that "he" can be sent on a rescue mission into a highly radioactive underground chamber. Dennett's cautionary tale leads to much futuristic speculation on the possibility for and implications of "remote sensing" and "telepresence" (Marvin Minsky's term), and a meditation on mind-body interaction, the nature of reality, and the location of the self. Such thought experiments, in fact, become increasingly common: The anthology in which "Where Am I?" appears collects several similar essays.

On the evening of October 17, 1989, my body, suffering from a bad cold, lay prone before the television on a sofa in the living room of my Memphis, Tennessee, apartment. When I had turned the set on, I tuned it to the local ABC affiliate to watch Game 3 of the World Series, but the remote control lay within reach on a nearby table. Then, during the pre-game show, ABC lost its feed from San Francisco. As I learned that the Bay Area had been hit by a strong earthquake, I remained with ABC for a time but then reached for the remote. Disembodied in Memphis, a couch potato, I was nevertheless able, via a kind of telepresence, to explore the effects of the quake on the Bay Area not from a single perspective but through the eyes and ears of NBC, CBS, ABC, and CNN. Safe in Memphis, my remote senses moved through this city at the touch of a button, walked across severed bridges, witnessed collapsed interstates, looked on from an aerial view at a raging fire in the Marina district. In January 1991, I found myself telepresent at the Persian Gulf war (or, I should say, at those scenes U.S. government censors chose to allow me to see), grazing my way through the first prime time war (Kirn 1990). In April 1992, I could remotely sense catastrophe unfolding—telepresent this time at the burning of Los Angeles, a distant voyeur at the horrible beating of a truck driver, a vicarious looter of stores, pushbutton torch of a city two thousand miles away.

"Our condition," writes Stanley Cavell (1971, 102), "has become one in which our natural mode of perception is to view, feeling unseen. We do not so much look at the world as look out at it, from behind the self." Nothing in the primal scene of grazing contradicts this notion. Indeed, everything about remote controlling encourages just such a stance.

If it is true, as Meyrowitz (1985) has argued, that electronic media in general and television in particular subtly alter—through a transformation of our customary "situational geography"—our sense of proper behavior in given social settings (bringing "backstage" behavior into the foreground, for example[10]), the proliferation of remote control can only accelerate the process. If, today, we often witness behavior once considered inappropriate for "mixed company," if we no longer "know our place" or understand the appropriate agenda of a given situation, it is, Meyrowitz shows, because media, like television, tear down the barriers that once segregated situations.

"It is extremely rare," Meyrowitz writes, "for there to be a sudden widespread change in walls, doors, the layout of a city, or in other architectural and geographical structures" (39). Such change, however, is the norm in the world of mass media, engineered not by architects or city planners but "by the flick of a microphone switch, the turning on of a television set, or the answering of a telephone" (40). Or the push of a button.

The specialness of time and place can be destroyed. "If we celebrate our child's wedding in an isolated situation where it is the sole 'experience' of the day," Meyrowitz writes, "then our joy may be unbounded" (310–11). However, the intervention of electronic media changes all that. When, on our way to the wedding, we hear over the car radio of a devastating earthquake, the death of a popular entertainer, or the assassination of a political figure, we lose not only our ability to rejoice fully but also our ability to mourn deeply. The electronic combination of many different styles of interaction from distinct regions leads to new "middle region" behaviors (which Meyrowitz describes, after McLuhan, as "cool") that, while containing elements of formerly distinct roles, are themselves new behavior patterns with new expectations and emotions. By allowing us to zap, zip, flip, and graze, remotes make even traditional televisual "place"—sticking with a particular network for an evening—seem passé.

The remote control, it should now be clear, is entirely post-modernist, a technological distillate, both cause and effect and exemplar of a new sensibility. The great modernist search for unity is now seemingly abandoned and the triumph of pastiche is now secure as the ultimate mode of the age (so Frederic Jameson argued in a seminal essay in 1984). In the words of Todd Gitlin, we are left only with

a cultivation of surfaces endlessly referring to, ricocheting from, reverberating onto other surfaces. The work calls attention to its arbitrariness, constructedness; it interrupts itself. Instead of a single center, there is pastiche and cultural recombination. Anything can be juxtaposed to anything else. In a spirit of aftermath and accommodation, post-Modernism demonstrates that originality is fraudulent by ripping it off and repeating it, endlessly. (1989, 56)

Post-modernism, Gitlin demonstrates convincingly, "only masquerades as avant-garde when, in fact, it is simply shouting that it has nothing to say" to an audience so habituated to the "experience of aftermath, privatization, weightlessness" that it seems worth listening and watching and grazing until, finally and irrevocably, they themselves are put out to pasture (58).

Apocalyptic-minded culture critics are fond of suggesting that as the century nears its end, we are "rearranging deck chairs on the Titanic." However accurate, the metaphor is now a cliché. Let me offer an alternative. To be more precise, we are chained in a state-of-the-art version of Plato's cave of illusion, remotes in hand, grazing shadows. As we come to live this life of allegory, as the myth becomes complete, it seems less and less likely that a philosophically minded couch potato—or even a semiotically inclined one, enraptured by TV's new, open textuality—will bother to get up to bring news from outside; it seems less and less likely that the shadows will be cross-checked against reality. As I write, new remote powers are on the horizon for the average consumer. Soon our RCDs will enable us to select camera angles on certain programs, track into the frame in search of other things to see, interact with the diegesis from the comfort of the sofa. In the near future we will be offered even greater control. With the likely late twentieth- or early twenty-first-century dissemination of virtual reality— described by William Gibson, the creator of cyberpunk science fiction, as potentially "lethal, like free-basing American TV" (Austin 1992, C–1)—the remoteness offered in the late 1980s and early 1990s will come to seem amateurish.

"It is possible," writes Mark Crispin Miller, "that no contrast, however violent, could jolt television's overseasoned audience, for whom discontinuity, disjointedness are themselves the norm; a spectacle that no stark images could shatter, because it comes already shattered. TV ceaselessly disrupts itself, not only through the sheer multiplicity of its offerings in the age of satellite and cable, but as a strategy to keep the viewer semi-hypnotized. Through its monotonous aesthetic of incessant change, TV may make actual change unrecognizable, offering, in every quiet living room, a cool parody of the Heraclitean fire" (1988, 13–14). Although we are unable to step into the same flow twice, remotes nevertheless inure us to this parody until it becomes indistinguishable from reality itself.

NOTES

1. Since 1963, the Korean-born Paik has demonstrated a "lifelong effort to deconstruct and demystify television" through unclassifiable works in which televisions—dislocated from their normal locales (placed in jungle settings, for example, or formed into new constellations in the sky) and distorted (Paik's "prepared" televisions alter normal picture reception in strange and unexpected ways—again become mysterious cultural objects. Roeg's *The Man Who Fell to Earth* (1976) tells the story of an alien being (played by David Bowie) who comes to this planet on a mission to secure water for his own, an arid wasteland, but becomes entrapped by American culture. One of his debilitating obsessions becomes the slavish watching of hundreds of television images at the same time, images that he finds numinous but enthralling. For a fuller discussion of Paik's work, see Hanhardt (1987); Youngblood (1978); and Jameson (1984). Jameson also notes the similarity of Paik's and Roeg's visions of TV.

2. Eco, it must be noted, is careful to distinguish between "works that were meant to be open" and the "patchwork" openness produced by a remote. Any critic tempted to theorize about remote control users as artists would do well to keep in mind the following sobering observation from McKibben (1992, 149):

Television, the culture's great instrument, speaks to eighty-year-olds and eighteen-year-olds with the same voice. I think of grandmother, spending her last years remote control in hand. She could watch what she felt like, of course, but almost all of the choices had been created for those with desirable demographics. Television never grows old, never ceases that small talk that may be innocuous when you're thirty but should be monstrous by the end of your life. Right to the last day of my grandmother's life it continued to offer her the sight of Donahue discussing sex changes and Cosby making faces and Vanna spinning letters.

3. Over a decade ago, before the widespread use of remote control, Susan Sontag (1973) issued an urgent call for an "ecology" of images. Any practicing ecologist in the 1990s will certainly have to contend with remotes, which mindlessly disseminate images into the cultural environment as widely and carelessly as fast food chains broadcast styrofoam.

4. This is a favorite, oft-quoted line from a surrealist precursor, the Comte de Lautreamont, written in the 1830s.

5. In a book that records the results of an experimental viewing of one day (over two thousand hours) of cable television compared with one day in nature, McKibben (1992) offers his own fascinating version of an exquisite corpse.

6. If we do discover people watching television on television, Ehrenreich observes, it is "only for a second, before the phone rings or a brand-new multiracial adopted child walks into the house." But "they are never really watching, hour after hour, the way real people do" (1987, 9).

7. Writing in *Esquire* (in a column called "The First Sex"), Bing (1990, 79), winking at his fellow males, confesses his own motives in using his RCD:

I love my remote, but I take it out of my mouth sometimes. During the day, for instance, I keep it holstered.... But late at night, when the children are in their warm, tousled beds and my wife is upstairs dreaming of upholstery,... when I can finally be with myself—not myself as a father or husband or son or commuter or aggressive pedestrian or angry restaurant patron or disappointed sports fan or corporate functionary, but myself as total human being on the face of the planet, the person known to myself and no other—I pick up my remote and watch TV like a man. "I can't stand the way you jump around," says my wife over the latest Anita Brookner as I move from giant trucks on ESPN to *King Lear* on PBS and back to Nick at Nite's continuing "Mr. Ed" festival.... As a man, I must graze in the broad and swampy fields of contemporary civilization. That's my karma. Call it kismet. The spectrum is the message. The medium is my program. So open that big electronic channel and come on down!

8. I have explored this flight, and the "spaciness" that results, at length in *Late for the Sky: The Mentality of the Space Age* (Lavery 1992).

9. "TV," to quote McKibben (1992, 189), "restricts the use of our senses—that is one of the ways it robs us of information. It asks us to use our eyes and ears, and only our eyes and ears. If it is doing its job 'correctly,' you lose consciousness of your body, at least until a sort of achy torpor begins to assert itself, and maybe after some hours a dull headache, and of course the insatiable hunger that you never really notice but that somehow demands a constant stream of chips and soda. If you cut off your nose to spite your face, or for any other reason, it wouldn't impair your ability to watch television."

10. Borrowing from sociologist Erving Goffman, Meyrowitz (1985) distinguishes

between "frontstage" and "backstage" behavior: the largely unwritten rules we follow (respectively) in public and behind the scenes. Teachers, for example, often behave quite differently—and talk differently about their students, for example—before a class (frontstage) than they do in the teachers' lounge (backstage).

16

Technoromancing the Clicker

Bruce E. Gronbeck

The story of Persephone lives in Greek as well as Indonesian myths and rites. The daughter of Zeus and Demeter, Persephone was a maiden playing in a meadow, where she was seduced by a plant with a hundred blossoms set out by Gaea, the earth goddess. As Persephone plucked the blossoms, the earth opened up and she was carried to the abyss of Hades, lord of the underworld, whose queen she became. Demeter and the moon-goddess Hekate heard Persephone's cries and, with the help of Phoebus the sun-god, discovered where she was. In grief and anger, Demeter quit the world of the gods, living out her years at the Well of the Virgin and as a nurse in Eleusis. She cursed the earth to bear no fruit for a year, until Zeus and the other Olympians begged her to relent. She refused. Zeus then caused Persephone to be released for two-thirds of each year, and so she returned to Olympus with her mother and Hekate, the fields once more covered with flowers and grain (Campbell [1959] 1987, 183–85).

The myth of Persephone had such circulation throughout the Western and oceanic worlds because it was a classic love-death myth, interrelating sex and death, death and rebirth, and hence the cycle of the fertile seasons and reproduction. As well, it is a prototypical romance in many ways, the story of a journey of discovery or rediscovery where failure seems sure until a hero (or, in this case, a heroine) is able to overcome adversaries in a battle that allows the hero/heroine to reclaim the desired object (or person). Romances are stories of search, struggle, death or near-death, and ultimate triumph by the forces of right (Campbell 1949), and the Persephone myth fits such literary criteria very well.

As a myth, the story of Persephone transmits to westerners what Northrop Frye called the "shared allusion to...culture" (1976, 9). The power of allusion or reference means that myth can be overlaid on events of the social world; hence, we reasonably could talk about the life and times of Patty Hearst in the 1970s as modelled by the myth of Persephone. The power of allusion, however, is also imperialistic. Myths can absorb secular stories and incorporate them into their mythic structures—something that occurred in biblical narratives (Frye 1976, 14). The myth of Persephone can absorb the story of the remote control device (RCD), the clicker.

THE TECHNOTRIUMPH OF THE CLICKER

"In [an] ideal text, the networks are many and interact, without any one of them being able to surpass the rest; this text is a galaxy of signifiers, not a struggle of signifieds; it has no beginning; it is reversible; we gain access to it by several entrances, none of which can be authoritatively declared to be the main one; the codes it mobilizes extend as far as the eye can reach, they are indeterminable" (Barthes 1974, 5–6).

Had Roland Barthes been discussing 36-, 72-, or 108-channel cable television accessed by an RCD, he could have used the same words. The openness of and accessibility to language that Barthes romanticized in his book, *S/Z*, have been found in the televisual world of remote control. Had Barthes known Theodore Nelson when he was writing, he might well have called that ideal discourse "hypertext"—the non-sequential writing in chunks and branches with computerized electronic pathways linking them together in near-endless variety (Landow 1992, 4).[1] The readerly abilities to control meaning-making that Barthes prized are available in the digitized world of computers.

The RCD is one of several technologies now depicted as capable of releasing Persephone from what Wicklein (1981) called an "electronic nightmare." Even his book jacket was as black as Hades; Wicklein described our home entertainment centers not as sources of play and delight, but as hundred-blossom plants that lure us into a marriage with the underworld of manipulated images. Today, however, rather than living the nightmare, Paul Traudt (Chapter 5 of this volume) sees us as conquerors of electronic hell: "As RCD users, we build a pattern of consumption probably characterized by unique and differentiated patterns, as unique as fingerprints but classifiable by a basic ontology of tempos influenced by user predisposition and programming availability. While it is true that we have virtually no direct control over programming, we do have great control over what we signify and how often we signify it."

Robert Bellamy (Chapter 14 of this volume) is quite sure that the RCD joins other technologies in the empowerment of the viewer: "The widespread diffusion of cable, satellites, and VCRs, along with the RCD that gives the user of such technology a great deal of control over the television medium, has fundamentally altered the power relationship of viewer (user) and medium." David Lavery (Chapter 15 of this volume) is even more ecstatic about his belief that "The remote control, it should be clear, is entirely postmodernist, a technological distillate, both cause and effect and exemplar of a new sensibility."

The clicker in these paeans to the liberated life is Zeus. The clicker has released the Persephones of the earth from bondage to the sinister forces of the media industry. No longer can signification systems bind our minds to predigested and formulated thought; no longer are we ruled by producerly texts (Fiske 1987). As Sony plays Demeter in demanding our release from the networks' nuptial bled, arming us in the mid–1970s with the technology for a functional infrared RCD, Zeus can be bestirred to action. Even as television itself grows at an alarming rate in the 1970s and early 1980s, with cable television taking control of distribution in most markets, the manufacture and sale of RCDs keeps pace; 96 percent of all color television sets now being sold in the United States come with clickers (Benjamin, Chapter 2 of this volume).

The technotriumph of you and me, the Persephones wed in Hades to the one-eyed monster called Cyclops, seems complete. Not really complete, of course; some (Bellamy and Walker 1990b) grumble that programming still is in the hands of the scions of the media political economy—"an increasingly international class of capitalists," in their terms. Even Persephone had to spend a third of her time in hell after liberation; complete freedom, even for a goddess, apparently is not possible.

Yet, our technotriumph, our release from bondage to producerly controlled televisual texts, is trumpeted. Thanks to the clicker we can make our own viewing experiences. In zapping the undesirable, zipping through the uninteresting, and grazing upon the multi-flavored grasses of independent cable producers, we assault the old signifying practices and, playing freely with the video signifiers, capture those practices for our own use. "We are what we watch" is transformed into "We watch what we are."

THE ETERNAL LURE OF ROMANCE

To Campbell the myth of Persephone is a primitive myth in that it deals with the tribulations of timeless gods. To Frye it is a naive (rather than sentimental) myth, a story from prehistoric, certainly preliterate, times that captured culture-defining mores. The mythoi of the preliterate times bounded societies together; they were marked by "a certain quality of importance or authority for the community." As authorities, they commanded consent: not conviction, not belief, but consent (Frye 1976, 16). Collectively, they comprised the doxastic, valuative, and ideological centers of societies. It is little wonder that Plato wanted to use Logoi, dialectically sharpened words, to drive out the emotionally powerful mythoi so as to radically reform Athens. The mythic stories had agglutinated thought itself and thus had become impossible to remove through any means but a process of rigorous truth-testing.

The stories of technology in America have attained a status much like the myths of the ancient Mediterranean city-states. I am not enough of an Americanist to know all the tales of harnessing technology for social and individual good, but I certainly know the ones we all were taught in grammar school:

- Benjamin Franklin flying a kite with a key on its string to draw down the power of the electric heavens in harmless form.
- Paul Bunyan building a plow big enough to cut the Mississippi River in a massive drainage project.
- Robert Fulton making a container strong enough to hold in steam so that it could be released in ways that would propel a boat.
- Eli Whitney constructing a machine to separate cotton fibers from seeds.
- Alexander Graham Bell learning how to run the human voice through a wire.
- Thomas Alva Edison managing to put that voice on an accessible disk, to add it to reproducible moving pictures, and to light the whole proceedings with a workable incandescent bulb.
- Madame Curie probing the inside of your body with Xrays rather than knives.
- A string of physicists harnessing the building blocks of life and the great agency of death, the atom.

These technological advances were real—no doubt about that. Yet what is fascinating is that each became a narrated story that turned into a great fable with a moral. The moral almost inevitably was that the human (at least American) spirit always rises to the challenges of nature and society and overcomes adversity through the construction and distribution of an empowering technology.

Especially since the beginning of the Industrial Revolution, the Western world has been dominated by a vision of homo faber, man the maker, and in this century, man the tool-making animal. This is to say that we live not only in a technological world, an environment with helpful things in it, but in a culture of technology. Not only does our world run on technologies, but they penetrate our ways of thinking about everything else. We "interface" not only with machines but with other people; a vice president of the United States not only fights his fellow citizens over family values but takes on a television character, Murphy Brown; computers arrange idealized dates between people; the clicker allows us to write our own visual-verbal-acoustic scripts out of the scripts of others.

The romantic myth holds center court in the great game of life because it is so hopeful. In the romance, sex may be followed by death but death is succeeded by rebirth. Periods of infertility and hibernation are cycled away by periods of life, growth, prosperity, and joy. The union of yin and yang is a perfect circle.

The anti-television critics (e.g., Macdonald [1953] 1968; Alley 1977; Goldsen 1977; Winn 1977; Mander 1978; Wicklein 1981) have been present during the medium's social history, but, at least in the United States, they have never held sway. Throughout our history with The Box, we have believed fervently that it brings good, not bad; that even when it's bad it can be controlled; and that when we cannot control ourselves a technology will arise to help us do it. In the 1950s we controlled viewing eye strain with panther lights on top of the machines. In the 1960s we controlled motion with stop-action video. In the 1970s we controlled the broadcasting networks with the narrowcasting that CATV represented. In the 1980s and early 1990s we are controlling the dominance of programmers and advertisers with the clicker.

American faith in technology is complete. American hope is eternal. America is technoromancing the clicker. Persephone frolics freely, choosing her favorite blossoms and arranging them with a click of a button. This will she do forever and ever, or at least until the abyss opens once more—and it will.

NOTE

1. Barthes very well might have been reacting to shifts in communication technology during his lifetime. His biographer, Annette Lavers, pooh-poohs the idea that "cybernetics, computers, and machine translation" played much of a role in his literary doctrines (1982, 138). However, Landow (1992, 167) does not agree.

References

Abel, J. D. (1976). The family and child television viewing. *Journal of Marriage and the Family* 38:331–335.

Adams, W. J. (1988). "Patterns in prime-time network television programs from 1948 to 1986: The influences of variety, churn, and content." Unpublished doctoral dissertation, Indiana University, Bloomington.

Adams, W. J., S. T. Eastman, and R. F. Lewine. (1993). Prime-time network television programming. In S. T. Eastman, ed., *Broadcast/cable programming: Strategies and practices*, 4th ed. (pp. 115–159). Belmont, CA: Wadsworth.

Adler, R. (1992, August 31). Personal communication.

Ainslie, P. (1985, February 28). Commercial zapping: TV tapers strike back. *Rolling Stone*, pp. 68–69.

———. (1988, September). Confronting a nation of grazers. *Channels*, pp. 54–57.

———. (1989). The new TV viewer. In *How Americans watch TV: A nation of grazers* (pp. 9–20). New York: C. C. Publishing.

Akhavan-Majid, R., and G. Wolf. (1991). American mass media and the myth of libertarianism: Toward an "elite power group" theory. *Critical Studies in Mass Communication* 8:139–151.

Alexander, A., M. S. Ryan, and P. Munoz. (1984). Creating a learning context: Investigations on the interaction of siblings during television viewing. *Critical Studies in Mass Communication* 1:345–364.

Allen, C. (1965). Photographing the TV audience. *Journal of Advertising Research* 5(1):2–8.

Alley, R. S. (1977). *Television: Ethics for hire?* Nashville: Abingdon.

Alvarez, M. M., A. C. Huston, J. C. Wright, and D. D. Kerkman. (1988). Gender differences in visual attention to television form and content. *Journal of Applied Developmental Psychology* 9:459–475.

Analysis: Interactive perspectives come home. (1992). *Interactive Update: The Journal of Interactive Entertainment*, p. 7.

Anderson, D. R. (1985). Online cognitive processing of television. In L. F. Alwitt and A. A. Mitchell, eds., *Psychological processes and advertising effects* (pp. 177–199). Hillsdale, NJ: Lawrence Erlbaum.

———. (1991, November). Personal communication.

Anderson, D. R., L. F. Allwitt, E. P. Lorch, and S. R. Levin. (1979). Watching children watch television. In G. A. Hale and M. Lewis, eds., *Attention and cognitive development* (pp. 331–361). New York: Plenum Press.

Anderson, D. R., D. Field, P. Collins, E. Lorch, and J. Nathan. (1985). Estimates of young children's time with television: A methodological comparison of parent reports with time-lapse video home observation. *Child Development* 56:1345–1357.

Anderson, D. R., E. P. Lorch, D. E. Field, P. A. Collins, and J. G. Nathan. (1986). Television viewing at home: Age trends in visual attention and time with TV. *Child Development* 57: 1024–1033.

Anderson, J. A. (1987). Commentary on qualitative research and mediated communication in the family. In T. R. Lindlof, ed., *Natural audiences: Qualitative research of media uses and effects* (pp. 161–171). Norwood, NJ: Ablex.

Arendt, H. (1958). *The human condition.* Chicago: University of Chicago Press.

Arrington, C. (1992, August 15). The zapper: All about the remote control. *TV Guide*, pp. 8–13.

Atkin, C. K., J. Galloway, and O. B. Nayman. (1976). News media exposure, political knowledge and campaign interest. *Journalism Quarterly* 53:231–237.

Austin, J. (1992, April 20). Imagine: Computer-created virtual reality lets voyagers enter, explore other worlds. *Memphis Commercial Appeal*, p. C–1.

Baldwin, A. (1952, January). Tune your TV set from across the room. *Popular Science*, pp. 167–170.

Banks, W. (1984, December). Look what's happened to the family TV. *Money*, pp. 187–198.

Barthes, R. (1957). *Mythologies.* Translated by Annette Levers. New York: Hill and Wang.

———. (1974). *S/Z.* Translated by A. Lavers and C. Smith. New York: Hill and Wang.

The battle (zap! click!) of the sexes. (1991, July 7). *New York Times* (editorial), section 4, p. 10.

Bechtel, R. B., C. Achelpohl, and R. Akers (1972). Correlates between observed behavior and questionnaire response on television viewing. In E. A. Rubenstein, G. A. Comstock, and J. P. Murray, eds., *Television and social behavior*, vol. 4. Washington, DC: Government Printing Office, 274–344.

Becker, L. B., and S. Dunwoody. (1982). Media use, public affairs knowledge and voting in a local election. *Journalism Quarterly* 59:212–218.

Becker, L. B., and K. Schoenbach. (1989). When media content diversifies: Anticipating audience behaviors. In L. B. Becker and K. Schoenbach, eds., *Audience responses to media diversification: Coping with plenty* (pp. 1–27). Hillsdale, NJ: Erlbaum.

Bellamy, R. V., Jr. (1988). Constraints on a broadcast innovation: Zenith's Phonevision system, 1931–1972. *Journal of Communication* 38(4):8–20.

———. (1992). Emerging images of product differentiation: Network television promotion in a time of industry change. *Feedback* 33(3):22–26.

Bellamy, R. V., Jr., and J. R. Walker. (1990a). The use of television remote control devices: A transactional study. *News Computing Journal* 6:1–18.

———. (1990b, November). "The diffusion of a tool technology: The political economy of the remote control device." Paper presented at the meeting of the Speech Communication Association, Chicago, IL.

Benjamin, L. (1989, November). "At the touch of a button: A history of remote control tuning." Paper presented at the meeting of the Speech Communication Association, San Francisco, CA.

Berger, I. (1980, June). Video cassette recorders: Rising stars of home entertainment. *Popular Electronics*, pp. 51–60.

Berringer, D., and J. Peterson. (1985). Underlying behavioral parameters of the operation of touch-input devices: Biases, models, feedback. *Human Factors* 27:445–458.

Beschloss, S. (1990, November 19). Go without the flow. *Channels*, pp. 14–15.

Bey, S. L. (1975). Androgyny versus the tight little lives of fluffy women and chesty men. *Psychology Today* 9:58–62.

Bey, S. L., W. Martyna, and C. Watson. (1976). Sex typing and androgyny: Further explorations of the expressive domain. *Journal of Personality and Social Psychology* 34:1016–1023.

Bing, S. (1990, August). I like to watch. *Esquire*, pp. 79–81.

Blood, R. O. (1961). Social class and family control of television viewing. *Merrill-Palmer Quarterly of Behavior and Development* 7:205–222.

Blumler, J. G. (1979). The role of theory in uses and gratifications studies. *Communication Research* 6:9–36.

Bollier, D. (1989). What grazing means for TV programmers and advertisers: A glimpse at the future. In *How Americans watch TV: A nation of grazers* (pp. 41–52). New York: C. C. Publishing.

Boyd, D. A., J. D. Straubhaar, and J. A. Lent, eds. (1989). *Videocassette recorders in the Third World*. New York: Longman.

Brandt, A. (1989). Created equal: Remote possibilities. *Self* 2(1):64–66.

Broadcasting & Cable Market Place. (1992). New Providence, NJ: R. R. Bowker.

Brown, C. (1988, March 7). Couch potato panic. *Forbes*, pp. 163–164.

Brown, M. (1989). Conclusion: How Americans watch TV. In *How Americans watch TV: A nation of grazers* (pp. 54–55). New York: C. C. Publishing.

Bryant, J. (1986). The road most traveled: Yet another cultivation critique. *Journal of Broadcasting & Electronic Media* 30:231–235.

———. (1989). Message features and entertainment effects. In J. J. Bradac, ed., *Message effects in communication science* (pp. 231–262). Newbury Park, CA: Sage.

Bryant, J., and S. C. Rockwell. (1990, November). "Remote control technologies and human factors in television program selection: Little things mean a lot." Paper presented at the 76th annual convention of the Speech Communication Association, Chicago, IL.

Bryant, J., and D. Zillmann. (1984). Using television to alleviate boredom and stress: Selective exposure as a function of induced excitational states. *Journal of Broadcasting* 28:1–20.

Bryce, J. W. (1987). Family time and television use. In T. R. Lindlof, ed., *Natural audiences: Qualitative research of media uses and effects* (pp. 121–138). Norwood, NJ: Ablex.

Buchsbaum, W. (1955, November). Remote control for TV. *Radio & Television News*, pp. 46–48.

———. (1957, November). TV remote controls for the technician. *Radio & Television News*, pp. 58–61.

Burger, J. M., and R. M. Arkin. (1980). Prediction, control, and learned helplessness. *Journal of Personality and Social Psychology*, 38(3):482–491.

Burger, J. M., and H. M. Cooper. (1979). The desirability of control. *Motivation and Emotion* 3(4):381–393.

Burgi, M. (1988, September). The remotest idea. *Channels*, p. 55.

Cable TV report and order. (1972). 36FCC2d 143.

Campbell, D., and J. Stanley (1966). *Experimental and quasi-experimental designs for research.* Chicago: Rand McNally.

Campbell, J. (1949). *The hero with a thousand faces.* New York: Pantheon.

———. ([1959] 1987). *The Masks of God: Primitive mythology.* New York: Viking Penguin.

Cantril, H. (1947). *The invasion from Mars: A study in the psychology of panic.* Princeton, NJ: Princeton University Press.

Carey, J. (1989). Consumer adoption of new communication technologies. *IEEE Communications Magazine* 28(8):28–32.

Carey, J., and M. L. Moss. (1985). The diffusion of new telecommunication technologies. *Telecommunications Policy* 9(2):145–158.

Carpenter, E. (1973). *Oh, what a blow that phantom gave me!* New York: Holt, Rinehart, & Winston.

Carragee, K. (1990). Interpretive media study and interpretive social science. *Critical Studies in Mass Communication* 7:81–96.

Carter, B. (1991, July 8). TV industry unfazed by rise in "zapping." *New York Times*, pp. D1, D6.

Cavell, S. (1971). *The world viewed.* New York: Viking.

Chaffee, S. H., J. M. McLeod, and C. K. Atkin. (1971). Parental influences on adolescent media use. *American Behavioral Scientist* 14:323–340.

Cheers & Jeers. (1991, August 24). *TV Guide*, p. 22.

Christ, W. G. (1985). The construct of arousal in communication research. *Human Communication Research* 11:575–592.

Clayton, K. (1990, January 1). Cable leaps and bounds into 1990s. *Electronic Media*, pp. 25, 88, 90.

Coe, S. (1992, June 8). ABC execs pressure affiliates on clearances. *Broadcasting*, p. 5.

Cohen, A. A., and L. Cohen. (1989). Big eyes but clumsy fingers: Knowing about and using technological features of home VCRs. In M. R. Levy, ed., *The VCR age: Home video and mass communication* (pp. 135–147). Newbury Park, CA: Sage.

Cohen, E. (1987, October). An analysis of the 1987 CONTAM/SRI television ownership study. In *Info-Pak.* Washington, DC: National Association of Broadcasters.

Cole, P. (1988, June 27). Zap! you're in control with a touch of the remote. *Business Week*, p. 108.

Collett, P., and R. Lamb. (1986). "Watching people watch TV." Report to the Independent Broadcasting Authority, London.

Color TVs with remote control. (1992, June 22). *Electronic Media*, p. 36.

Comstock, G., S. Chaffee, N. Katzman, M. McCombs, and D. Roberts. (1978). *Television and human behavior*. New York: Columbia University Press.

Conway, J. C., and A. M. Rubin. (1991). Psychological predictors of television viewing motivation. *Communication Research* 18:443–463.

Copeland, G. (1989, November). "The impact of remote control devices on family viewing." Paper presented at the meeting of Speech Communication Association, San Francisco, CA.

Cott, J. (1973). *Stockhausen: Conversations with the composer*. New York: Simon and Schuster.

Culbertson, H. M., and G. H. Stempel, III. (1986). How media use and reliance affect knowledge level. *Communication Research* 13:579–602.

Curran, J. (1990). The new revisionism in mass communication research: A reappraisal. *European Journal of Communication* 5(2–3):135–164.

Curran, J., M. Gurevitch, and J. Woollacott. (1982). The study of the media: Theoretical approaches. In M. Gurevitch et al., eds., *Culture, society, and the media* (pp. 11–29). London: Methuen.

Cutler, N. E., and J. A. Danowski. (1980). Process gratification in aging cohorts. *Journalism Quarterly* 57:269–276.

Dalton, M. (1992, May). Of universal interest. *Dealerscope*, pp. 41–42, 43.

Davis, D. M., and J. R. Walker. (1990). Countering the new media: The resurgence of share maintenance in primetime network television. *Journal of Broadcasting & Electronic Media* 34:487–493.

Dawson, K. (1989, September 1). Selling second sets and remotes. *Cable Television Business*, pp. 36–37, 40.

Deaux, K. (1976). *The behavior of women and men*. Monterey, CA: Brooks/Cole.

Dennett, D. (1981). Who am I? In D. R. Hofstadter and D. Dennett, eds., *The mind's I: Fantasies and reflections of self and soul* (pp. 217–231). New York: Basic Books.

Dick, P. K. (1968). *Do androids dream of electric sheep?* New York: Ballantine.

Diebold, T. (1989, May 29). Family decline wrought by remote control. *Memphis Commercial Appeal*, p. A–9.

Dizard, W. P., Jr. (1982). *The coming information age*. New York: Longman.

Domestic communication satellite facilities. (1972). 35 FCC2d 844.

Donahue, J. (1992, June 22). Personal interview via telephone. In *Communication, Social Cognition, and Affect*. Hillsdale, NJ: Erlbaum.

Donnelly, William J. (1986). *The confetti generation: How the new communications technology is fragmenting America*. New York: Henry Holt.

Donohew, L., H. E. Sypher, and E. T. Higgins, eds. (1988). *Communication, social cognition, and affect*. Hillsdale, NJ: Erlbaum.

Dordick, H. S. (1987). The emerging information societies. In J. I. Schement and L. Lievrouw, eds. *Competing visions, complex realities* (pp. 13–22). Norwood, NJ: Ablex.

Dorr, A. (1986). *Television and children: A special medium for a special audience*. Beverly Hills, CA: Sage.

Eakins, B. W., and R. G. Eakins. (1978). *Sex differences in human communication.* Boston: Houghton Mifflin.

Eastman, S. T. (1991). The scope of promotion. In S. T. Eastman and R. Klein, eds., *Promotion and marketing for broadcasting and cable,* 2d ed. (pp. 3–38). Prospect Heights, IL: Waveland.

———. (1993). Cable system programming. In S. T. Eastman, ed., *Broadcast/cable programming: Strategies and practices,* 4th ed. (pp. 245–283). Belmont, CA: Wadsworth.

Eastman, S. T., and J. Neal-Lunsford. (1992). "Programming and grazing." Unpublished paper, Indiana University, Bloomington.

Eastman, S. T., and L. P. Trufelman. (1991). Cable television promotion. In S. T. Eastman and R. Klein, eds., *Promotion and marketing for broadcasting and cable,* 2d ed. (pp. 280–308). Prospect Heights, IL: Waveland.

Eco, U. (1986). *Travels in hyper-reality.* Translated by William Weaver. New York: Harcourt, Brace, Jovanovich.

Edwards, E. D. (1991). The ecstasy of horrible expectations: Morbid curiosity, sensation seeking, and interest in horror movies. In B. A. Austin, ed., *Current research in film: Audience, economics, and law,* vol. 5 (pp. 19–38). Norwood, NJ: Ablex.

Ehrenreich, B. (1987, April). Ode to a couch potato. *Mother Jones,* p. 9.

Eisener, E. W. (1991). *The enlightened eye: Qualitative inquiry and the enhancement of educational practice.* New York: Macmillan.

Electronics Industries Association. (1986). *Electronic market data book.* Washington, DC.

———. (1991). *Electronic market data book.* Washington, DC.

Emberson, M. (1992, October 13). "An overview of the Cerritos project." Paper presented to the 1992 National Communications Forum, Chicago.

Engle, J. F., and R. D. Blackwell. (1982). *Consumer Behavior,* 4th ed. Chicago: Dryden Press.

Epstein, N. B., L. M. Baldwin, and D. S. Bishop. (1983). The McMaster family assessment device. *Journal of Marital and Family Therapy* 9:171–180.

Epstein, N. B., D. S. Bishop, and L. M. Baldwin. (1982). McMaster model of family functioning: A view of the normal family. In F. Walsh, ed., *Normal family processes* (pp. 115–141). New York: Guilford.

Epstein, N. B., D. S. Bishop, and S. Levin. (1978). The McMaster model of family functioning. *Journal of Marriage and Family Counseling* 4:19–31.

Equipment reports: Universal wireless remote control and stereo TV tuner. (1987, May) *Radio-Electronics,* pp. 24–26.

Eskin, G. (1985). Tracking advertising and promotion performance with single-source data. *Journal of Advertising Research* 25(1):31–39.

Everett, S. C. (1992). "Nomads of the air: Television viewing behavior in a multi-channel environment." Paper presented at the annual convention of the Association for Education in Journalism and Mass Communication, Montreal.

Ferguson, D. A. (1990a, November). "Selective exposure to television: An exploratory study of VCR usage." Paper presented at the annual meeting of the Speech Communication Association, Chicago.

———. (1990b, November). "Selective exposure to television: Predicting inheritance effects from VCR and cable penetration." Paper presented at the annual meeting of the Speech Communication Association, Chicago.

———. (1992a). Channel repertoire in the presence of remote control devices, VCRs, and cable television. *Journal of Broadcasting & Electronic Media* 36:83–91.

———. (1992b, April). "Measurement of mundane TV behaviors: Remote control device flipping frequency." Paper presented at the meeting of the Broadcast Education Association, Las Vegas.

Ferguson, D. A., and E. M. Perse. (1991, November). "Gender differences in the use of remote control devices." Paper presented at the meeting of the Speech Communication Association, Atlanta, GA.

———. (1993). Media and audience influences on channel repertoire. *Journal of Broadcasting & Electronic Media* 37(1): 31–47.

Fiske, J. (1987). *Television culture*. London: Methuen.

Fleischmann, M. (1990, January 15). Man and machine in the 21st century. *Audio/Video Interiors*, pp. 98–103.

Forkan, J. P. (1989, October 30). Selling U.S. news and sports abroad a changing game. *Television/Radio Age*, pp. 38–39.

Fountas, A. (1985, January). Commercial audiences: Measuring what we're buying. *Marketing & Media Decisions*, pp 75–76.

Frank, B. (1984, July). "And now a word from our ... " zap (revisited). *Marketing & Media Decisions*, pp. 162, 164, 166.

Franklin, N. (1992, June 1). Managing your TV household. *Electronic Media*, p. 14.

Free, J. (1977, April). Programmable color TV changes channels automatically. *Popular Science*, p. 30.

Freedman, D. H. (1988, February 20). Why you watch some commercials—Whether you mean to or not. *TV Guide*, pp. 4–7.

Frey, J. H. (1983). *Survey research by telephone*. Beverly Hills, CA: Sage.

Friedman, L. (1989, August/September). How good is the seven-day diary now? *Advertising Research*, p. RC3–5.

Frye, N. (1976). *The secular scripture: A study of the structure of romance*. Cambridge, MA: Harvard University Press.

Fuller, J. (1993). National public television programming. In S. T. Eastman, ed., *Broadcast/cable programming: Strategies and practices*, 4th ed. (pp. 473–493). Belmont, CA: Wadsworth.

Gantz, W. (1985). Exploring the role of television in married life. *Journal of Broadcasting & Electronic Media* 29:65–78.

Garron, B. (1992, July 16). ABC not so quick to pull plug on dramas. *Kansas City Star*, p. F–2.

Geller, M., ed. (1991). *From receiver to remote control: The TV set*. New York: The New Museum of Contemporary Art.

Gerbner, G., and L. Gross. (1976). Living with television: The violence profile. *Journal of Communication* 26(2):173–199.

GE's bid to turn TV sets into command posts. (1983, April 25). *Business Week*, p. 34.

Gilbert, R. (1989). Introduction. In *How Americans watch TV: A nation of grazers* (pp. 4–8). New York: C. C. Publishing.

Gillespie, A., and K. Robins. (1989). Geographical inequalities: The spatial bias of the new communications technologies. *Journal of Communication* 39:7–18.

Gilligan, C. (1982). *In a different voice*. Cambridge, MA: Harvard University Press.

Gitlin, T. (1989, Spring). Post-modernism: The stenography of surfaces. *New Perspectives Quarterly*, pp. 56–59.

Goldsen, R. K. (1977). *The show and tell machine: How television works and works you over*. New York: Dial Press.

Gomery, D. (1989). Media economics: Terms of analysis. *Critical Studies in Mass Communication* 6:43–60.

Gottlieb, I. (1952, April). A remote-control for your TV set. *Radio & Television News*, p. 100.

Gould, S. J. (1987). Gender differences in advertising response and self-consciousness variables. *Sex Roles* 16(5/6):215–225.

Gray, A. (1987). Behind closed doors: Video recorders in the home. In H. Baehr and G. Dyer, eds., *Boxed in: Women and television* (pp. 38–54). New York: Pandora.

Greenberg, B. S., and C. Heeter. (1987). VCRs and young people. *American Behavioral Scientist* 30:509–521.

Greenberg, B. S., K. W. Simmons, L. Hogan, and C. K. Atkin. (1980). The demography of fictional TV characters. In B. S. Greenberg, ed., *Life on television*. Norwood, NJ: Ablex.

Greene, W. F. (1988). Maybe the valley of the shadow isn't so dark after all. *Journal of Advertising Research* 28(5):11–15.

Greenstein, J. (1990, June 4). TNT moving to conquer new territory. *Electronic Media*, p. 35.

Gross, M. (1988, October). Television—some thoughts on flipping. *Marketing and Media Decisions*, pp. 94–97.

Grotta, G. L., and D. Newsom. (1982). How does cable television in the home relate to other media use patterns? *Journalism Quarterly* 59:588–591, 609.

Gunter, B., and J. L. McAleer. (1990). *Children and television: The one-eyed monster?* London: Routledge.

Halley, R. D. (1975). Distractability of males and females in competing aural message situations: A research note. *Human Communication Research* 2:79–82.

Halonen, D. (1990, February 26). Industry flares up over DBS. *Electronic Media*, pp. 1, 31.

———. (1992a, June 22). FCC votes to let Big 3 into cable. *Electronic Media*, pp. 3, 38.

———. (1992b, June 29). FCC set to allow telcos to carry TV. *Electronic Media*, pp. 1, 2.

Hanhardt, J. G., ed. (1987). *Video culture: A critical investigation*. Layton, UT: Gibbs M. Smith.

Harvey, M. G., and J. T. Rothe. (1986). Video cassette recorders: Their impact on viewers and advertisers. *Journal of Advertising Research* 25(6):19–27.

Head, S. W., S. T. Eastman, and L. Klein. (1993). A framework for programming strategies. In S. T. Eastman, ed., *Broadcast/cable programming: Strategies and practices* 4th ed. (pp. 4–40). Belmont, CA: Wadsworth.

Heeter, C. (1985). Program selection with abundance of choice: A process model. *Human Communication Research* 12(1):126–152.

————. (1988a). The choice process model. In C. Heeter and B. S. Greenberg, eds., *Cableviewing* (pp. 11–32). Norwood, NJ: Ablex.

————. (1988b). Gender differences in viewing styles. In C. Heeter and B. S. Greenberg, eds., *Cableviewing* (pp. 151–166). Norwood, NJ: Ablex.

Heeter, C., and T. F. Baldwin. (1988). Channel type and viewing styles. In C. Heeter and B. S. Greenberg eds., *Cableviewing* (pp. 167–176). Norwood, NJ: Ablex.

Heeter, C., D. D'Alessio, B. S. Greenberg, and D. S. McVoy. (1988). Cableviewing behaviors: An electronic assessment. In C. Heeter and B. S. Greenberg, eds., *Cableviewing* (pp. 51–63). Norwood, NJ: Ablex.

Heeter, C., and B. S. Greenberg. (1985a). Cable and program choice. In D. Zillmann and J. Bryant, eds., *Selective exposure to communication* (pp. 203–224). Hillsdale, NJ: Erlbaum.

————. (1985). Profiling the zappers. *Journal of Advertising Research* 25(2):15–19.

————. eds. (1988a). *Cableviewing*. Norwood, NJ: Ablex.

————. (1988b). Profiling the zappers. In C. Heeter and B. S. Greenberg, eds., *Cableviewing* (pp. 67–73). Norwood, NJ: Ablex.

————. (1988c). A theoretical overview of the program choice process. In C. Heeter and B. S. Greenberg, eds., *Cableviewing* (pp. 33–50). Norwood, NJ: Ablex.

Hindus, L. (1992, January 23). VLSI chip cuts cost of wireless remote cursor control. *EDN*, p. 3.

Hirschman, E. C. (1987). Consumer preferences in literature, motion pictures and television programs. *Empirical Studies of the Arts* 5(1):31–46.

Horwitz, R. B. (1989). *The irony of regulatory reform*. New York: Oxford.

Hovland, C. I., and W. Mandell. (1957). Is there a law of primacy in persuasion? In C. I. Hovland, ed., *Order of presentation in persuasion* (pp. 13–22). New Haven, CT: Yale University Press.

How Americans watch TV: A nation of grazers. (1989). New York: C. C. Publishing.

Hsia, H. J. (1989). Introduction. In J. L. Salvaggio and J. Bryant, eds., *Media use in the information age: Emerging patterns of adoption and consumer use* (pp. xv–xxviii). Hillsdale, NJ: Erlbaum.

Husserl, E. (1931). *Ideas: Pure phenomenology*. London: George Allen & Unwin.

Hyde, J. S. (1990). Meta-analysis and the psychology of gender differences. *Signs: Journal of Women in Culture and Society* 16(1):55–73.

Ihde, D. (1982). The experience of media. In J. Pilotta, ed., *Interpersonal communication: Essays in phenomenology and hermeneutics* (pp. 69–80). Washington, DC: University Press of America.

Industry Sales. (1992). Press release. Chicago: Zenith Electronics Corporation.

Jaccoma, R. (1992, August). A 21st century outlook. *Dealerscope*, pp. 52–53.

Jameson, F. (1984, July/August). Postmodernism, or the cultural logic of late capitalism. *New Left Review* 146:53–94.

Johnson, S. (1986, August 27). Zap! *Chicago Tribune*, Tempo Section, pp. 1, 7.

Jordon, A. B. (1990). A family systems approach to the use of the VCR in the home. In J. R. Dobrow, ed., *Social and cultural aspects of VCR use* (pp. 163–179). Hillsdale, NJ: Lawrence Erlbaum.

Kabacoff, R. I., I. W. Miller, D. S. Bishop, N. B. Epstein, and G. I. Keitner. (1990). A psychometric study of the McMaster family assessment device in psychiatric, medical, and nonclinical samples. *Journal of Family Psychology* 3:431–439.

Kaplan, A. G. (1976). Androgyny as a model of mental health for women: From theory to therapy. In A. G. Kaplan and J. P. Bean, eds., *Beyond sex-role stereotypes: Readings toward a psychology of androgyny* (pp. 352–362). Boston: Little, Brown.

Kaplan, B. M. (1985). Zapping—The real issue is communication. *Journal of Advertising Research* 25(2):9–12.

Katz, E., and P. F. Lazarsfeld. (1955). *Personal influence: The part played by people in the flow of mass communications.* New York: The Free Press.

Keitner, G. I., et al. (1990). Family functioning, social adjustment, and recurrence of suicidality. *Psychiatry* 53:17–30.

Kill that commercial! (1950, November 20). *Newsweek*, pp. 95–96.

Kirn, W. (1990, October 16). The La-Z-Boy war: Tuning in the Persian Gulf crisis from middle America. *Village Voice*, p. 32.

Kissinger, D. (1991, February 25). Zap-happy fellas widen ratings gender gap. *Variety*, pp. 59, 63.

Klapper, J. T. (1960). *The effects of mass communication.* New York: Free Press.

Klein, J. (1992, June 8). Whose values? *Newsweek*, pp. 18–22.

Klein, P. (1976). Programming. In S. Morgenstern, ed., *Inside the TV business* (pp. 11–36). New York: Sterling.

Klein, P. L. (1978). Why you watch what you watch when you watch. In J. S. Harris, ed., *TV Guide: The first 25 years* (pp. 186–188). New York: Simon and Schuster.

Klopfenstein, B. C. (1989). The diffusion of the VCR in the United States. In Mark Levy, ed., *The VCR Age* (pp. 21–39). Beverly Hills, CA: Sage.

Knopf, T. A. (1992, June 22). Preparing for a TV revolution. *Electronic Media*, pp. 14, 30.

Kosinski, J. (1977). *Being there.* New York: Bantam.

Krasnow, E., and L. D. Longley. (1976). *The politics of broadcast regulation.* New York: St. Martin's.

Kruger, B. (1987). Remote control. In Brian Wallis, ed., *Blasted allegories* (pp. 395–405) Cambridge, MA: MIT Press.

Laban, R. (1988). *The mastery of movement,* 4th ed. Plymouth, England: Northcote House.

Landow, G. P. (1992). *Hypertext: The convergence of contemporary critical theory and technology.* Baltimore: Johns Hopkins University Press.

Lanigan, R. L. (1988). *Phenomenology of communication.* Pittsburgh: Duquesne University Press.

Larson, E. (1992, March). Watching Americans watch television. *Atlantic Monthly*, pp. 66–80.

Lavers, A. (1982). *Roland Barthes: Structuralism and after.* Cambridge, MA: Harvard University Press.

Lavery, D. (1992). *Late for the sky: The mentality of the space age.* Carbondale: Southern Illinois University Press.

Lawrence, F. C. and P. H. Wozniak. (1989). Children's television viewing with family members. *Psychological Reports* 65:395–400.

Lawrence, P. A. (1990). "Arousal needs and gratifications sought from theatrical movies." Unpublished doctoral dissertation, University of Kentucky.

Lee, E., and J. MaGregor (1985). Maximizing user search time in menu retrieval systems. *Human Factors* 27:335–343.

Leichter, H. J., D. Ahmed, L. Barrios, J. Bryce, E. Larsen, and L. Moe. (1985). Family contexts of television. *Educational Communication & Technology Journal* 33:26–40.

LeRoy, D., and J. LeRoy. (1988, October 12). Coping with cable by going local. *Current*, p. 4.

Levy, M. R. (1980a). Home video recorders: A user survey. *Journal of Communication* 30(4):23–27.

———. (1980b). Program playback preferences in VCR households. *Journal of Broadcasting* 24:327–36.

———. (1981). Home video recorders and time shifting. *Journalism Quarterly* 58:401–405.

———. (1987). Some problems of VCR research. *American Behavioral Scientist* 30:461–470.

———. ed. (1989). *The VCR age: Home video and mass communication*. Newbury Park, CA: Sage.

Levy, M. R., and B. Gunter. (1988). *Home video and the changing nature of the television audience*. London: John Libbey.

Lewis, C. (1991). "Television and the family: A qualitative study." Paper presented to the Radio-TV Division of the *Association for Education in Journalism and Mass Communication*, Boston.

Lilienthal, L. (1986, March). Videostudy: Continued fast forward with no end in sight. *Mart*, p. 9.

Lindheim, R. (1992, April 6). Big 3 networks most evolve or die. *Electronic Media*, p. 18.

Lindlof, T. R., and G. A. Copeland. (1982). Television rules of prepartum new families. In M. Burgoon, ed., *Communication Yearbook* 6:555–582. Beverly Hills, CA.: Sage.

Lindlof, T. R., M. J. Shatzer, and D. Wilkison. (1988). Accommodation of video and television in the American family. In J. Lull, ed., *World families watch television* (pp. 158–192). Newbury Park, CA: Sage.

Lipman, J. (1992, April 29). Commercials are cluttering cable shows. *Wall Street Journal*, pp. B1, B7.

Loftus, J. (1988, November 14). U.S. TV sky-high over Europe. *Television/Radio Age*, p. 53.

Lull, J. T. (1978). Choosing television programs by family vote. *Communication Quarterly* 26(4):53–57.

———. (1980a). The social uses of television. *Human Communication Research* 6:197–209.

———. (1980b). Family communication patterns and the social uses of television. *Communication Research* 7:319–334.

———. (1982). How families select television programs: A mass observational study. *Journal of Broadcasting* 26:801–811.

———. (1990). *Inside family viewing: Ethnographic research on television's audiences*. London: Comedia.

McCroskey, J. C., and T. J. Young. (1979). The use and abuse of factor analysis in communication research. *Human Communication Research* 5:375–382.

Macdonald, D. ([1953] 1968). A theory of mass culture. In A. Casty, ed., *Mass media and mass man* (pp. 12–24). New York: Holt, Rinehart & Winston.

McDonald, D. G. (1986). Generational aspects of television coviewing. *Journal of Broadcasting & Electronic Media* 30:75–85.

McGuire, W. J. (1974). Psychological motives and communication gratification. In J. G. Blumler and E. Katz, eds., *The uses of mass communications: Current perspectives on gratifications research* (pp. 167–196). Beverly Hills, CA: Sage.

McKibben, B. (1992). *The age of missing information.* New York: Random House.

McLeod, J. M. and J. D. Brown. (1976). The family environment and adolescent television use. In R. Brown, ed., *Children and television* (pp. 199–233). Beverly Hills, CA: Sage.

McLeod, J. M., and S. H. Chaffee. (1972). The construction of social reality. In J. T. Tedeschi, ed., *The social influence process* (pp. 50–99). Beverly Hills, CA: Sage.

McLeod, J. M., M. A. Fitzpatrick, C. J. Glynn, and S. F. Fallis. (1982). Television and social relations: Family influences and consequences for interpersonal behavior. In *National Institute of Mental Health, Television and behavior: Ten years of scientific progress and implications for the eighties* (DHHS Publication No. ADM 82–1196) (pp. 272–286). Washington, DC: U.S. Government Printing Office.

McMahon, J. J. (1992, October 13). "An overview of the Cascades project." Paper presented to the 1992 National Communications Forum, Chicago.

McNamara, K. and C. Loveman. (1990). Differences in family functioning among bulimics, repeat dieters, and nondieters. *Journal of Clinical Psychology* 46:518–523.

McQuail, D. (1987). *Mass communication theory.* Beverly Hills: Sage.

McQuail, D., and Euromedia Research Group. (1990). Caging the beast: Constructing a framework for the analysis of media change in Western Europe. *European Journal of Communication* 5(2–3):285–311.

Maddox, K. (1992a, May 18). Interactive programming seen for TV sports. *Electronic Media*, p. 4.

———. (1992b, September 28). Putting a price on retransmission. *Electronic Media*, pp. 1, 39.

Mahoney, W. (1989a, February 27). New World bought by foreign firm. *Electronic Media*, pp. 1, 31.

———. (1989b, April 17). Japanese firm moves into U.S. market. *Electronic Media*, p. 52.

———. (1989c, April 24). Buying Hollywood: Foreign investors go after U.S. studios. *Electronic Media*, pp. 1, 69.

———. (1990, January 1). Big 3 erosion of ratings power. *Electronic Media*, pp. 26, 94, 101.

Manchester, W. (1973). *The glory and the dream*, vol. 1. Boston: Little, Brown.

Mander, J. (1978). *Four arguments for the elimination of television.* New York: Morrow.

Mandese, J. (1988, February). A deluge of data, too. *Marketing and Media Decisions*, p. 95.

———. (1992, March 9). Video technology foils measurement. *Advertising Age*, p. 30.

Markoff, J. (1991, December 29). Denser, faster, cheaper: The microchip in the 21st Century; The exponential growth of transistor capacity will continue to have a high impact. *New York Times*, p. F5.

Merleau-Ponty, M. (1964). *The primacy of perception and other essays on phenomenological psychology, the philosophy of art, history and politics*, edited by James M. Edie. Evanston, IL: Northwestern University Press.

Mermigas, D. (1984, July 23). Opinions splinter over zap's sting. *Advertising Age*, pp. 3, 83.

———. (1989, March 13). Time-Warner deal rocks industry. *Electronic Media*, pp. 1, 3, 30.

———. (1990, January 1). '80s bring free-for-all TV competition. *Electronic Media*, pp. 1, 25, 40.

Meyers-Levy, J. (1989). Gender differences in information processing: A selectivity interpretation. In P. Cafferata and A. M. Tybout, eds., *Cognitive and affective responses to advertising* (pp. 219–260). Lexington, MA: Lexington Books.

Meyrowitz, J. (1985). *No sense of place: The impact of electronic media on social behavior*. New York: Oxford.

Miller, D. C. (1983). *Handbook of research design and social measurement* (pp. 300–308). New York: Longman.

Miller, I. W., N. B. Epstein, D. S. Bishop, and G. I. Keitner. (1985). The McMaster family assessment device: Reliability and validity. *Journal of Marital and Family Therapy* 11:345–356.

Miller, M. C. (1988). *Boxed in: The culture of television*. Evanston, IL: Northwestern University Press.

Minnucci, G. (1991). Promoting the news. In S. T. Eastman and R. Klein, eds., *Promotion and marketing for broadcasting and cable* 2d ed. (pp. 222–248). Prospect Heights, IL: Waveland.

Mitnick, B. M. (1980). *The political economy of regulation*. New York: Columbia University Press.

Modleski, T. (1983). The rhythms of reception: Daytime television and women's work. In E. A. Kaplan, ed., *Regarding television* (pp. 67–75). Los Angeles: University Publications of America.

Moriarty, S. (1991). "Explorations into the commercial encounter." Paper presented at the American Academy of Advertising Conference, Reno.

Morley, D. (1986). *Family television: Cultural power and domestic leisure*. London: Comedia.

MTV announces its move to multiplexing. (1991, August 5). *Broadcasting*, p. 39–41.

Murdock, G., and P. Golding. (1979). Capitalism, communication, and class relations. In J. Curran, M. Gurevitch, J. Woollacott, J. Marriott, and C. Roberts, eds., *Mass communication and society* (pp. 12–43). Beverly Hills, CA: Sage.

Nelson, J. (1989). Eyes out of your head: On televisual experience. *Critical Studies in Mass Communication* 6:387–403.

Network rating/share trend. (1992, August 31). *Electronic Media*, p. 20.

New methods make remote control popular. (1934, January). *Popular Science Monthly*, p. 54.

Niven, H. (1960). Who in the family selects the TV program? *Journalism Quarterly* 37:110–111.

Nunnally, J. (1978). *Psychometric theory*, 2d ed. New York: McGraw-Hill.

O'Connelly, J. (1989, April/May). Balancing research and creativity. *BPME Image*, pp. 16, 20.

Own, B. M., and S. S. Wildman. (1992). *Video economics*. Cambridge, MA: Harvard University Press.

Palmgreen, P., L. A. Wenner, and K. E. Rosengren. (1985). Uses and gratifications research: The past ten years. In K. E. Rosengren, L. A. Wenner, and P. Palmgreen, eds., *Media gratifications research: Current perspectives* (pp 11–37). Beverly Hills, CA: Sage.

Patterson, T. E., and R. D. McClure. (1976). *The unseeing eye: The myth of television power in national politics*. New York: Putnam.

Patton, M. Q. (1990). *Qualitative evaluation and research methods*, 2d ed. Newbury Park, CA: Sage.

Patzer, G. (1991). Multiple dimensions of performance for 30-second and 15-second commercials. *Journal of Advertising Research* 31(4):18–25.

Pearson, P. H. (1970). Relationships between global and specified measures of novelty seeking. *Journal of Consulting and Clinical Psychology* 34(2):199–204.

———. (1971). Differential relationships of four forms of novelty experiencing. *Journal of Consulting and Clinical Psychology* 37:23–30.

Perse, E. M. (1990). Audience selectivity and involvement in the newer media environment. *Communication Research* 17:675–697.

Peters, D. (1958, April). The complete TV remote control. *Radio & Television News*, pp. 55–57.

Picard, R. G. (1989). *Media economics: Concepts and issues*. Newbury Park, CA: Sage.

Pilotta, J., ed. (1982). *Interpersonal communication: Essays in phenomenology and hermeneutics*. Washington, DC: Center for Advanced Research in Phenomenology and University Press of America.

Polan, D. (1986). Brief encounters: Mass culture and the evacuation of sense. In T. Modleski, ed., *Studies in entertainment: Critical approaches to mass culture* (pp. 167–187). Bloomington: Indiana University Press.

Postman, N. (1985). *Amusing ourselves to death: Public discourse in the age of show business*. New York: Penguin.

A practical remote control for VHF-UHF channels (1978, February). *Consumer Reports*, pp. 65–66.

Prentiss, S. (1977, June). TV remote control uses infrared signal. *Popular Science*, p. 141.

Radio or record controlled from any room. (1933, April). *Popular Mechanics*, p. 603.

Radway, J. A. (1984). *Reading the romance: Women, patriarchy, and popular literature*. Chapel Hill: University of North Carolina Press.

Remote control for television. (1955, November). *Popular Mechanics*, p. 160.

Remote control for television set employs ultrasonic commands. (1956, October). *Popular Mechanics*, p. 153.

Remote controls. (1991, March). *Consumer Reports*, pp 157–159.

Remote controls for radio and TV. (1956, March). *Consumer Reports*, pp. 165–166.

Reynolds, M. (1992, March 18). Cable sports gets lathered up. *Inside Media*, p. 29.

Rice, M. L., and J. Sell. (1990). "Exploration of the uses and effectiveness of Sesame Street home videocassettes." Report to Children's Television Workshop, New York.

Rice, R. E. (1984). *The New Media: Communication, research and technology.* Beverly Hills, CA: Sage.

Rogers, E. M. (1983). *Diffusion of innovations,* 3d ed. New York: Free Press.

———. (1986). *Communication technology: The new media in society.* New York: Free Press.

Rogers, E. M., and F. Balle, eds. (1985). *The media revolution in America and in Western Europe.* Norwood, NJ: Ablex.

Rogers, E. M., and F. F. Shoemaker. (1971). *Communication of innovations.* New York: Free Press.

Rothstein, E. (1990a, October 10). Paradise in the palm of the hand. *New York Times,* pp. B1, B6.

———. (1990b, October 21). New remote controls on fast forward. *Tuscaloosa News,* p. 23.

Rotter, J. B. (1966). Generalized expectancies for internal vs. external control of reinforcement. *Psychological Bulletin* 80:1–28.

———. (1982). *The development and applications of social learning theory: Selected papers.* New York: Praeger.

Rubin, A. M. (1981). An examination of television viewing motivations. *Communication Research* 8:141–165.

Rubin, A. M., and C. R. Bantz. (1987). Utility of videocassette recorders. *American Behavioral Scientist* 30:471–485.

Rubin, A. M., and R. B. Rubin. (1982). Older persons' TV viewing patterns and motivations. *Communication Research* 9:287–313.

Ruotolo, A. C. (1988). A typology of newspaper readers. *Journalism Quarterly* 65:126–130.

Saayman, G. S., and R. V. Saayman. (1989). The adversarial legal process and divorce: Negative effects upon the psychological adjustment of children. *Journal of Divorce* 12:329–348.

Sanoff, A. P., and C. Kyle. (1987, June 1). Zapping the TV networks. *U.S. News & World Report,* pp. 56–57.

Sarnoff, D. (1937, August 11). Letter to RCA stockholders. Owen D. Young Papers, St. Lawrence University, Box 92, File 11-14-6, January 1, 1937, to July 1, 1939.

Sawyer, D. (Reporter). (1991, May 30). "Primetime live" (Television program). New York: ABC Television Network.

Schement, J. I., and L. Lievrouw, eds. (1987). *Competing visions, complex realities: Social aspects of the information society.* Norwood, NJ: Ablex.

Schiller, H. I. (1987). Old foundations for a new (information) age. In J. I. Schement and L. Lievrouw, eds., *Competing visions, complex realities: Social aspects of the information society.* (pp. 23–31). Norwood, NJ: Ablex.

Schlosberg, J. (1987, February). Who watches television sports? *American Demographics,* pp. 45–49, 59.

Schwartz, E., I. Beldie, and S. Pastoor (1983). A comparison of page scrolling for changing screen contents by inexperienced users. *Human Factors* 25:279–282.

Sculley, J. (1992, February). Address at the Technology Entertainment and Design Conference, Monterey, CA.

Seavy, M. (1992a, April). Universal remote-control tags to dip again. *HFD*, pp. 180–181, 183.

———. (1992b, August). Philips to ship TV-only remote at $14.95. *HFD*, p. 83.

———. (1992c, August). Rampant price-slashing continues on three-function universal remotes. *HFD*, pp. 60, 63.

———. (1992d, October 5). Voice recognition: Firm targets mass. *HFD*, pp. 116, 118.

Secunda, E. (1990). VCRs and viewer control over programming: A historical perspective. In J. R. Dobrow, ed., *Social and cultural aspects of VCR use* (pp. 9–24). Hillsdale, NJ: Erlbaum.

Selnow, G. (1989). A look at the record: Why grazing can't be ignored and what to do about it. In *How Americans watch TV: A nation of grazers* (pp. 31–40). New York: C. C. Publishing.

Shales, T. (1989, December 31). Television's shattering decade. *Washington Post*, pp. G–1, G–12.

Sheneman, P. (1956, December). Push-button remote TV tuning. *Radio & Television News*, pp. 94–95.

Signorielli, N., and M. Morgan, eds. (1989). *Cultivation analysis: New directions in media effects research*. Newbury Park, CA: Sage.

Silverstone, R. (1989). Let us then return to the murmuring of everyday practices: A note on Michel de Certeau, television and everyday life. *Theory, Culture & Society* 6:77–94.

Simatos, A., and K. Spencer. (1992). *Children and media: Learning from Television*. Liverpool: Manutius.

Sims, J. B. (1982). VCR viewing patterns: An electronic and passive investigation. *Journal of Advertising Research* 22(5):35–39.

Singer, J. L., and D. G. Singer. (1983). Psychologists look at television: Cognitive, developmental, personality, and social implications. *American Psychologist* 38:826–834.

Slakoff, M. A., L. A. Helper, and J. Neal-Lunsford. (1991). Independent television station promotion. In S. T. Eastman and R. Klein, eds., *Promotion and marketing for broadcasting and cable*, 2d ed. (pp. 204–221). Prospect Heights, IL: Waveland.

Slater, P. (1974). *Earthwalk*. New York: Bantam.

The smart TV age. (1992, May 4). *Broadcasting*, p. 64.

Smith, D. C. (1961). The selectors of television programs. *Journal of Broadcasting* 6:35–44.

Snyder, A. (1988, September). In search of greener pastures. *Channels*, p. 58.

———. (1989a). I can't get no.... In *How Americans watch TV: A nation of grazers* (p. 21). New York: C. C. Publishing.

———. (1989b). In search of greener pastures. In *How Americans watch TV: A nation of grazers* (p. 22). New York: C. C. Publishing.

Sontag, S. (1973). *On photography*. New York: Farrar.

Sorkin, M. (1987). Faking it. In T. Gitlin, ed., *Watching television* (pp. 162–182). New York: Pantheon.

Sparkes, V. M. (1983). Public perception of and reaction to multichannel cable television service. *Journal of Broadcasting* 27:163–175.

Spigel, L. (1992). *Make room for TV: Television and the family ideal in postwar America*. Chicago: University of Chicago Press.

Spracklen, J., and P.C.J. Desmares. (1956, October). Ultrasonic remote control. *Radio & Television News*, pp 68–69, 161.

Spradley, J. (1979). *The ethnographic interview*. New York: Holt, Rinehart and Winston.

Stauffer, J., R. Frost, and W. Rybolt. (1983). The attention factor in recalling network television news. *Journal of Communication* 33(1):29–37.

Steeves, H. L. (1987). Feminist theories and media studies. *Critical Studies in Mass Communication* 4:95–135.

Stephenson, W. (1967). *The play theory of mass communication*. Chicago: University of Chicago Press.

Steven Bochco: Taking risks with television. At-large interview. (1991, May 6). *Broadcasting*, pp. 25–28, 53.

Stilson, J. (1989a, February 20). ABC buys into German media firms. *Electronic Media*, pp. 1, 37.

———. (1989b, February 20). CBS to sell European shows. *Electronic Media*, pp. 3, 27.

———. (1989c, March 20). Status quo seen in Europe. *Electronic Media*, pp. 1, 43.

Stipp, H. (1989). New technologies and new viewers: A different perspective. In *How Americans watch TV: A nation of grazers* (pp. 24–30). New York: C. C. Publishing.

Stokes, G. (1990, January 8). Eco Eco Eco Eco. *Village Voice*, p. 40.

Stout, P. A., and B. L. Burda. (1989). Zipped commercials: Are they effective? *Journal of Advertising* 18(4):23–32.

Streeter, T. (1987). The cable fable revisited: Discourse, policy, and the making of cable television. *Critical Studies in Mass Communication* 4:174–200.

Svennevig, M., and R. Wynberg (1986, May). Viewing is viewing...or is it? A broader approach to television research. *Admap*, pp. 267–274.

Sweeny, D. (1989, April 17). Remote possibilities. *Audio/Video Interiors*, pp. 55–59.

Sylvester, A. K. (1990, February). Controlling remote. *Marketing & Media Decisions*, p. 54.

Taylor, J. I. (1992, June 24). Personal interview via telephone.

Technology projections: 2001. (1992, May). *Direct Marketing*, pp. 23–25.

Television and Cable Factbook. No. 51. (1983). Washington, DC: Television Digest.

———. No. 52. (1984). Washington, DC: Television Digest.

———. No. 53. (1985). Washington, DC: Television Digest.

———. No. 54. (1986). Washington, DC: Television Digest.

———. No. 55. (1987). Washington, DC: Television Digest.

———. No. 56. (1988). Washington, DC: Television Digest.

———. No. 57. (1989). Washington, DC: Television Digest.

———. No. 58. (1990). Washington, DC: Television Digest.

———. No. 59. (1991). Washington, DC: Television Digest.

———. No. 60. (1992). Washington, DC: Television Digest.

Television Digest with Consumer Electronics. (various issues). Washington, D.C.:
Television Digest, Inc.

Traudt, P., J. Anderson, and T. Meyer. (1987). Phenomenology, empiricism, and
media experience. *Critical Studies in Mass Communication* 4:302–310.

Trends in Viewing. (1988, March). New York: Television Bureau of Advertising.

Tuning the radio from your arm chair (1930, February). *The Canadian Magazine*,
p. 40.

TV remote control penetration. (1992, April 27). *Electronic Media*, p. 28.

Tydeman, J., H. Lipinski, R. Adler, M. Nyhan, and L. Zwimpfer (1982). *Teletext
and videotex in the United States: Market potential, technology, public policy
issues.* New York: McGraw-Hill.

Tyrer, T. (1991, July 29). Networks must adapt to survive, Iger says. *Electronic
Media*, p. 8.

———. (1992, May 4). CBS-made film to debut on Showtime. *Electronic Media*,
pp. 3, 43.

———. (1992b, May 4). Warner details global sales status of "Kung Fu." *Electronic
Media*, pp. 8, 28.

United States Bureau of the Census. (1991). *Statistical abstract of the United States:
1991*, 111th ed. Washington, DC: Government Printing Office.

Universal to unveil upgradable VCR remote. (1992, May 25). *HFD*, p. 84.

van Zoonen, L. (1991). Feminist perspectives on the media. In J. Curran and M.
Gurevitch, eds., *Mass media and society* (pp. 33–54). London: Edward Ar-
nold.

VPT offers speech controlled VCR. (1992). *Interactive Update: The Journal of
Interactive Entertainment*, p. 2.

Wakshlag, J., V. Vial, and R. Tamborini. (1983). Selecting crime drama and ap-
prehension about crime. *Human Communication Research* 10:227–242.

Walker, C. L. (1953, November) How to stop objectionable TV commercials. *Reader's Digest*, p. 72.

Walker, J. R. (1988). Inheritance effects in the new media environment. *Journal of
Broadcasting & Electronic Media* 32:391–401.

———. (1992). Grazing, source shifting, and time shifting: Television viewing styles
in the 1990s. *Feedback* 33(2):2–5.

Walker, J. R., and R. V. Bellamy, Jr. (1990, March). The gratifications of grazing:
Why flippers flip. *Resources in Education*, ED311523.

———. (1991a). The gratifications of grazing: An exploratory study of remote
control use. *Journalism Quarterly* 68, 422–431.

———. (1991b). Remote control grazing as diversionary viewing. *Feedback* 32(1):
2–4.

———. (1992). "Gratifications derived from remote control devices: A survey of
adult RCD use." Paper presented at the annual meeting of the International
Communication Association, Miami, FL.

Walley, W. (1992a, March 30). Pay-per-view boom luring new players. *Electronic
Media*, pp. 16, 26.

———. (1992b, September 14). "No necktie" network for truckers set to roll.
Electronic Media, pp. 8, 47.

Wand, B. (1968). Television viewing and family choice differences. *Public Opinion
Quarterly* 32: 84–94.

Warner, W. L., M. Meeker, and K. Eells. (1949). *Social class in America*. Chicago: Science Research Associates.

Weaver, J. B. (1991). Exploring the links between personality and media preferences. *Personality and Individual Differences* 12: 1293–1299.

Webb, E. T., D. T. Campbell, R. D. Schwartz, L. Sechrest, and J. B. Grove. (1981). *Nonreactive measures in the social sciences*, 2d ed. Boston, MA: Houghton Mifflin Company.

Webster, J. G. (1986). Audience behavior in the new media environment. *Journal of Communication* 36(3):77–91.

———. (1989a). Assessing exposure to the new media. In J. L. Salvaggio and J. Bryant, eds., *Media use in the information age: Emerging patterns of adoption and consumer use* (pp. 3–19). Hillsdale, NJ: Erlbaum.

———. (1989b). Television audience behavior: Patterns of exposure in the new media environment. In J. L. Salvaggio and J. Bryant, eds., *Media use in the information age: Emerging patterns of adoption and consumer use* (pp. 197–216). Hillsdale, NJ: Erlbaum.

Webster, J. G., and L. W. Lichty. (1991). *Ratings analysis: Theory and practice*. Hillsdale, NJ: Erlbaum.

Webster, J. G., and J. J. Wakshlag. (1983). A theory of television program choice. *Communication Research* 10:430–446.

Weinstein, S. B. (1986). *Getting the picture: A guide to CATV and the new electronic media*. New York: The Institute of Electrical and Electronics Engineers.

Wenner, L. A. (1982). Gratifications sought and obtained in program dependency: A study of network evening news programs and "60 Minutes." *Communication Research* 9:539–560.

———. (1983). Political news on television: A reconsideration of audience orientations. *Western Journal of Speech Communication* 47(4):380–395.

———. (1985). Transaction and media gratifications research. In K. E. Rosengren, L. A. Wenner, and P. Palmgreen, eds., *Media gratifications research* (pp. 73–94). Beverly Hills, CA: Sage.

———. (1986). Model specification and theoretical development in gratifications sought and obtained research: A comparison of discrepancy and transactional approaches. *Communication Monographs* 53:160–179.

Wenner, L. A., and M. Dennehy. (1990, November). "In our lives, in our hands: Towards an understanding of remote control use." Paper presented at the meeting of the Speech Communication Association, Chicago, IL.

Westrum, R. (1991). *Technologies and Society: The shaping of people and things*. Belmont, CA: Wadsworth.

Wicklein, J. (1981). *Electronic nightmare: The new communications and freedom*. New York: Viking.

Will, G. (1990, January 2). *Northern Virginia Daily*, p. 4.

Williams, F. (1983). *The new communications*. Belmont, CA: Wadsworth.

———. (1989). *The new communications*, 2d ed. Belmont, CA: Wadsworth.

Williams, F., A. F. Phillips, and P. Lum. (1985). Gratifications associated with new communication technologies. In K. E. Rosengren, L. A. Wenner, and P. Palmgreen, eds., *Media gratifications research: Current perspectives* (pp. 241–252). Beverly Hills, CA: Sage.

Williams, F., R. E. Rice, and E. M. Rogers. (1988). *Research methods and the new media*. New York: Free Press.

Winn, M. (1977). *The plug-in drug*. New York: Viking.

Winston, B. (1986). *Misunderstanding media*. Cambridge, MA: Harvard University Press.

Yorke, D. A., and P. J. Kitchen. (1985). Channel flickers and video speeders. *Journal of Advertising Research* 25(2):21–25.

Youngblood, G. (1978). *Expanded cinema*. New York: Dutton.

Zahradnik, R. (1986, June). Rewinding VCR penetration. *Marketing and Media Decisions*, p. 28.

———. (1987, April). Zap busters. *Marketing & Media Decisions*, p. 10.

Zenith gets InSight program guide for line of TVs, VCRs and decoders. (1992, May 11). *HFD*, p. 102.

Zillmann, D., and J. Bryant. (1985a). Affect, mood, and emotion as determinants of selective exposure. In D. Zillmann and J. Bryant, eds., *Selective exposure to communication*. Hillsdale, NJ: Erlbaum.

———. eds. (1985b). *Selective exposure to communication*. Hillsdale, NJ: Erlbaum.

Zillmann, D., R. T. Hezel, and N. J. Medoff. (1980). The effect of affective states on selective exposure to televised entertainment fare. *Journal of Applied Social Psychology* 10:323–339.

Zuckerman, M. (1971). Dimensions of sensation seeking. *Journal of Consulting and Clinical Psychology* 36:45–52.

———. (1974). The sensation seeking motive. *Progress in Experimental Personality Research* 7:79–148.

———. (1979). *Sensation-seeking: Beyond the Optimal level of arousal*. Hillsdale, NJ: Erlbaum.

Zuckerman, M., E. A. Kolin, L. Price, and I. Zoob. (1964). Development of a sensation-seeking scale. *Journal of Consulting Psychology* 28(6):477–482.

Index

About the Editors
and Contributors

ROBERT V. BELLAMY, JR. is Associate Professor of Communication at Duquesne University. His research interests include media programming, sports and media, and the impact of technological change on media industries. His work has appeared in such publications as the *Journal of Broadcasting and Electronic Media*, *Journal of Communication*, and *Journalism Quarterly*.

LOUISE BENJAMIN is Assistant Professor of Telecommunications at the University of Georgia. Her research interests are in telecommunications history, law, and policy. Her work has appeared in such publications as the *Journal of Broadcasting and Electronic Media*, *Journalism Quarterly*, and the *Free Speech Yearbook*.

JENNINGS BRYANT is Professor of Communication, holder of the endowed Reagan Chair of Broadcasting, and Director of the Institute for Communication Research at the University of Alabama. His research interests include human aspects of telecommunications theory, media effects, entertainment theory, and practical social applications of intelligent networks. His work has appeared in such publications as the *Journal of Broadcasting and Electronic Media*, *Journal of Communication*, *Human Communication Research*, and *Journal of Personality and Social Psychology*.

GINGER CLARK is Assistant Professor of Radio-Television-Film at Texas Christian University. Her research interests are in qualitative audience research and the social and cultural history of television.

GARY A. COPELAND is Associate Professor of Telecommunications and Film at the University of Alabama. His research interests include psychological correlates of individual responses to mass media content, the effects and effectiveness of political communication, and media technologies within the home. He is co-author of *Negative Political Advertising: A Coming of Age* and *Broadcast/Cable and Beyond*. His work also has appeared in such publications as *Critical Studies in Mass Communication, Journal of Broadcasting and Electronic Media,* and *Journalism Quarterly.*

NANCY C. CORNWELL is a doctoral student in Media Studies at the University of Colorado. She has worked in cable television and in broadcast news production. Her research interests involve telecommunications technology and policy, and First Amendment theory.

ROBERT DAWSON is Associate Instructor of Telecommunications and a doctoral student at Indiana University. His research interests include ethnographic approaches to media and everyday life. He is co-author of a chapter in *Towards a Comprehensive Theory of the Audience.*

MARYANN O'REILLY DENNEHY, at the time the study was undertaken, was Undergraduate Student of the Year in the Department of Psychology at the University of San Francisco.

SUSAN TYLER EASTMAN is Associate Professor of Telecommunications at Indiana University. Her research interests include television programming and promotion, sports and media, and children's use of computer technologies. She has authored many book chapters and textbooks, including *Broadcast/Cable Programming: Strategy and Practices,* 4th ed. (1993), and *Promotion and Marketing for Broadcast & Cable,* 2d ed. (1991). Her articles have appeared in such publications as the *Journal of Broadcasting and Electronic Media* and *Journal of Communication.*

SHU-LING EVERETT is Assistant Professor in the Center for Mass Media Research at the University of Colorado. Her primary research interests are media and socialization, multicultural communication, and technology and society. She has worked in the television and research industries.

STEPHEN E. EVERETT is Assistant Professor in the Center for Mass Media Research at the University of Colorado. His main research interests are audience processes in a complex media environment, health care marketing/communication, and new technology. He has worked in the radio industry.

DOUGLAS A. FERGUSON is Assistant Professor of Telecommunications at Bowling Green State University. His research interests are media management and television viewing behavior. His work has appeared in such publications as the *Journal of Broadcasting and Electronic Media* and *Journalism Quarterly*.

BRUCE E. GRONBECK is Professor of Communication Studies at the University of Iowa. He specializes in rhetorical studies, particularly in the area of media, politics, and culture. His books include *Writing Television Criticism* (1984), *Spheres of Argument* (1989), *Communication, Consciousness, and Culture* (1991), and *The Velvet Glove and the Mailed Fist: Socio-Cultural Dimensions of Rhetoric and Communication* (1993).

CARRIE HEETER is Communication Technology Lab Director and Associate Professor of Telecommunications at Michigan State University. Her research interests are in design of emerging media with particular emphasis on virtual reality and hypertext. Her virtual reality and hypermedia designs have been exhibited in juried national and international shows such as SIGGRAPH and CYBERARTS. Her research has appeared in such publications as the *Journal of Educational Hypermedia*, *IEEE Computer Graphics and Applications*, and *Presence*.

BRUCE C. KLOPFENSTEIN is Associate Professor and Chair of the Department of Telecommunications at Bowling Green State University. His research interests are in the diffusion of new communication technologies, the impact of new technologies on media industries, and the future of telecommunications technologies and services. His work has appeared in the *Journal of Broadcasting and Electronic Media*, *Journal of the American Society for Information Science*, and as chapters in several books in mass communication.

KATHY A. KRENDL is Associate Professor and Chair of the Department of Telecommunications at Indiana University. Her research interests are in the ways audience members respond to, and learn from, media in both formal and informal contexts. Her work has appeared in the *Journal of Communication*, *Journal of Educational Computing Research*, *Journal of Educational Technology Systems*, *Educational Communication and Technology Journal*, and *Journalism Quarterly*, among others.

DAVID LAVERY is Associate Professor of Communication at Memphis State University. His work has appeared in such publications as the *Georgia Review* and *Journal of Popular Film and Television*. He is the author of *Late for the Sky: The Mentality of the Space Age* (1992).

SANDRA MORIARTY has been involved with the Viewing Behavior project at the University of Colorado since 1989. In addition to more general questions about grazing, she is interested in the visual impact of video and viewers' response to video aesthetics and commercial encounters.

JEFFREY NEAL-LUNSFORD is Assistant Professor of Journalism and Mass Communication at Kansas State University. His research interests include television programming and promotion, cartoon animation, television production, and sports and media. His work has appeared in the *Journal of Sport History* and in *Promotion and Marketing for Broadcasting & Cable*, 2d ed. (1991).

ELIZABETH M. PERSE is Associate Professor of Communication at the University of Delaware. Her research interests are the uses and effects of newer communication technologies, as well as the application of interpersonal communication theories to the mass communication context. Her recent work has appeared in *Communication Research*, *Journal of Broadcasting and Electronic Media*, and *Human Communication Research*.

STEVEN C. ROCKWELL is a Research Fellow in the Institute for Communication Research at the University of Alabama. His research interests include new communication technologies, media effects, entertainment theory, and educational media.

JOSEPH A. RUSSOMANNO is a doctoral student in Journalism and Mass Communication at the University of Colorado. His current research interests include television and politics, mass media law, and First Amendment theory. He previously worked as a television news producer.

JAMES SAMPSON is a market researcher for Information Resources in San Francisco. His research interests include the ever-widening gap between the amount of information available and the amount of information any one person can or does know.

KARLA SCHWEITZER is a doctoral student in Mass Communication at the University of Alabama. Her research interests include psychological correlates of individual response to mass media content.

MICHAEL TRACEY is Director of the Center for Mass Media Research at the University of Colorado. He researches and writes about television-related issues. From 1981 to 1988 he was Director of the Broadcasting Research Unit in London.

ROBERT TRAGER is Professor of Journalism and Mass Communication at the University of Colorado. Previously he practiced communication law with a major mass media company and with a private firm in Washington, DC.

PAUL J. TRAUDT is Associate Professor of Communication at Duquesne University. His research interests include mass media messages and the construction of everyday experience. His work has appeared in such publications as *Critical Studies in Mass Communication*.

CATHRYN TROIANO is a doctoral student in Telecommunications at Indiana University. She is interested in issues related to gender and media. Her dissertation focuses on women and VCRs.

JAMES R. WALKER is Associate Professor of Communication at Memphis State University. His research interests are in studies of media audiences and the impact of developing technologies on telecommunications industries. His work has appeared in such publications as the *Journal of Broadcasting and Electronic Media* and *Journalism Quarterly*.

LAWRENCE A. WENNER is Professor of Communication at the University of San Francisco. His books include *Media Gratifications Research* (1985) and *Television Criticism* (1991). He is editor of the *Journal of Sport and Social Issues*.

KAK YOON is Assistant Professor of Journalism and Mass Communication at Florida International University. His research interests include advertising and how advertisements are cognitively and affectively processed, the role of brand cognition and attitude, and cross-cultural comparisons.